THE
WHY
AXIS

THE
WHY
AXIS

HIDDEN MOTIVES AND THE UNDISCOVERED
ECONOMICS OF EVERYDAY LIFE

URI GNEEZY
AND JOHN A. LIST

With a Foreword by STEVEN D. LEVITT
coauthor, *Freakonomics* and *SuperFreakonomics*

PublicAffairs
New York

Published in the United States by PublicAffairs™,
an imprint of Perseus Books, LLC.,
a subsidiary of Hachette Book Group, Inc.

PublicAffairs books are available at special discounts for bulk purchases in the United States by corporations, institutions, and other organizations. For more information, please contact the Special Markets Department at Perseus Books, 2300 Chestnut Street, Suite 200, Philadelphia, PA 19103, call (800) 810-4145, ext. 5000, or e-mail special.markets@perseusbooks. com.

Book Design by Pauline Brown.

Library of Congress Cataloging-in-Publication Data

Gneezy, Uri.

The why axis : hidden motives and the undiscovered economics of everyday life / Uri Gneezy and John A. List ; with a foreword by Steven D. Levitt.

pages cm

Includes bibliographical references and index.

ISBN 978-1-61039-311-9 (hardcover)—ISBN 978-1-61039-312-6 (e-book) 1. Economics—Psychological aspects. 2. Motivation (Psychology)—Economic aspects. I. List, John A., 1968-II. Title.

HB74.P8G56 2013

330.01'9—dc23

2013024592

ISBN 978-1-61039-8374 (paperback)

First Edition

10 9 8 7 6 5 4 3 2 1

*For our most important field
experiments—our amazing children:*

*Annika, Eli, Noah, Greta,
and Mason*

Noam, Netta, and Ron

||||||||||||||||||||||||||||||||||||||||||||||| CONTENTS

CONTENTS

Sometimes the things that *should* be completely obvious turn out to be the hardest ones to see.

That was certainly the case for me as a young economist in the late 1990s. It was an exciting time in the economics world. I had the good fortune to be spending my time at Harvard and MIT, two revered institutions that were at the epicenter of the new wave in economics.

Historically, economics had been a discipline dominated by *theory*. The big advances had mostly come from impossibly smart people writing down complicated mathematical models that generated abstract theorems about how the world worked. With the explosion in computing power and big data sets, however, the economics profession was transformed in the 1980s and 1990s. *Empirical* research—the analysis of real-world data—increasingly became the focus of many economists. It became respectable for a young economist like me, having figured out I was not nearly smart enough to come up with fancy theoretical insights, to spend my time toiling in the data looking for interesting facts.

The big challenge then (and now) was how to figure out whether a relationship between two variables was truly causal, or whether it was merely correlation. Why did it matter? If a relationship was *causal*, then there was a role for public policy. If a relationship was *causal*, then you learned something important about how the world worked.

Causality, however, is very hard to prove. The best way to get at causality is through randomized experiments. That is why, for instance, the Food and Drug Administration requires randomized experiments before approving new drugs. The problem was that the sort of laboratory experiments used to test drugs weren't all that applicable to the kinds of questions economists like me wanted to answer. Consequently, we spent our energy trying to find "accidental experiments"—quirky things that happen more or less by chance in the real world that vaguely mimic randomized experiments. For instance, when a hurricane happens to devastate one city and leave another untouched, one might think that it was more or less random which city got hit. Or consider the legalization of abortion with the Supreme Court's *Roe v. Wade* decision in 1973. The likelihood a fetus got aborted changed dramatically with that decision in some states, but not in others. A comparison of life outcomes for babies born around that time in different states tells us something about the impact of the policy and maybe also about deeper questions, like how being born unwanted affects a person's life.

So that is how I, along with a lot of other economists, spent my days: looking for accidental experiments.

Everything changed for me, though, when I one day met an economist a few years younger than me. He had a very different pedigree than my own. He hadn't attended Harvard or MIT, but rather, had received his undergraduate degree at the University of Wisconsin–Stevens Point and then his Ph.D. from the University of Wyoming. His first job teaching was at the University of Central Florida—not the most prestigious place.

His name was John List. Unlike me and the other big-name economists, he was pioneering something that in retrospect was completely sensible and obvious: running randomized economics experiments in the real world. But for some reason, almost no one else was doing it. Somehow, because of the traditions of the profession and what the economists before us had done, it just never occurred to us that we *could* run randomized experiments on real people in real economic settings without these people even knowing they were part of an experiment. It was a truck driver's son showing us the way.

Think about prejudice, for example. If a person acts in a biased way toward another, everyone has always assumed such a person is racist, sexist, homophobic, or what have you. But nobody has ever teased apart the underlying motives in behaviors that appear, on the surface, to be based on dislike, distaste, or flat-out hatred of other people in the way that John List and Uri Gneezy have. Their experiments—which they describe in Chapters 6 and 7—have shown that the hidden motive behind discrimination is not always hatred, but it is sometimes simply to make more money.

To me, the sign of true genius is the ability to see things that are completely obvious but to which everyone else is blind. And by that measure, John List and Uri Gneezy are definitely geniuses. They are true trailblazers in one of the greatest innovations in economics of the past fifty years. This book is their story of how the experimental approach, in the hands of incredibly thoughtful and creative researchers, can shed light on just about any problem under the sun. The only limit is the imagination of the person designing the experiment.

Not only are randomized field experiments (as John and Uri's approach has come to be known) a powerful tool, it turns out they can be a whole lot of fun, too, as you will soon discover. I hope you enjoy reading this book as much as I have.

—*Steven Levitt*

Getting Beyond Assumptions
What Makes People Do What They Do?

The sign on the road leading to the city of Shilong in the Khasi hills of northeast India had a puzzling message: "Equitable distribution of self-acquired property rights." We asked Minott, our driver, what it meant.

Minott had met us at the Guwahati airport after the long flight from the United States. He was an informative, enjoyable guide as we traveled over impossible roads through these beautiful, quiet villages situated in ginger-scented green hills, surrounded by lush rice and pineapple fields. A short, skinny, grinning twenty-eight-year-old, full of wound-up eager-to-please energy, Minott spoke seven dialects and reasonably good English, and he won us over immediately.

"I do not work in the rice fields, like most men of my tribe," he told us proudly. "I work as a translator. And a driver. And I operate a gas station in my sister's house. And I trade goods at the market. You see! I work very hard!"

We nodded in agreement. He certainly seemed like a natural-born entrepreneur. In the United States, Minott would undoubtedly have operated a successful franchise, or even, given the blessing of a good education, a Silicon Valley–style software startup.

But Minott's life was constricted. "I can't get married," he sighed. When we asked why, he explained that, as a Khasi man, he would have to live either with his sister or with his wife's family, and he did not want to do that. He wanted to have a house of his own, but this was impossible in his society. He was not allowed to own property. Many of the things he wanted to do required his sister's permission, because in the matrilineal Khasi society, women hold the economic power. Even the most able, enterprising men, such as Minott, are relegated to second-class citizenship. The sign on the road, Minott explained, was part of a nascent men's movement, as the men in Khasi society began to articulate their resentment over being treated as "breeding bulls and babysitters."[1]

Here was a parallel universe—one we believed might help us solve one of the most vexing economic questions in Western society: *Why are women less economically successful than men?*

If you're like most people, you have an *opinion* about the reasons why gender inequality—and other problems such as discrimination, the education gap between rich and poor students, and poverty—exist. But how do you *really know* why? Anecdotes? Gut feelings? Introspection?

As you'll see, this book is about moving beyond anecdotes and urban legends. In these pages, you will be our co-explorer, discovering why everyday people behave as they do. To get at the real underbelly of human motivation, we run experiments in the wild, where we can observe people going about their business in their natural environments when they're not aware that they're being observed. Then we crunch the results to come up with conclusions that will change the way you view humanity, and yourself. Our unique approach culls new lessons from observations of everyday life, yielding an understanding of the incentives that motivate people—whether these take the form of money, social recognition, or something else.

———————

So how do we learn about underlying motivations and the right incentives? How do we get at the real underbelly of human motivation? For the last twenty years, we've left the confines of our offices to try to figure out what motivates people to do what they do in their natural environments. Our reason for doing this is simple: if you put a bigot in a laboratory where he knows he's being observed, he won't act like a bigot—he'll say what he thinks the scientist wants to hear, or he'll act the way he knows society expects him to because he is motivated to behave as the researcher wishes. But if you watch his behavior in his own neighborhood bar as someone "different" walks in (or give him an opportunity to converse with someone who looks and talks like a boorish Borat), you'll witness simple discrimination.

For that reason, our research has taken us on a journey from the foothills of Kilimanjaro to California wineries, from sultry northern India to the chilly streets of Chicago, from the playgrounds of schools in Israel to the boardrooms of some of the largest corporations in the world. Venturing out into the real world has provided us with a unique understanding of what's really going on with people.

By observing the way people behave in everyday markets, we can better understand their motives. One of our key discoveries is that self-interest lies at the root of human motivation—not necessarily selfishness, but self-interest. These may seem like the same thing, but in fact they are very different. This is a key insight, because once we establish what people really value—money, altruism, relationships, praise, what have you—then we can more accurately figure out the triggers or mechanisms needed to induce them to get better grades at school, stay out of trouble with the law, perform better on the job, give more to charity, discriminate less against others, and so on.

How did we develop this approach? As a sports-card dealer in the 1980s, John would often experiment with different negotiation tactics and pricing policies to discover what worked best. And later on, as a sports-card-dealing undergraduate studying economics at the University of Wisconsin–Stevens Point, he often wondered whether he could learn something important about economics by using field experiments. Could the laws of economics be tested in the real world? Thousands of miles away, Uri was wondering how to incentivize employees who collect donations for a charity. In the process, he discovered that when motivating volunteers, the traditional pay-per-performance model can actually be worse than not paying them at all.

In the past, economists have been skeptical about running *controlled field experiments*. For an experiment to be valid, everything else but the item under investigation has to be held constant. This is how researchers test their theories: if they want to determine whether Diet Coke causes cancer in rats, they will hold "other things equal" and only vary the amount of Diet Coke consumed. Same air, same light, same type of rat. For years, economists believed that there was no possible way to perform such tests in the "real world" because they could not easily control other important factors.

But in reality, the economic world is not a chemistry test tube—there are billions of people and thousands of firms. At odds with received economic wisdom, we will show that if you have "dirtiness"—that is, if you are looking at the way things work in an uncontrolled, quirky, real world—then randomized field experiments yield real answers. In fact, field experiments have become one of the most important empirical innovations in decades. Our methodology permits us not only to measure something that is happening but also to ascertain *why* it happens. We offer examples of the way our methodology can solve many of the world's most vexing economic problems, including the following:

- Why, in most modern economies, do women still earn less than men for equal work, and occupy fewer of the top management positions?
- Why are some people charged more than others for products and services?
- Why do people discriminate against one another, and how can we get them to stop—and avoid it ourselves?
- Despite the fact that the United States spends far more on public education than most other developed countries, the high school dropout rate is higher than 50 percent in some places. Do expensive, faddish educational programs make any difference at all? How can we close the education gap between rich and poor students in a cost-effective manner?
- How can businesses innovate more creatively, improve productivity, and create more value, opportunities, and jobs in an increasingly global, competitive world?
- How can nonprofit organizations encourage more people to give back to society, and how can you make your favorite charity more effective?

You may think that these questions have little or nothing in common. But from where we sit, all of these questions can be considered from an economic perspective—and all of them are amenable to simple economic solutions. Field experiments can unlock these solutions. It's all a matter of understanding the right incentives and of figuring out what really makes people do what they do.

Correlation vs. Causality

People love to say, "This causes that," whether we know it to be a fact or not. But in the absence of experimental data gathered in the real world, we are all pretty much talking through our hats when we infer causality this way.

Not long ago, with fellow University of Chicago economists Steve Levitt and Chad Syverson, we chatted with executives at a big and well-known retailer about how they could boost sales. A high-ranking marketing executive showed us the following picture in an effort to demonstrate that his company's retail advertisements were effective in generating sales (for confidentiality purposes the numbers are changed, but the relationship is similar):

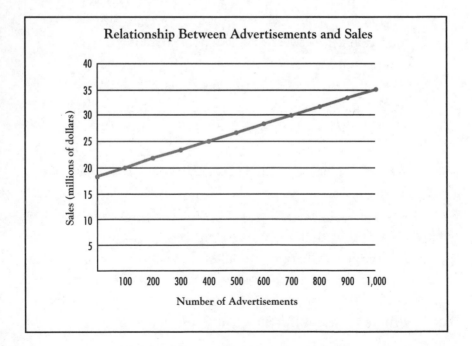

"This is the smoking gun," he said proudly. "It shows a clear positive relationship between ads and sales. When we placed 1,000 ads, sales were roughly $35 million. But see how sales dipped to roughly $20 million when we placed only 100 ads?"

To see why the relationship between ad placements and sales might not be as clear-cut as the executive believed, take a look at a similar figure that we have produced:

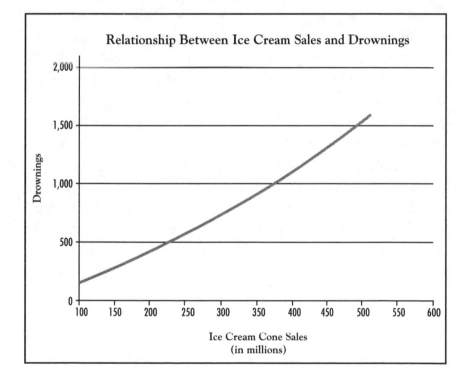

This second chart shows two very different phenomena: the number of drowning incidents from 1999 to 2005, and the number of retail ice cream cone sales (in millions) from one of the biggest ice cream companies in the United States over the same time period. Of course, it's shocking to see such a relationship between these two variables.

Parents persuaded by charts like this might believe that the correlation is causal, and never let their kids eat ice cream near open water. But, of course, there is a hidden third variable lurking in the background. In the summertime, people eat more ice cream *and* swim more. More swimming leads to more drownings. Even though people do eat more ice cream cones in the summer, eating ice cream doesn't *cause* people to drown. Swimming does.

So what was the hidden variable lurking in the background of the chart the marketing executive showed us? We learned later that the retailer placed a lot of ads during the November and December holiday shopping season when, not surprisingly, the company sold a lot of products. This gave the illusion that ads and sales were related causally. But when we dug deeper into the data and took account of the fact of when the ads were placed, we found no causality in the data—just correlation. Consumers bought more products because of the holidays, not necessarily because of the retail ads.

Our world is beleaguered by mistakes like this. In cases where we think a causal relationship could exist, it's easy to mistake simple correlations with causality. In so doing, we stand to waste a lot of money and effort for nothing. The problem is that the world is filled with complicated relationships, and it's difficult to find true causal relationships.

Then there's the current trend "big data." By gathering mounds and mounds of data and observing the patterns, people using big data can draw interesting conclusions. Big data is important, but it also suffers from big problems. The underlying approach relies heavily on correlations, not causality. As David Brooks has noted, "A zillion things can correlate with each other, depending on how you structure the data and what you compare. To discern meaningful correlations from meaningless ones, you often have to rely on some causal hypothesis about what is leading to what. You wind up back in the land of human theorizing."[2]

The other problem with big data is that it is so big that it's hard to find your way in it. Companies have so much data that they don't know what to look at. They collect everything, and then become overwhelmed because they have so many possible permutations of variables of interest that they really don't even know where to start. Because our work focuses on using field experiments to infer causal relationships, and because we think hard about those causal relationships of interest *before* generating the data, we go well beyond what "big data" can ever deliver.

Fortunately, field experiments can provide the kind of hard data that citizens, educators, philanthropists, policy makers, and CEOs need in order to not only avoid making big mistakes but also to develop a better understanding of the people they are supposed to serve: *What really motivates people and why?*

What kinds of incentives cause people to do the "right" things? When do incentives in the form of punishments and sanctions steer people away from undesirable behaviors? And when do incentives just plain not work?

As economists, we clearly believe that there's more to motivation than meets the eye, and that when one does find a *causal* relationship between variables, the implication can be profound. In fact, incentives are not simple blunt instruments. Hidden motives are actually very complex, and they don't always operate the way we think they should. Until one fully understands what incentives motivate people, it is impossible to predict how new policies, or changes, will actually work.

In this book, we show the many ways that incentives *can* work to change ourselves, our businesses, our schools, and the world for the better; but before we try to apply them, we need to understand *how* these incentives change our hidden motives.

We[3] are also fueled by our personal interests and passions. For example, consider how we got interested in the question: *Why do people discriminate against each other?* It wasn't just because discrimination hurts society in general, or because it is a murky issue that has vexed researchers for years. We chose to study it because we, and our loved ones, have been on the receiving end.

Uri will never forget the nightmarish stories his father, Jacob, a Holocaust survivor from Budapest, told him about what happened to his tight-knit neighborhood. When the Nazis took over Hungary and the Holocaust swept into Budapest in 1944, Jacob was no longer allowed to work. His mother, Magda, managed to move the family into one of three safe houses run by the Swedish diplomat Raoul Wallenberg outside the Jewish ghetto. But the houses turned out to be not so safe after all.

One night, members of the pro-Nazi Arrowcross party flushed their Jewish neighbors from their homes, marched them to the Danube river, and shot every man, woman, and child. The next night, the same thing happened to the people in the second building. On the next night, Uri's father and his family were expecting to go to a similar destination. But instead the Nazi sympathizers forced them at gunpoint into the ghetto, where Magda fended off the family's starvation by fighting over the decidedly un-Kosher meat of dead horses. They escaped death by sheer luck. Many years later, not far from the sites of those roundups, Uri lectured at Budapest University—the same institution from which his grandfather was summarily ejected on the basis of his religion. Uri could not help shuddering as he stood at the lectern.

When we think of discrimination, these are the types of ugly, virulent prejudice that we think about. But John faced a much different kind of discrimination when he entered the job market as a newly minted Ph.D. in 1995. Although he applied to more than 150 academic jobs and had completed several field experiments, he was given only one interview. He later learned that other nearly identical applicants received thirty interviews from just forty or so applications. The main difference between John and these other applicants was that John received his Ph.D. from the University of Wyoming, whereas they had received theirs from "brand-name" schools like Harvard and Princeton. Employers were using that bit of information to screen their applicants—effectively discriminating between the "haves" and the "have-nots."

You, too, have likely experienced this type of discrimination—maybe without even knowing it. And like most people, you may think that human beings treat each other unfairly because we're simply wired that way. It's easy to understand why most of us assume the worst of each other. All around us, every day, accusations of racism fly. President Obama's supporters accuse his detractors of racism and vice versa; bloggers, news organizations, politicians, and other public officials routinely jump to conclusions about people's motivations before the facts are out.

What does all this have to do with economics? The answer is this: rather than accept that humans are hardwired to be racists or bigots, we wanted to learn more about the underlying motivations for why people actually discriminate. Clearly discrimination has serious, long-term effects on people's lives, and we wanted to understand how discrimination works in real markets, where people function every day. What causes it? Is it driven by deep-seated prejudice alone, or is there another explanation?

Using various field experiments in real markets, we have learned that the kind of discrimination that John faced is today much more common than the kind that Uri's family faced. Unabashed hatred and pure animus are not as pervasive as most of us believe. As a result, if you really want to end discrimination, don't just focus on the ugly, racist side of things—that's the wrong culprit. Instead, consider the *economic* incentive for the discrimination, and then look through the microscope. As it turns out, most cases of modern-day discrimination are caused by people or companies trying to increase their profits.

But that does not mean that outright hatred is dead. As it turns out, people often discriminate in a bigoted way when they perceive others as *having a choice in the matter*. As Archie Bunker, the racist protagonist of the old television sitcom *All in the Family*, asked Sammy Davis Jr. in one famous episode: "Your bein' colored, now, I know you had no choice in that. But whatever made you turn Jew?"[4]

These insights turn out to be important not only for society, but also for you. Furthermore, policy makers cannot begin to battle something that they don't understand. If you are someone who designs laws, understanding how *not* to be discriminated against is invaluably important.

———————

Another issue that really bothered us was the gender gap in labor markets. Women still earn less than equally skilled men do, and are still too scarce in boardrooms and the C-level offices of companies.

Between us, we have four smart daughters (and four beautiful sons). Like you, we want all of our kids to get a fair shake as they grow up, go to college, and compete for jobs. But from their earliest years, we noticed that fair shakes weren't always happening for our daughters. Why did one of our girl's teachers seem to be telling her that she wasn't as good at math as the boys, even though it was clear that she had mathematical talent? Why did the sports coaches at her school berate the boys in her class to "stop playing kickball like a girl"? And why were Uri's two daughters—one competitive, one not so much so—so different?

We both wondered whether our daughters would be able to compete for great schools and great jobs, or whether they would be discouraged and sidelined along the way. After combining our observations from their early days in school with the facts about the great differences between men's and women's ability to command high salaries, climb the corporate ladder, and hold prominent public positions, we wondered if differences in competitiveness could help to explain the gender gap. So we asked a simple question: *Are women different than men in terms of competitiveness?* After finding important differences, we asked the age-old question: *Is this difference in competitiveness because of nature or nurture?*

To find answers, we boarded planes, helicopters, trains, and automobiles and went to the far corners of the earth to investigate gender competitiveness among the most and least patriarchal societies on the planet (that's how we met Minott). The results of our research come down strongly on the side of nurture. In the right environment—one in which women are not deterred from competitive situations and are accepted by their society as powerful individuals—women grow up to be just as competitive as men, and sometimes even more so. This has important implications for our daughters and yours, and for policy makers who want to reduce the gender gap in labor markets. If you set the incentives correctly, the gender gap can be reduced drastically.

Another question we've explored is: *How can we get people to donate more money to charity?* Beyond our desire to be good citizens, we each had selfish reasons for our curiosity.

For his part, John has been interested in the economics of charity since he was a wet-behind-the-ears professor at the University of Central Florida, where he discovered that an integral part of our economy—the charitable sector—was largely driven by anecdotes and outdated rules of thumb devoid of scientific validation. Along the way, he came to know Brian Mullaney, the founder and CEO of Smile Train and WonderWork.org—whose ubiquitous magazine ads and direct-mail envelopes appeal for donations that can correct cleft lips and palates (and, through WonderWork.org, other maladies) with a simple surgery.

A large-scale field experiment touching roughly 800,000 direct-mail recipients revealed something about giving that no one would have guessed: allowing people to check a box saying "never contact me again" actually lead to *higher* levels of gifts, not lower. Many fundraising experts thought the idea was crazy; why on earth would any charity invite people to *stop* contributing? But as it turned out, people loved it. We raised much more money using the opt-out rather than the standard treatment, and only 39 percent of recipients opted out. Smile Train and WonderWork.org ended up saving money on postage, because they only needed to re-mail to those who were interested in giving in the future. It was a true win-win.

For his part, Uri became intrigued by the idea of getting people to give more to charity while experimenting with a new pricing mechanism at various companies—"pay what you want." Under pay-what-you-want pricing, a company tells its customers that they can have the goods or services they need for any price they set (including $0). We were able to convince Disney to test this new and unusual pricing mechanism in one of its large theme parks. We found that when a charitable donation is combined with pay-what-you-want pricing, people pay a lot—much more, in fact, than they do according to the traditional pricing models.

And, as we discovered, human beings have more complicated and, yes, more complex reasons to give than simple altruism. When we looked at all kinds of techniques—door-to-door campaigns, direct-mail solicitations, matching grants, and so on—we found out what works best in setting the right incentives and convincing people to open their hearts and wallets. As you will see, a running theme throughout the book is this: once we discover what people value, then we can design useful policies that influence their behavior and induce change.

Here's another dilemma that has grabbed us: *How can you use incentives to keep kids in school and curtail youth gun violence?*

This question is anything but abstract. Public schools in some areas of Chicago have horrendous attrition rates, in some cases as high as 50 percent, and one out of every thousand public school student gets shot. When the mayor of Chicago Heights asked John for some help, John responded as any good citizen would—and he brought the tool kit of an economist to the job. The large-scale experiments we describe in this book—the first of their kind anywhere in the country—are demonstrating that certain kinds of incentives, offered in the right way, can go a long way toward improving student performance. They can save lives, too.

In investigating student performance, we had to delve deep into motivation. What really happens when you use money as an incentive? When do incentives work and when don't they? These questions first started to bother us years ago, when our children were in day care. The principal of the preschool, frustrated by parents who failed to pick up their kids at the appointed time, decided to impose a small fine for late pickups. The fine actually acted as a counterincentive, because it put a price—and a fairly low one at that—on inconveniencing the teachers and staff. Parents might have felt guilty about being late before, but once the fine was instituted, they decided it was downright silly to show up on time. Why rush through traffic like a crazy person for the sake of saving a few bucks? We did more research, and concluded that if you want someone to do something, you had better be pretty careful about the details—the who, what, when, where, why, and how much you motivate. Money works, but only at the right levels.

As you might have gathered by now, we're not like most economists. While we use important insights from economic theories, we didn't develop our thinking in intellectual hothouses.

For example, John, as we mention above, took his first forays into the business world as a hungry college student, when he learned to buy, sell, and trade sports memorabilia. He received an unforgettable lesson about cutthroat competition and capitalism when he traded a valuable collection of his own sports cards for a set of worthless counterfeits. But through the process he learned how to bargain more effectively, and even how to price his goods correctly. To his surprise, he later observed that most firms—even international corporations—haven't the foggiest idea about how to set prices for their goods and services.

Uri loves good California wine. Often, when visiting wineries, he wondered how owners priced their wines—a particularly tricky task, since quality is hard to judge objectively. When a vintner asked him to help with just that, Uri told him that he had no clue how much the wine should cost—but he did have a tool that could do the job of finding out simply and cheaply. We conducted a small field experiment in the winery, and few weeks later we were able to find the best price—one that raised the winery's profits considerably. Our field experiments in companies have shown how to raise both productivity and profits in a way that increases everyone's share of the pie.

Often, businesspeople think that running experiments is a costly undertaking, but we believe it's prohibitively costly *not* to experiment. How many product and pricing failures can be laid at the feet of insufficient investigations and tests? Just ask the people at Netflix, who blundered badly in 2011 when they introduced new pricing that substantially damaged both their brand and their stock value.

Every transaction is an opportunity to learn something about customers. Companies that learn to run field experiments, and run them well, will lead in their markets. In the past, skilled managers could rely on intuition and received wisdom from their predecessors. But tomorrow's successful manager will generate her own data via field experiments and use those insights to drive the bottom line.

So there you have it. By the time you finish this book, we hope you will come away with a much better idea of what works—and what doesn't. We also hope that you will see economics as a *passionate* science, not a "dismal science," the name conferred on it by Victorian historian Thomas Carlyle.[5]

To us, economics is a discipline fully engaged with the entire spectrum of human emotions, with a laboratory as big as the whole world, and with the capacity to produce results that can change society for the better. We believe you'll find that our field experiments are not just eye-opening, but fun and full of surprises. We hope you'll discover that economics is not boring or dismal at all. We think you'll come away with new understanding of the hidden motives that drive people to behave the way they do and of how we can all achieve better outcomes for ourselves, our companies, our customers, and society in general.

Finally, we hope you'll come to a new understanding of how incentives can be used as a way of framing questions and gathering insights that are not only interesting, but important and useful.

We hope you enjoy the adventure.

How Can You Get People to Do What You Want?

When Incentives (Don't) Work and Why[1]

If you want people to do what you want, incentives can be incredibly handy. When you were little and your mom promised you a toy for cleaning your room, you probably cleaned your room. And if you didn't clean it the next week, she took away the toy until you did. Much of what we learn from the time we can say our first words is largely based on an application of carrots to reward and sticks to punish. Negative incentives in the form of punishments and fines can steer people away from undesirable behaviors. Positive incentives—often in the form of monetary enticements—can cause people to move mountains, clean up their acts, and do the "right" things.

But incentives are trickier than they seem. They are sophisticated tools, and they don't always operate the way we think they will. Before putting an incentive scheme into place, you first need to understand *how* it works and then use it to understand *why* people behave as they do. Once we understand what people value and why, we can develop effective incentives and use them to change our kids' behavior, motivate employees, attract customers, and even convince ourselves to do things. Field experiments are a powerful tool to understand how and why incentives work.

In some cases, incentives can even backfire, causing people to behave in the opposite way you would expect them to.

This lesson hit home some years ago when Ayelet (Uri's wife) and Uri were late in picking up their kids from day care. Ayelet and Uri had enjoyed a beautiful day at the beach in Tel Aviv, a nice lunch, and good conversation that caused them to lose track of time. It was almost four o'clock, and they had less than fifteen minutes to pick up their daughters from the day-care center a good half an hour away. When they finally got there, their girls greeted them like excited puppies. Then they saw Rebecca.

Dear Rebecca. She was a kind, warm woman, the owner, principal, and matriarch of the day-care center. For years, she had worked hard and saved her money until she had enough to open her own center, situated in a beautiful old suburban house, about twenty minutes from Tel Aviv. Each room was colorful and filled with light, and the kids shrieked with happiness in the play yard. Rebecca had hired a dream team of teachers to look after the little ones, and the center quickly gained a reputation as one of the best in the city. She was proud of her center, and for good reason.

But when she saw Uri and Ayelet, she pursed her lips.

"I'm so sorry we're late," Uri ventured. "The traffic. . . ."

Rebecca nodded her head. She said nothing as Uri and Ayelet scooped up their daughters. What was she thinking? They knew she had to be upset, but *how* upset was she? It was hard to figure out, as Rebecca was always so nice. Uri and Ayelet felt awful for showing up late, wondering whether she might even treat their kids a little more poorly because of their tardiness.

Rebecca gave Uri and Ayelet a little insight into how she felt about their tardiness when, a few weeks later, she announced that her day care would begin charging a NIS10 (about $3) fine to parents who picked up a child more than ten minutes late. In saying this, she made it clear exactly how bad it was to be late: $3.

So how did Rebecca's incentive work? Not very well. Since she only charged $3 for coming late, Uri and Ayelet figured that was a pretty good deal for some extra day care. Next time they were at work or enjoying a day at the beach and knew they would be late, they didn't drive like crazy to get to the center as soon as possible. After all, they didn't have to face the wrath of Rebecca. Now that she'd imposed a $3 late fee, they would gladly pay it and continue with what they were doing without worrying or feeling guilty.

The experience with Rebecca and her fine for tardiness inspired us to work, together with Aldo Rustichini, with ten day-care centers in Israel to measure the effect of a small fine on late-coming parents over a period of twenty weeks. First we measured what happened when there was no fine. Then, in six of the centers, we introduced a flat $3 fine for parents who were more than ten minutes late. As you might have guessed by now, the number of parents who came late *increased* drastically. Even after the day-care centers removed the fine, the number of parents coming late remained higher in the centers that had initially introduced it.[2]

So what was going on? When Rebecca imposed the fine, she *changed the meaning* of a late pickup. Before the fine, parents operated under a simple unspoken agreement, according to which arriving on time was "the right thing to do" for the sake of the children, Rebecca, and her team.

Yet that contract with Rebecca was incomplete. It said that parents should pick up their kids by four in the afternoon, but it didn't specify what would happen if they failed to do so. Would Rebecca and her teachers be content to remain with the children until all the parents arrived? Or would Rebecca and her team be upset and treat the children badly as a result? We just didn't know.

But once Rebecca introduced the fine, the meaning of the agreement between the parents and the teachers changed. The parents realized that they didn't have to drive recklessly through traffic to arrive on time. Furthermore, Rebecca set a clear price—a low one, but a price nonetheless—on lateness. Accordingly, being late no longer involved breaking any tacit agreement. The teachers' overtime simply became a commodity, like a parking space or a Snickers bar. The market-based incentive completed the contract: now everyone knew exactly how bad it was to be late. If you were Rebecca, you would quickly realize that imposing a fine was a lot less effective than a simple guilt trip.

Changing meaning in this way turns out to be a big deal. Let's say that you are the parent of a teenager. You talk with your child about drugs in the hope of convincing her that taking them is bad. If you're lucky, she listens to you. But if you have suspicions, you might demand that she take a drug test. How does this sort of demand change your relationship with your teen? You are no longer just a parent; you are also a cop. And your teen might now focus on finding ways to cheat the drug test instead of questioning the use of drugs in general.

Negative incentives in the form of day-care fines and drug tests change meaning, but of course rewards change meaning too. We all assume that offering people money will get them to do what we want. But let's say you go into a bar after work. You meet someone attractive, and you sense the feeling is mutual. You buy each other drinks and have an interesting conversation. After a while, you say, "Hey, I really like you! Want to come back to my place?" Who knows? You might get lucky. But what will happen if you add, "I'm even willing to pay you $100"? You've completely changed the meaning of the interaction and insulted the other person by effectively turning him or her into a prostitute. By adding a monetary value to your interaction, you've essentially destroyed what might have blossomed into a nice relationship.

The Devil's in the Details

The rub of the episode with Rebecca is that if you are going to use incentives, you have to make sure that they really work. In fact, if you use incentives that involve money, you'd better be pretty careful about the details, because incentives can easily change our perception of the relationship.

Consider the following two scenarios involving a policy aimed at encouraging people to recycle soda cans.

Scenario 1: Let's say you live in a place where people aren't paid to recycle soda cans. On a freezing morning you see a neighbor carrying a large bag, full of cans, on her way to the recycling center.

Scenario 2: Your town has changed its policy. Now people can receive a five-cent reward for each recycled soda can. You see your neighbor carrying a large bag of soda cans to the recycling center.

What do you think of your neighbor in Scenario 1? In Scenario 2?

In the first scenario, you probably think that your neighbor is an environmental steward—a citizen of high character, doing her part for the environment.

But once the small, five-cent-per-can reward is in place, you might think that she is either cheap or really down on her luck. "Why," you might ask yourself, "is she going through so much effort for such a small compensation? Is she a miser?"

In fact, the five-cent incentive might have changed the meaning of what your neighbor thinks she is doing. Before the policy changed, her can-collecting was all about protecting the environment. But after the change, she might be aware that she looks cheap or desperate. "What's next," she might say to herself, "Dumpster diving? In that case, my can-collecting ain't worth it." Given this shift in her self-perception, she might eventually stop recycling.

Another example of how using money as an incentive can backfire took place during Israel's widely publicized "donation days."[3] Every year, high school students go door-to-door to collect donations for a charitable organization supporting, say, cancer research or aid to disabled children. On average, the more houses the students visit, the more money they collect.

Our experimental objective was to determine whether a monetary incentive would increase the amount collected and, if so, how much money it would take to maximize the students' performance. So we divided 180 students into three different groups (none of the participants knew that they were taking part in an experiment). The first group listened to the leader talk about the importance of the donations to the charity, explaining that the charity wanted to motivate them to collect as much money as possible. For the second group, the leader added that each student would receive a token 1 percent of the amount he or she collected (we made it clear that the bonus would not come from the donations). This 1 percent added an external monetary motivation to the intrinsic do-good one. The third group was told they would be given 10 percent of the donated amount.

The group that garnered the most donations was the one receiving no payment at all. Basically, this group wanted to do good for others. But apparently, when the monetary compensation was introduced, the students in the other two groups stopped thinking about the good they were doing, and concentrated instead on a simple cost-benefit calculation with respect to their monetary payments. The group offered the 10 percent payment came in second. Those offered 1 percent garnered the fewest donations. Why? Because in this case, the money didn't support the intrinsic, do-gooding incentive—instead, like Rebecca's day-care fine, it crowded out the higher motivation. That is, the money became more relevant than the desire to do good.

When you're deciding whether to motivate someone, you should first think about whether your incentive might crowd out the will-ingness to perform well without an incentive (to help the environment by recycling soda cans, to help with cancer research, and so on). Crowding out could occur because of a change in the perception of what you are doing, or because you have insulted the person you are trying to encourage or discourage. When you decide to take the incentive route, you should make sure that the incentive is large enough to reap gains. Think of an incentive as a price. If you charge a lot (for example, if Rebecca had charged late parents, say, $5 per minute, as occurs in some places in the United States), people will be more likely to behave the way you want them to. So, the moral of the story is to either pay enough, or don't pay at all.

Cash, in the end, really isn't king; some things can't be bought. Rewarding people on the basis of what they *really* value—their time, their self-image as good citizens, even candy—is often much more motivating than just slapping down, or taking away, a couple of bills. In short, not all incentives are created equal.[4]

I'll Have What She's Having

Incentives can influence behavior in other strange ways too. Con-sider, for example, what happens in an episode of the sitcom *Friends* when all the friends go out to dinner at a nice restaurant. Monica, Ross, and Chandler, who make decent livings, order full-course dinners with all the trimmings, but Rachel, who doesn't earn much money, only orders a side salad. Phoebe, similarly short in her bank account, orders a cup of soup, and Joey, who is no trust-fund baby either, chooses a miniature pizza. When the bill arrives at the end of the meal, Ross announces they will split it—and the final tally comes to $33.50 a piece. A pall falls over the table. "No way," Phoebe resentfully retorts. So much for the nice evening out with friends.

Splitting the bill makes a lot of sense on the surface: after all, sitting around figuring out exactly who ate what and how much sales tax they owe is an unpleasant way to end an otherwise nice experience. Indeed, in some cultures it's considered pretty gauche to do so. In Germany, diners will figure out the price of their individual bills to the last cent, and no one feels bothered. But in Israel, and in many places in the United States, such behavior is considered rude. When a group of people jointly enjoys a meal at a restaurant, there is often an unspoken agreement to divide the bill equally. So how does splitting the bill really affect behavior?

We conducted a study to see what would happen when different groups of diners—students who didn't know each other—were faced with different ways of paying the bill.[5] We divided our participants into three types of groups and changed the way they paid for the bill. In one case, six diners (three men and three women) paid individually; in the second, they split the bill evenly. In the last case, we paid for the whole meal. How did the payment scheme affect what each person ordered?

Now, imagine you are one of six students going to lunch in our experiment, and you are told that you are going to split the tab with the other five. You're pretty hungry, so you order a lobster roll ($20), a side of fries ($3.50), and a beer ($5). The person sitting next to you isn't very hungry, so she just orders a salad ($8) and an iced tea ($2.50). After you all eat your lunch, you and a few others at the table decide to top it off with a piece of pie ($4) and a cappuccino ($5.50), whereas others abstain.

Then the waiter comes along and delivers the bill: the total comes to $125, including tax, and tip, which means each of you pays $25. This is no problem for you because, if you had paid individually, your share would have come close to $40. But it is a problem for the woman who only ordered $10.50 worth of food.

It turns out that the way you split the bill actually affects what you order. We found that people ate the most when we footed the bill for the whole meal. No surprise there. But when it came to the bill-splitting group, people tended to order more expensive items than they did when each person paid for his or her own meal. You have to wonder about the people who "ordered up." They weren't "bad" people who took advantage of others; they just reacted to the incentives they were facing. After all, for every extra dollar they ordered, they had to pay only one-sixth of the cost. So why not order the $20 lobster roll, if all you have to pay for is less than $4 extra? Of course, there are no free lunches (apart from those in our experiments). Someone has to pay for the other $16 for the lobster roll.

This is an example of a "negative externality"—that is, someone else's behavior that affects your well-being. Let's say you're a non-smoker, and a smoker sitting near you decides to light up. He enjoys his cigarette, but you are also "consuming" his smoke. The guy smoking has bestowed a negative externality on you. Simply put, the party consuming the good is not paying all of its cost. In a bill-splitting situation, the person enjoying the large, expensive lunch while others consume less is doing the same thing. People simply react to the incentives they are facing.

What Works?

Throughout this book, we look at significant issues such as discrimination, gender and education gaps, charitable fundraising, and business profitability. The lesson that recurs is this: incentives shape outcomes. But it's crucial to set them up right and to finely tune them to match the underlying motivations of people.

Consider, for example, what it might take to get people to lose weight. The last decade has seen a dramatic rise in obesity in the United States. And obesity is a major risk factor for heart disease, diabetes, and other health problems. Can incentives help people get control of their weight?

After yet another holiday season of too much food and drink—all those Christmas cookies, fried Hanukah latkes topped with sour cream, that New Year's Eve champagne-and-caviar extravaganza—you look in the mirror, stand on the scale, and see that you've reached what might be generously referred to as "critical mass." You have to cinch your belt more loosely. You feel pretty guilty about this, and you vow to slim down.

The local gym is offering a discount on an annual membership, so you forgo the pay-as-you-go option of $10, and sign a year-long contract. If you are like many people, you go to the gym a few times in January, less frequently in February, and not so often after that.[6] You have several reasons (excuses?) for absenting yourself: you lack the time; you are too embarrassed to show up in your Spandex with that belly roll; you're out of shape anyway, so you aren't able to exercise vigorously; maybe you just plain don't like sweating. Because you don't go to the gym more than a few times, your decision to pay the annual membership fee costs you a lot more money than simply using the pay-as-you-go option would have.

Your failure to stick to an exercise routine once you've signed up for an annual membership could be because you were too optimistic—you truly believed you were going to exercise much more than you did in the end. Another, more sophisticated, explanation is that you have "played a game with your future self." That is, you have a hunch that you may be less willing to exercise in the future. You know that with the current pay-as-you go option, you have a choice. You imagine, for example, that you could use the $10 for a one-time visit, or you could go to a movie instead of the gym. You have a feeling you'd choose the movie. So you pay the annual membership now in order to reduce the perceived cost in the future. If you pay now, you figure, then later on you will not give your lazy, future self another reason (saving the $10) to not go exercise.

Other people and organizations may also care about your health—often because it can save them money. Consider the incentives some employers and insurers use to try to encourage employees to exercise. Say you're called in to get yourself weighed and measured. You're also asked if you smoke. If you're deemed to be the right weight, you don't smoke, and you have normal cholesterol and blood pressure, your company reduces or refunds the co-pays and deductibles you're paying in your health care premium, saving you $750 a year. Not bad, right?

This is exactly what Safeway supermarkets tried to do with its Healthy Measures program, which it rolled out with great fanfare to its nonunion workforce (mostly people who work in offices). "By our calculation, if the nation had adopted our approach in 2005, the nation's direct health care bill would be $550 billion less than it is today," CEO Steven Burd boasted in a 2009 editorial in the *Wall Street Journal*.[7] Burd claimed healthcare costs for his company stayed flat.

Following the publication of his article, Burd became a celebrity. Companies and insurers began exploring similar programs. In Washington, D.C., Safeway became a poster child for healthcare reform. President Obama talked of Safeway's cutting its healthcare spending by 13 percent. The House and Senate worked on a so-called Safeway Amendment, which could save families with average health benefits thousands a year.

One needs to be careful when extrapolating Safeway's claims to possible savings for the nation. First, the statistics Mr. Burd reported were problematic.[8] It is always hard to conclude what works and what doesn't when the people providing the data have an interest in the conclusion. Additionally, the Safeway gambit was not a controlled experiment. For example, we don't know what fraction of the change was due to healthy people deciding to stay on the payroll or to join Safeway as a result of this policy. The less fit people may have simply chosen to work for a different company. Either way, Safeway saves money—which is great—but from a global perspective, the problem just ends up being rolled somewhere else.

None of this means Safeway's incentive scheme was bad. But from a practical perspective, designing incentives that truly change behavior is challenging. In recent years, we have been involved in a large project with a major health insurance company that tries to use incentives to help its members. Theirs is a win-win situation: the members get in better shape, and the company saves money. The problem is that the incentives come on top of strong, already existing motivations. Think about the amounts of money and effort that people spend on dieting in frustrated efforts to lose weight. They are already motivated to shed pounds. Could paying them a little help get them to change their exercise habits?

The trick in using money, of course, is to entice people to change their habits. Here's an example of an incentive scheme that we designed and tested.[9] We wanted to use the simplest incentive possible, so we invited students to our lab, and then randomly divided them into two groups. One group was simply used as a control; we "bribed" the other by offering to pay each participant $100 to go to the gym eight times during a month. Following the principle of "paying enough," there are very few things you can't get students to do for the right amount of money. Not surprisingly, the participants came to the lab and went to the gym as required.

But we weren't after temporary compliance. The important question was whether the incentive led to habit formation: what would happen once the month was over and we stopped paying the bribe?

Would the incentive backfire, as happened in the day-care study? Would it make any kind of difference at all? Or would the students form some kind of habit of visiting the gym—enough so that they might continue to visit the gym after we stopped paying them?

The results were encouraging. We found that attendance, even after we stopped paying, doubled for the group we'd paid to visit the gym eight times. The incentive seemed to help these people "get over the hump" of exercising regularly. Those who said they didn't exercise because they didn't have time "found" the time after we "forced" them (with incentives) to find it, and they continued to find the time afterwards. Others may have noticed that they just felt a lot better. Still others might have looked forward to seeing new friends. Whatever the reasons, the important thing was that they managed to change their habits, and they were rewarded with better health as a result.

What can we learn from this study? Many of us want to exercise more than we do. The experiment told us that the hardest part of doing this is not the sweating, panting, and changing clothes; it's adapting to the routine. Adaptation, indeed, is what it's all about. Think about this for a moment. There are certain routines you probably can't see yourself living without—your morning cup of coffee, brushing your teeth at night, and so on. So if you give yourself enough time to get over the hump and adapt to a new routine of exercising, it will become a habit.

Start by committing to going to the gym a couple of times a week for a month. Even if you initially feel the cost of exercising will be higher than the benefit, you'll find that after just those four weeks, you'll have gotten used to the effects of exercise. You'll notice your pumping heart, the psychological lift, the feeling of accomplishment. After this month of exercising you'll find that the effort of heading to the gym is much less difficult than it was during the first week or two of your personal experiment. In fact, you'll have become so used to the way you feel afterwards that you'll start to miss that feeling if you skip a gym visit. At this point, you'll decide that either the cost of going to the gym is lower, the benefit is higher, or both—such that exercising will become a net positive.

Now, it's too simplistic to think we can throw money or other positive incentives at people over time and expect them to do what we hope they will do. Changing deeply embedded habits is difficult for most people. After all, some people keep smoking or eating the wrong things even when they are faced with the prospect of death.

As you can see, making assumptions about how people react to incentives is pretty risky. We assume that people respond in predictable, knee-jerk ways to incentives like money, but they don't. Sometimes incentives work in the short term but not in the long run. And sometimes they make people behave in the opposite way you would expect them to. Higher incentives don't necessarily lead to better performance.

Here is the truth: if you want people to do something, you really need to understand what motivates them. That is the key: once you understand what people value, then you can use incentives to work in predictable ways, and you can get people (including yourself) to behave in ways that you want them to.

As economists, it's our job to look under the hood. We have to learn what can happen in different scenarios. And we must try to understand, as best we can, which incentives work, which ones don't, and why, so that individuals, businesses, and governments can achieve their goals.

In the next two chapters, we'll look into how deeply held cultural worldviews might play into the age-old question of why women continue to earn less than men.

What Can Craigslist, Mazes, and a Ball and Bucket Teach Us About Why Women Earn Less Than Men?

On the Plains Below Kilimanjaro

In January 2005, Larry Summers, then president of Harvard University, offered a lunchtime address to participants at the Conference on Diversifying the Science & Engineering Workforce. Introducing his talk as an "attempt at provocation," he proceeded to lob a heavy grenade into the ancient war of the sexes. Specifically, he wondered aloud whether an innate, gender-related difference in aptitude between men and women was the culprit behind the huge gender disparity observed among hard-core scientists.

Citing research showing that women make up just 20 percent of US professors in science and engineering, Summers questioned whether, "in the special case of science and engineering, there are issues of intrinsic aptitude, and particularly of the variability of aptitude, and that those considerations are reinforced by what are in fact lesser factors involving socialization and continuing discrimination." In other words, he wondered whether women might be at an inherent intellectual disadvantage when it comes to getting to the top in the hard sciences.[1]

The reaction against Summers's comment was swift, huge, and harsh. A top biologist from MIT, Nancy Hopkins, exited the room in a huff. "For him to say that 'aptitude' is the second most important reason that women don't get to the top when he leads an institution that is 50 percent women students—that's profoundly disturbing to me," Hopkins told reporters. "He shouldn't admit women to Harvard if he's going to announce when they come that, hey, we don't feel that you can make it to the top."[2] The local and national media went wild, and a campaign quickly ensued to fire Summers. The following year, he resigned his post at Harvard—partly because of the reactions to his comments at the conference.

Summers's comments—viewed as sexist at worst, tone-deaf at best, and utterly politically incorrect (and he apologized for them several times)—at least did fit with eons of tradition. For millennia, culture and science have colluded to explain why women aren't as competitive and ambitious as men. In the book of Genesis, Adam's role was to be Eve's master. In ancient Rome, women were citizens, but they could not vote or hold public office. Many religions, laws, and cultures around the world persist in subjugating women and forbidding them from competing in a "man's world."

Summers's comments also bore the stamp of Charles Darwin, who more than 150 years ago proposed that successful males evolved to win the mating race. Since then, Darwin's theory of natural selection has helped to explain why males are generally more aggressive and violent than females. After all, men had to go out and compete with men from other tribes to kill animals, while women raised and nurtured the young. The main idea is that the females' cost of producing and raising offspring (such as pregnancy, birth, and nursing) is much higher than for males. Hence, males should compete to have as many offspring as they can, while females need to be choosy in their selection of the right male.

If, as Darwin suggested, evolution is responsible for a comparative lack of competitiveness in females (Darwin didn't write only about humans), a few hundred years of cultural changes would not make a difference. Evolution could help explain why the number of women in high-profile jobs still pales in comparison to that of their male counterparts, or why US women still only earn, on average, 80 cents for every dollar earned by a man.

After citing the research and mentioning his "innate differences" hypothesis, Summers explicitly told his audience: "I'd like to be proven wrong on this one."

In this chapter and the one following, we will take up this challenge. In particular, we will examine what part of the gender gap in labor markets is due to culture. We couldn't just take for granted, in the absence of data, that women were innately less competitive than men. We decided to start collecting evidence by looking at ordinary men and women in their natural habitats and doing things people do every day—say, participating in a gym class or answering job ads on Craigslist—and we used the full gamut of experimental tools at our disposal to answer these questions: *To what degree are the differences between men and women (such as levels of aggression, competitive drive, and wage-earning power) truly innate? To what degree are they culturally learned?* In the end, we've come up with a unique explanation for the persistent differences we observe between men and women, particularly when it comes to competition.

But first, let's take a closer look at why women, despite massive advances, still seem to be held back.

How Much Do Women Compete?

Our interest in gender roles and competitiveness began with the births of our own children. Soon after they were born, we began to notice differences among the girls, and between the girls and their brothers. While one of Uri's girls was much more competitive than her sister, all of our girls always preferred dolls to their brothers' trucks and baseballs. We began to ask ourselves the same question most parents of daughters ask: *In a man's world, what sort of chances would they have? Would they be able to play, and succeed in a culture in which the opportunities are still unequal, despite all the strides women have made?*[3]

The sad fact is that while women are doing better than men in some areas, such as higher education, there is no reason to celebrate an upending of the millennia-old, male-dominated order of things just yet. In the United States and around the world, men still occupy the highest ranks of society. The proportion of women in the market workforce has risen from 48 percent in 1970 to 64 percent in 2011,[4] but only one in five senior management positions are held by women, and fewer than 4 percent of CEO positions in Fortune 500 companies. Some consider these facts as an achievement, since they are the highest in US history. Yet, women are still paid less than men for equivalent jobs. Even in public positions women still have not achieved parity. In Congress, for example, they still hold fewer than 17 percent of seats.

Scholars have theorized for decades about the reasons why women can't seem to make faster progress in breaking through the glass ceiling. Personally, we think that much of it boils down to this: men and women have different preferences for competitiveness, and they respond differently to incentives. Our research shows that many women tend to avoid competitive settings and jobs in which salary is determined by relative rankings.

To illustrate, consider the following large-scale field experiment that we conducted on Craigslist.[5] In this experiment, we wanted to *directly* discover the factors that drive people to apply for entry-level jobs. How would men and women respond to different compensation scenarios? Would women go after jobs that required some competitiveness and risk-taking if the salary offered were higher?

To get some answers, we placed two ads on Internet job boards in sixteen cities for an administrative assistant, one of the most common jobs in the United States. An example of one of our job postings in Seattle read as follows:

POSTING CATEGORY: admin/office jobs
TITLE: Seeking Sports News Assistant
The Becker Center is seeking a Seattle-area administrative assistant to help gather information on sports stories in the Seattle region. While the Becker Center is based in Chicago, we have a satellite project in Seattle. The assistant will provide us with up-to-date information on local news and views on basketball, football, baseball, soccer, Nascar, golf, tennis, hockey and other sports. Responsibilities for the position include reading local sports-related news coverage (pro, semi-pro, and college) and preparing short reports. The successful candidate will also be comfortable with typical administrative duties—light correspondence, proofreading, filing, email and phone communication, etc.
COMPENSATION: Hourly

Our second job description looked almost identical to this one, but it didn't mention sports. Instead, the description noted, "The assistant will provide us with up-to-date information on community events, arts and culture, business, entertainment, policy issues, crime, and other stories. Responsibilities for the position include seeking out, reading, and summarizing local news stories and preparing short reports."

Over a period of four months, nearly 7,000 interested job seekers applied for these jobs listed in the various cities.[6] Upon responding to our ad, some were told that they would be paid on an hourly basis, while others were told that their pay would depend on how they performed compared to a coworker.

Our goal was to see if the competitive aspect influenced one sex more than the other.[7] What do you think we found after placing several months of ads on Craigslist? Which sex continued to show interest in our job after being told of the wage structure?

Not surprisingly, guys were more interested in the sports-oriented ad and women responded to the non-sports-oriented ad: whereas 53.8 percent of the job seekers for the sports-related job were women, 80.5 percent of those responding to the alternate job were female.

But the real differences showed up when we described the compensation schemes. According to one scheme, the job would pay a flat $15 per hour. Not too shabby for an entry-level office administration gig. The competitive pay scheme, on the other hand, rewarded the workers based on how they performed in relation to a coworker. Applicants were told that they would be paid $12 per hour but would be compared to another worker, and whichever of the two performed better would receive a bonus of $6 per hour in addition to the $12-per-hour base pay. In this way, each of the two compensation schemes paid an average of $15 per worker, but one was highly incentivized, whereas the other was not.

You might be surprised (and saddened) by the actual gender breakdown of who applied for each kind of job. In general, women didn't like the competitive option; in fact, they were 70 percent less likely than men to go after the competitive job. Further, the women who *did* apply for the highly incentivized job tended to have more impressive resumes than the men who applied for those same jobs.

These findings seemed to underscore the fact that, when it comes to competition, men aren't nearly as shy as women.[8]

A successful career as a CEO demands a high level of engagement and responsiveness to competitive situations. No wonder, then, that so few women are at the top. Just Google the phrase "every man has his price," and you'll get lots of nice quotes about how every man can be bribed to do almost everything. But if you Google "every woman has her price"—well, that has a very different meaning.

Girls Against Boys

Larry Summers was not talking about entry-level jobs. He was talking about scientists. So what happens when smart female mathematicians and scientists compete against men? To find out, we asked groups of three men and three women to solve a series of mazes on a computer in exchange for money.[9] The setting was the Technion, the so-called MIT of Israel. It's a tough school to get into, and men constitute 60 percent of the student body. The women at the Technion have to prove from their earliest years that they are every bit as good at math and science as the guys, the implicit assumption being that women have to work harder to show that they can be Einsteins, too.

One of the women in the experimental group was Ira (a common girls' name for Russian immigrants in Israel). Ira was a brilliant student who had played computer games all her life, and she enjoyed technology and sophisticated technical concepts. She was born in Moscow and immigrated to Israel with her parents and older brother when she was ten. Even when she was young, math was her passion, so her decision to try to get into the Technion was not surprising. But being there wasn't easy; she was the star of her math class in high school, but at the Technion, everyone was smart. She had to work extra hard and compete with other students to pass the courses. Many less-committed students failed along the way and switched to less competitive fields. But Ira did well. She worked diligently, sleeping only four hours at night, and gave up her ballet practice. She knew she was going to make it.

Unlike some of her female peers, Ira didn't feel discouraged by the idea of a career in science and technology.[10] Nevertheless, we wanted to know whether her gender-identification as a woman would affect her desire to compete for money in our experiment. Would she go all-out in a competitive game if incentives were involved?

In the experiments, participants were asked to solve as many mazes as they could in fifteen minutes, and receiving a dollar for every maze solved. When we then measured how well participants in these groups did, we found that the women performed pretty much the same as the men. But other groups of participants were given a competitive incentive: the person who solved the most mazes was paid proportionally more. In the heat of the battle, would Ira increase her effort?

It turned out that the male participants responded to the competitive incentive by significantly increasing the number of mazes they solved during the fifteen minutes, but Ira and the other women did not perform as well. In the competitive condition, the women solved, on average, the same number of mazes as they did in the noncompetitive one. The hypothesis that women are less competitive than men seemed to hold firm, even for Ira and the other bright women of the Technion.

In a later experiment, we mimicked something you might remember from your childhood.[11] Think about running as fast as you can alone, or next to someone else. If you are competitive, just having someone running next to you might motivate you to run faster and win an imaginary "race." You just transformed an innocent situation into a competition. And if you're less competitive, maybe you don't care who's next to you—you just run fast.

As you might have guessed, we wanted to test whether young boys and girls would have different competitive tendencies. To do so, we went to visit some fourth-grade schoolkids in Israel. In a physical education class, we first asked kids to run forty meters on a track, one at a time. After the teacher timed the individual students' results, the students who ran at similar speeds raced against each other. We didn't offer incentives, and we didn't even tell the kids that this was a competition. The kids simply had to run neck and neck.

As we found in the Technion maze experiment, the boys ended up reacting more strongly to the competitive environment, running faster than when they had run alone. The girls, again, didn't seem to react to the heightened competition. They ran about as fast as when they had run alone—even when they were competing against only against girls. Once more, it looked like girls didn't do as well in a competitive context.

Eventually our research led us to visit the most patriarchal and matrilineal societies in the world. This approach was meant to provide some preliminary insights on how cultural influences shape competitive preferences.

One frosty night a few years back, in a heavy dose of male bonding, we were sitting around playing poker with a bunch of other guys in College Park, Maryland. Between cigar chomps and shots of whisky, we asked ourselves why most women didn't seem to enjoy these oh-so-fun activities as much as we did. But, more importantly, we also wondered about the results of the experiments conducted at the Technion and in the school. Were women simply born to dislike competition, or did society influence their tastes and preferences? Was the lack of competitiveness inherent in women or a learned behavior? If the latter, exactly what did nurture—or the fact that culture might be linked to their competitive inclinations—have to do with their learning? And if the differences turned out to be socialized, would our daughters have a fair shot at succeeding in a competitive society?

There was only one way to find out. We had to get away from Western society. With support from the National Science Foundation, we set out to test assumptions about biologically based competitiveness in two of the most culturally different places on the planet. We conducted experiments in a society in which women held virtually no power, and in one in which they ran the show. We literally went to the ends of the earth to tease out the question that Freud, Darwin, and numerous other psychologists, sociologists, and anthropologists after them have theorized about, but have had difficulty testing.

In the process, we were able to develop scientific experiments that permitted us a unique glimpse into women's behavior in markets across extremely different societies that held women in diametrically opposite roles. In exploring the underpinnings of their behavior, we gained insight into this question: *Are women from every walk of life less competitively inclined than men?*

With the help of some anthropologist friends, we identified two polar-opposite tribes—the ultra-patriarchal Masai tribe of Tanzania, and the matrilineal Khasi of northeast India (the latter of which we'll encounter more in the following chapter). What would happen if we compared the way men and women in these tribes competed under the same experimental conditions?[12]

A Trip to Tanzania

On the plains below Kilimanjaro, the tallest mountain in Africa, proud Masai tribesmen, dressed in brightly colored robes and carrying their spears, follow the calling of their cattle-herding ancestors.

The more cattle a man has, the more wealth he possesses. A man's cows are more important to a Masai man than his wives. A cattle-wealthy Masai man can have as many as ten wives.

The Masai culture is very unkind to its women. The men, who tend not to wed until they are around thirty years old, marry women who are in their early teens. If you ask a man, "How many children do you have?" he will count only his sons. Women are taught from birth to be subservient. A wife is confined to working in her home and her village. If her husband is absent, a woman must ask an elder male for permission to travel, seek health care, or make any important decision.

On a bright Sunday morning, we made our way to one of the Masai villages to coordinate the week's experiments. We passed lots of families walking to the market more than ten miles away. In every group, the man walked first, carrying only his stick. About ten feet behind him walked his wife, a huge, heavily-loaded basket balanced on her head. The woman typically had a baby strapped to her back; with her free hands, she led her older children along. The men didn't even look back to see how their wives and children were faring.

Basically, Masai women are chattel. "Men treat us like donkeys," one Masai woman told some other researchers.[13]

When we pulled up to the Masai village, we were greeted by a wonderful call-and-response chanting of the women (the Masai seem to sing this way almost constantly). Koinet Sankale, the Masai chief whose first name, we were told, means "the tall one," came out to greet us. Handsome and broad-browed, he was an honored warrior who had proved his bravery as a pubescent boy by spearing a lion. The beast had left distinct teeth-marks on his face, his upper chest, and both arms. He walked up to us with a long, loping stride and shook our hands. Then he turned and introduced us to thirty of his tribesmen, who squinted at us suspiciously. The men wore colorful, loose, plaid or solid-colored cloaklike garments that they threw over their shoulders. They wore draping earrings and neck-laces made of shiny beads, and had marked their arms and faces with slashes of red ochre. Most of them were missing some teeth.

After the introductions, we enjoyed a meal of barbequed goat together in the midst of a circle of their flat-roofed homes, called bomas, and listened to the sounds of the mooing cattle, with whom the Masai appear to have a symbiotic relationship.

After sleeping in a less-than-wonderful local hotel, we woke the next day and discovered bad news. We had come to Tanzania to run a pilot test using the same maze experiment we'd used with Ira, except without computers. The Masai participants were supposed to solve the mazes on paper, using pens. But when confronted with these simplest of tools, the village women scratched their heads. The women had never held a pen, and were not willing to start now.

We were clearly in trouble.

Someone suggested building mazes out of wood so the villagers could solve them by moving a small piece of wood in them. Our collaborator on the project, Ken Leonard, who is an expert on the Masai, knew a fellow who had a workshop in town. The next day, with the assistance of a local car mechanic and a carpenter, we spent twelve hours sweating under the blazing African sun building a maze out of wood. The villagers watched as we worked, staring and laughing at the funny white men who were apparently attempt-ing to build a child's toy. After a long day of hard work, we had one maze built. Unfortunately, it was indicative of our talent as carpen-ters. The maze was unsolvable. So now we were in even more trouble. How could we show up at the village the next day with nothing for the throng of assembled tribespeople to do?

Then came the eureka moment. On his way to the hotel, Uri saw a store that sold tennis balls and buckets. The task we decided to use (and that we have used in many other experiments since then) was simple—we asked our participants to toss a tennis ball into a bucket.

The villagers had never before done anything like shooting baskets, so there was no practice advantage or gender advantage. In addition, we thought this task would provide us with a quick indication of an individual's initial proclivity to compete. All it would take to land a ball in a bucket was good aim.

In the morning, our team returned to the village, armed with several cans of tennis balls, small toy buckets, and lots of money. We found the people waiting for us, and we divided them into two groups. We then invited participants—one from each group—to step over to a private place where a member of the research team waited for them. They were told the task involved throwing a tennis ball into a bucket from a distance of three meters, or about ten feet. Each participant would get ten tries to land the ball in the bucket so that it stayed there.

We next asked the villagers to choose one of two payment options: in the first option, participants would receive the equivalent of $1.50—a full day's wage—each time they landed a ball in the bucket. In the second option, they would receive the equivalent of $4.50 for each successful pitch, but only if they were better than their opponent. If both participants succeeded the same number of times, they would both get $1.50 for each success. But if their opponent proved more apt, they received no payment for the experiment. *That is, we asked the participants to choose between two options: one in which their payment depended only on their success, and one in which they would compete with someone else.*

The young people—especially the men—seemed to be excited by this idea, whereas the older people, regardless of gender, seemed a bit suspicious. (You would probably be suspicious, too. After all, imagine someone coming over to your leafy suburb and offering you and your neighbors a week's pay to play what appeared to be nothing more than a silly game.)

The first man to step up was a large, burly fellow named Murunga, who looked to be somewhere in his late fifties. Murunga was a true tribal patriarch, with six wives, thirty children, and an unfathomable number of grandchildren. He chose to compete. He drew back his arm and aimed the ball at the bucket. Tossing the ball a little too hard, he missed the first try and roared his disappointment. On the second try, the ball skipped off the lip of the bucket. But he landed the third ball and grinned from ear to ear. And so he continued throwing the remaining seven balls. After having landed a few successful tosses and learning that he had been successful with more tosses than his competitor, he collected his money and walked off looking pleased.

It wasn't long before word got around that some ridiculous Americans were doling out wads of money. Ultimately, 155 preselected people came to play the game. By the end of the day, the villagers didn't want to let us leave. We managed to escape by jumping into our car with the remainder of our money—which we needed in order to conduct similar experiments in other villages—and we tore away from the scene, the people chasing at our heels.

After a couple of weeks of such experiments in various villages, we tallied the data. Would these patriarchal men show themselves to be more competitive than those in the United States, Israel, or any other developed nation? Would the women show themselves to be less so?

The figure on page 46 tells the story. In short, we found that the men and women in Tanzania were a lot like the men and women we studied in developed nations. Whereas 50 percent of the Masai men chose to compete, only 26 percent of the women did.

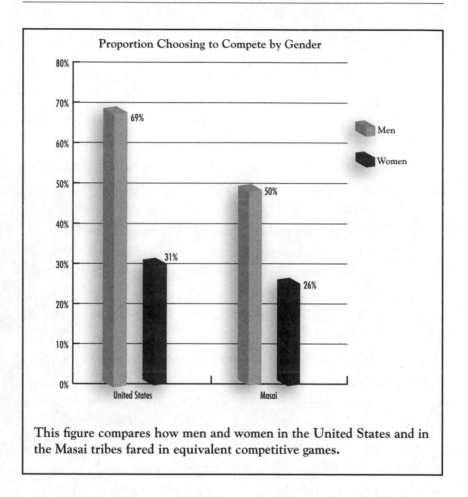

Proportion Choosing to Compete by Gender

This figure compares how men and women in the United States and in the Masai tribes fared in equivalent competitive games.

Again, it looked as if most of the women just didn't want to compete—but, perhaps surprisingly, they were not much *less* competitive than women in Western cultures everywhere.

The Right Person for the Job

Meanwhile, back in the United States, Liz was trying to land a job.

Liz was a forty-two-year-old woman who applied for a job as creative head for a New York–based direct marketing company. Liz had lots of experience as the former head of a creative department, and she came with all the right qualifications and abilities. But the hiring process was long and competitive, and hundreds of people had applied.

To sort the wheat from the chaff, the hiring manager and human resources department asked top candidates, including Liz, to participate in multiple interviews. As the process became more competitive, the candidates were asked to design an outer envelope for a direct mail package within an hour. If done correctly, this chore would actually have taken much longer, and it had little to do with the actual job of managing an in-house team of twenty designers. The test had more to do with testing an ability to work fast in a competitive environment—more appropriate to, say, a position working on a trading floor—than it had to do with the actual work of getting people to open envelopes.

At the end of the day, the company hired a man who did better in the competitive process. Without having specific competencies in mind, the company screened out the better candidate. For Liz, it meant that she "lost" to someone who was less qualified. For the company, it meant that they passed on the more talented applicant in favor of the more competitive one.

As it turns out, many hiring managers base their hiring decisions on intuition and what was done in the past (typically how it was done by their old boss). In many such cases, these old hiring practices were based on a notion that was either misconceived or has now changed—and usually favored men. In study after study, it's been shown that when members of an all-male board have to pick a new board member or a CEO, they usually hire someone who looks like them.[14] A 2012 University of Dayton Law School paper noted that "virtually every recent report or study describes women's progress in achieving greater representation on corporate boards of directors as 'stalled' or some similar adjective,"[15] despite the fact that when women do serve on boards, their companies' stock values rise.[16]

But you can only keep top talent down for so long in markets. Soon, the time will come for women to enjoy their rightful places at the helms of organizations, and companies that act sooner rather than later will benefit.

In the next chapter, we'll get to the bottom of all this.

What Can a Matrilineal Society Teach Us About Women and Competition?

A Visit to the Khasi

As you saw in the previous chapter, all of our experiments—from those we conducted online with Craigslist, to the Technion, to the races with the schoolkids, to our visit to the Masai—confirmed that women just don't like to compete as much as men and react to competitive scenarios differently than men do. This, in and of itself, provides an intriguing explanation for the gender gap.

But, we still wanted to know, *why* is this so? Is there an important innate difference between the sexes that would lead them to act this way regardless of how they are raised? Or do societal influences play a vital role in our competitive inclinations?

Our visit to the matrilineal society of the Khasi helped to answer these foundational questions. Let's explore the exotic life of the Khasi. Put on your seatbelt, because you are in for an incredible ride.

Minott (the driver who picked us up at the airport after we landed in India, whom you met in our Introduction) was our initial guide into the matrilineal society of the Khasi people. With him, we crossed over into a bizarre world of reverse sexism. By our standards, of course, it seemed unfair that Minott could not own a house, even if he could have afforded one, and that his personal opportunities were stymied. At the same time, we got a fabulous window into what happens when women hold their culture's economic purse strings.

When Minott first drove us from Guwahati airport into the city of Shillong, every square foot of the road was filled with people—women in colorful saris, dark-haired men in cotton shirts, half-naked beggars, children—all pushing and pulsing against one another in the sweltering heat. The next day, when Uri went to a local bank for the cash we needed for the experiments, the people behind him crowded over his shoulders as if they were trying to board a train. (Once again, he was a rich Westerner, parachuting into a foreign culture.) When he made the request to cash $60,000 worth of travelers' checks, the cashier went to speak to his manager and, hours of negotiations and discussions later, Uri got a huge bag full of rupees and proceeded to count them out in front of everyone.

Fearing that the people pushing behind him would tear the bag right out of his hands, he turned and pushed his way through the crowd, then fled as fast as he could. (We now understood the exhilaration that the famous bank robbers Bonnie and Clyde must have felt after each heist.)

Minott drove us up impossible roads to our destination—a peaceful village in the midst of verdant hills and fecund fields. Though rich in natural amenities, the village was economically poor. We dropped our gear, including the bag holding all that money, in our unlocked, rented house. Then we set out to meet the villagers. Instead of being greeted by suspicious, red-robed Masai warriors who stood squinting at us, we met warm, welcoming, smiling people.

We discovered that life is considerably better for Khasi women than it is for their Masai counterparts. The Khasi are one of the world's few matrilineal societies; inheritance flows through mothers to the youngest daughter. When a woman marries, she doesn't move into her husband's home; rather, he moves into hers (and out of his mother's). The mother's house is therefore the center of the family, and the grandmother is the head of the household. Khasi women don't do much of the farming, but as the holders of the economic power they wield a great deal of authority over men.

Over the following weeks, we conducted ball-throwing experiments identical to those we conducted in Tanzania.

On one side of the village school building, the Khasi men dutifully queued up, and the researchers wrote down their survey data, just as we had done in Tanzania. One young man named Kyrham, who chose not to compete, was dressed in a simple white shirt and jeans. He smiled gently as he took hold of the first tennis ball. He seemed a little tentative at first, and his first attempt missed the bucket by a couple of feet. On the next try, he threw a bit more strenuously, and the ball landed on the other side of the bucket. He was clearly disappointed, and bit his lip. On the third try, he managed to land the ball squarely inside the bucket.

On the other side of the building, a woman stepped up to the line. Her assertiveness impressed us. Shaihun didn't hesitate to choose the competitive option. She pulled up her sleeves, grasped

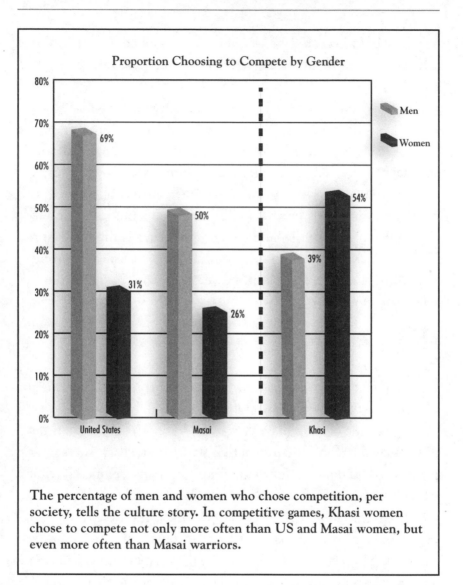

Proportion Choosing to Compete by Gender

The percentage of men and women who chose competition, per society, tells the culture story. In competitive games, Khasi women chose to compete not only more often than US and Masai women, but even more often than Masai warriors.

a tennis ball, and squinted, ready for battle, at the plastic toy bucket ten feet in front of her. Confidently extending her bangled arm, she tossed the ball toward the target. She missed, but that didn't lower her spirit. As the second ball landed inside the bucket, she shouted with joy. In fact, she sank the ball five times and in so doing won plenty of money for a few minutes' worth of games. She was totally, wonderfully competent, sure of herself, and in command. It was time for her competitors to move over.

We had landed in a world turned on its head, gender-wise. Our results, summarized on the previous page, showed that 54 percent of the Khasi women chose to compete, whereas only 39 percent of the Khasi men did. Khasi women were *more* likely to choose to compete than even the super-patriarchal Masai men. Generally speaking, the Khasi women behaved more like the Masai (or US) men.

The Khasi experiment sheds some insight—in this domain—into the long-standing debates about sex differences. Of course, we looked at the behavior of women in a society unlike most others in the world. But that was the point: to strip away, as much as possible, the cultural influences of a patriarchal society. In the case of the Khasi, the average woman chose to compete much more often than the average man. Or, put more simply, nature was not the only player in town. For the Khasi, nurture is king—or queen, as the case may be.

Our study suggests that given the right culture, women are as competitively inclined as men, and even more so in many situations. Competitiveness, then, is not only set by evolutionary forces that dictate that men are naturally more so inclined than women. The average woman will compete more than the average man if the right cultural incentives are in place.

Can Women Negotiate Effectively?

So how does this interest in competing affect Khasi women's be- havior in the marketplace, where strong economic incentives rule? To find out, we visited an open-air market in Shillong, where Khasi and non-Khasi people live side by side.

The Shillong open-air market—one of the largest in the world—
is a lively affair. As you walk among the crowds, you take in the
odor of rotting meat and blood; the fresh smell of tomatoes, onions,
and peppers; the scent of flowers, straw hats, and cotton shirts.
Cheap electronics and shoes flood the stalls.

To see how culture affects negotiation style, we gave Khasi and
non-Khasi men and women money to buy two kilos of tomatoes in
the market. Prices ranged between 20 and 40 rupees per kilo, depending on how well they haggled; our participants earned more if
they negotiated a lower price. For every tomato-buying negotiation,
we recorded the starting price, how long the bargaining lasted, and
the ending price.

We discovered two important things. First, Khasi women, trained
from birth to be assertive and self-confident, proved to be successful
negotiators; our ball-tossing experiment had proven to be a good
predictor of real life behavior in these markets. Our second finding
was no less interesting. The market functioned very differently,
depending on whether the pricing rules were set by women from
the matrilineal tribe or not.

When the Khasi women entered a section of the market in which
non-Khasi people set the price, men and women sold goods and
haggled side by side, and the Khasi women proved themselves to be
forces of nature. Shaihun was among them. She was a fantastic
bargainer, reaching excellent prices for such items as tomatoes or
cotton shirts for her sons. Interestingly, when Shaihun and her
peers entered a section of the market in which *only* the Khasi set
the price and *only* women bought and sold goods, we noticed that
there was not much haggling. The shopping prices appeared, as it is
in the West, to be more set than negotiated. It seemed that the
surroundings and socialization were instrumental in dictating how
people behaved.

The two observations are related. Women can be nurtured to react to incentives in similar ways as men and to negotiate just as well as men. But given the option, Khasi women set the incentives in their part of the market differently than men. By setting standard prices, they simply made the environment less competitive and aggressive, and they reacted to the social incentives that they themselves set.

Can Women Save Mankind from Itself?

Another lesson we learned from the Khasi is this: when women are in power, everyone seems to benefit.

In 1968, ecologist Garrett Hardin published a paper called "The Tragedy of the Commons," in which he described what happens when a public resource becomes depleted because too many people are taking advantage of it.[1] In the article, he described a situation in medieval Europe in which herders shared a common parcel of land on which everyone was allowed to graze cattle. As long as herders didn't allow too many cattle on the land at once, everything was fine. But if one greedy herder brought additional cows to graze, the damage to the pasture increased, eventually depleting the parcel so much that none of the cattle could graze at all. (Remember the discussion of negative externalities when splitting the bill?)

Think, for example, about coastal fishing rights. In many places, overfishing has so depleted stocks that the future of a number of fish species is in serious question. Given the high demand for fish, each fisherman has an incentive to fish as much as he can; but if everyone does the same, nothing will be left for future generations—at some point the fish population decreases so much that it doesn't recover.

One conventional assumption about women is that they tend to care more about public goods, like fish stocks and grasslands, than men do. We set out to investigate this assumption with the Khasi, as well as in a neighboring village of Assamese, a patriarchal tribe, using a standard game from economics called the "public goods game" (so named because it emulates what happens when we contribute money to provide public goods for all, such as well-cared for national parks and clean air).

We gave each group the same set of instructions: "In this game, you can choose to invest in the community, or to invest in yourself." We told some of the participants the following: "Every rupee you invest in yourself will yield you a return of one. Every rupee invested in the group exchange will yield a return of one-half for every member of the group, not just the person who invested it."[2]

Given what you know now about their society, you might guess that the Khasi people were more inclined to spend their rupees to invest in the group. And you would be correct. Khasi men and women invested more in the group than did their Assamese counterparts. Basically, our results found fewer selfish people, regardless of gender, among the Khasi. These results open up a question—would a society "ruled" by women be very different than the one we live in today?

What Can We Do?

The edgy television series *Mad Men* shows us how far gender relations have advanced in American society since the 1960s, when public discourse held that women were supposed to look and act like Marilyn Monroe, and men were supposed to look and act like Rat Pack predators. The series offers an important look at the way society dictated male and female behavior before anyone dreamed of a women's movement, black power, or gay liberation. People may not have been sure of who they were, but they knew who it wasn't safe to be.

Fast-forward to the twenty-first century. Now we know that men and women react differently to competitive incentives; and this difference in reaction to incentives is strongly influenced by culture. Together, such social factors help to explain the gap between men's and women's job status and earnings. As the Khasi taught us, once women hold economic power and can express their true preferences without risking public scorn, they can learn how to react to competitive incentives to achieve considerable economic gain, and become true leaders in their societies.

The implications of our two key findings—(a) that women can be just as competitive, or even more competitive, than men; and (b) that when women have stronger economic influence, the society becomes more consensual and public-spirited—are profound. When we watched women haggle over tomatoes, we thought about American women who don't apply for competitive jobs or ask for raises. We thought about the structural problems in Western societies that prevent women from achieving everything they can. And when we watched the women's market operate with less friction, we thought about the US Congress, where bickering and grandstanding are the norm.

So if we want to encourage women and girls to be more competitive and to increase their earning power, what changes should we bring about to make that happen? What does all this mean for our daughters and yours?

Uri's nineteen-year-old daughter, for example, believes that she can be successful in her future career. Her parents have encouraged her to believe that the sky is the limit and that she can achieve whatever she desires. At the same time, she feels that, at least in the culture of San Diego today, she can't go out and compete as freely as her male peers. So how can she get to the top without behaving as aggressively they do?

Meanwhile, John's South Side Chicago girls likewise notice that boys in their gym class who do not perform to their peak get scolded by coaches who, as we said before, tell them to "stop playing like a girl." "Should we play like girls or boys?" John's daughters ask. "Should we be nice, or grab what we can?"

As we noted at the opening of this chapter, women tend to avoid salary negotiations; laboratory research has shown, for example, that men are nine times more likely than women to ask for more money when applying for a fictitious job. But do such tendencies manifest themselves in the real world? And, if so, why?[3]

To find out, we ran a field experiment that was similar to the Craigslist experiment we described in Chapter 2. Between November 2011 and February 2012, we placed eighteen online "help wanted" postings for administrative assistants in nine major metropolitan areas in the United States. The jobs were either for a gender-neutral position in fundraising, or for positions in a sports environment, a situation that again prompted more male applicants. One ad said that that the job paid $17.60 and that the salary was negotiable. The other noted that the job paid a flat $17.60.[4]

We received interest from 2,422 people. What happened?

First, we discovered that when there was no explicit statement that wages were negotiable—the ambiguous case—men were much more likely to negotiate for a higher wage than women. However, when we explicitly mentioned the possibility that wages were negotiable, this difference disappeared, and even tended to reverse—in this case, women bargained slightly more than men.

In other words, when employers say that salaries are negotiable, women step up to the negotiating plate. But when employers don't say this, and the rules determining wage are left ambiguous, men are more likely to negotiate for higher salaries.

And who applies for these positions? We found that by merely adding the information that the wage was "negotiable," the gender gap in job applications shrank by approximately 45 percent. This was true even for so-called masculine jobs (our sports ad), where one would expect more applicants to be men.

These results show that women avoid job postings that are not explicit about the rules of the game, whereas men embrace such postings. Clearly, if they want a healthy applicant pool of both men and women, prospective employers should be explicit in the details of the job and the wage/benefit offering. We turn to further ideas in this spirit now.

What Employers Can Do

While our "salary negotiable" experiment had to do with responses to job descriptions, it didn't involve face time between job seekers and employers. Nevertheless, it's important to realize that when job descriptions are vague about whether salaries are negotiable or not, women should still "go for it."

Women shouldn't simply accept the first offer that's on the table; they should counteroffer, and not be afraid to simply say, "I want more money," without explaining why. That's what men do, after all.[5]

Also, hiring managers should realize that many women have been acculturated to be risk-averse, which can pull them off the corporate ladder. All too often, women fail to ask for raises, or take on new projects—not because they lack talent, but because their cultural worldview has taught them that being assertive is not "lady-like." Companies need to think about ways to encourage women to fight for the top corporate spots. One example to follow is the consulting firm Deloitte, which tries to ensure that female employees get considered for top assignments, and where at least 23 percent of senior management personnel are female.[6] Firms like Deloitte will soon find themselves better off for doing so, because they will be able to uncover the true top talent in their organization, a move that will positively affect their bottom line.

Additionally, talent recruiters need to get on board. Instead of truly understanding what a candidate does and doesn't bring to the table, recruiters typically rely on their intuition. Sometimes companies hire people because they feel the applicant would "fit" in a job without realizing that they may be biased in favor of men.

Companies that are aware of such biases can include processes that work against this tendency. For example, at Campbell Soup Company (where a woman, Denise Morrison, is CEO), gender diversity is part and parcel of the company's selling proposition because most of the people who buy its products are women. For that reason, the firm made a conscious decision to make sure that its leadership reflected people who looked like their customers.

Companies that understand why women react less to competitive incentives can use this information to their benefit, too. For example, the no-haggling Khasi market reminded us of a different market—auto dealerships in the United States. Many women hate the back-and-forth of "let me check with my manager" hassles that accompany a visit to buy a car. To address this, companies like Honda have tried to follow an idea first put forward by General Motors' Saturn division, making no-haggle pricing part of its sales pitch. Though the Saturn division is gone, during its time its cars became very popular with women, who amounted to 63 percent of Saturn owners.

Policy Makers, Educators, and Parents

Policy makers, too, can do something to close the gender gap. If you are a policy maker, don't apply bandages to old injuries when what we need is early, corrective surgery. For example, we are not sure Title IX, designed to level the playing field for female athletes, is the way to correct imbalances. Rather, ask yourself, "If we are going to create a more equitable society, what is the right point for intervention?" Given that differences in competitiveness spring partly from cultural influences, our investment in gender equality would probably be better spent on early childhood education and socialization than on making sure women's basketball teams receive the same funding as men's.

And if you are a parent, our studies have implications for the way you raise your kids. We are now convinced that investing in the self-confidence of our own girls is a lot like investing in retirement. Exposing our daughters to more competitive environments as they grow up, and especially early on, is vital. Such exposure is particularly important around the age of puberty.

When children are in school, gender biases can manifest themselves even with the most diligent parenting. Our work has shown that gender biases run deep and begin at an early age.[7] Educators and parents should raise their level of awareness of sex-typing with very young children, and take measures to combat it. Don't be shy in encouraging kids, and in particular girls, to be competitive. Parents, teachers, and anyone who works with kids should really come to understand that socialization, and not only biology, determines competitive outcomes. There is nothing preordained about being good at math, playing with pink dolls or black trucks, competing in school or in sports, or anything else. Change the way children are socialized to react to incentives, and you change their future.

One silver bullet that has been proposed to completely change the face of socializing boys and girls is a return to single-sex schools. It might seem odd to return to our puritanical roots in an effort to encourage female competitiveness, but on an intuitive level, the idea does make sense. The research shows that boys, after all, still receive more attention from their teachers than girls do.

Finally, it's important to note that although the ability to compete effectively is important, it's hardly the key to happiness. Peace isn't found in what we own or in our titles, but in the life we live as citizens, parents, and neighbors. It is our personal hope, above all, that our girls (and everyone) learn this lesson.

In the next two chapters, we will expand the discussion of inequity to something much broader—education in general—and discover that when incentives are properly applied, they can help to close the gap between rich and poor students.

How Can Sad Silver Medalists and Happy Bronze Medalists Help Us Close the Achievement Gap?

Public Education: The $627 Billion Problem

So far, we've learned the importance of understanding why people behave as they do. We've learned that incentives are tricky and that they can backfire if we do not understand people's motivations. We have also learned that women will respond every bit as strongly to competitive incentives as men do, provided their surroundings do not dictate that they should do otherwise.

In this chapter and the one that follows, we show how field experiments can further our understanding of one of society's most difficult problems—educating kids. The United States alone spends over $600 billion annually on public elementary and secondary education. With 54.7 million students, that's an average spending of $11,467 per student, with less than spectacular results.

By turning our schools into laboratories of innovation, we can reverse the decades-long decline of our education system. In this way, we learn alongside our children: we learn what works and why, and kids master the tools they need to succeed in life. We show through the lens of field experiments how schools can be used to educate our kids effectively and at the same time serve as a useful learning venue for adults who care about education.

On one early fall afternoon, our research assistant Joe Seidel visited Wentworth Elementary School on Chicago's South Side. Joe was checking in with the school's administrators on a project we were running. As he walked down a stairwell, Joe heard a bang. He thought it sounded like someone had dropped a stack of books, but then the sound repeated several times. He stopped and looked at the face of a teacher in the stairwell. Her eyes had grown wide and her face was blank. Joe had never heard gunshots before, but she clearly had.

A moment later, a voice over the PA system announced the school would be going into lockdown. Over the next hour, police gathered outside, questioning witnesses, while inside the schoolrooms, teachers carried on as usual. Shooting or no shooting, they still had to go over the antebellum period, pre-algebra, and paragraph structures. Could the students possibly pay attention under such circumstances?

For too many students in low-income areas of the United States, getting a decent public education is more a matter of luck than anything else. This is not only tragic but also horribly ironic, given the fact that America is one of the most prosperous countries in the world. Despite the blows delivered by the 2008 financial crisis and subsequent recession, the United States still ranks near the top in general economic measures—life expectancy, income, the quality of medical care, and the number of technologies that make people's routine tasks easier and more fun.

It's no coincidence that this historic prosperity has come hand-in-hand with unprecedented achievements in education. When Thomas Jefferson advocated a public education system at the nation's birth, the goal was for all Americans to receive a quality high school education. By the time the public education system began to take shape in the last half of the nineteenth century, US policy makers had made a winning bet on improving the country's level of education. For decades, American primary schools were as impressive as its colleges and universities. In fact, the latter remain the envy of the world, as today thousands of non-Americans arrive at their gates to earn bachelor's, master's, and Ph.D. degrees.

Over the past several decades, however, the United States has developed two educational systems for precollege students: one for the haves, and one for the have-nots. Students whose parents can afford to send them to a generously endowed high school receive a well-rounded education (the haves); those who aren't so fortunate often attend schools where shootings occur, and where half the students fail to graduate (the have-nots). Dropout rates for low-income Americans hover four to five times higher than for students from high-income families. For example, in 2008, 2 percent of high-income students dropped out, compared to 9 percent of low-income students. And dropout rates for inner-city schools often exceed 50 percent.

American taxpayers continue to pour massive resources into the public education system. The country ranks fifth in the world in per pupil spending. Despite this level of investment, the primary system has soured for many children. The average ninth grader in Chicago or New York City Public Schools reads about as well as the average third or fourth grader in better endowed school systems.

Student reading, math, and science scores in the United States have fallen below the top ten in the world. In fact, when it comes to teaching basic grammar and high school math, the United States is considered mediocre at best. The system has gotten so bad that American students' high school graduation rates have slipped close to those of Mexico and Turkey, countries that spend far less to educate their youth.

Something is obviously very wrong with urban education in America. Many efforts to correct the problem through policy—from the 1954 Supreme Court *Brown vs. Board of Education* ruling to the No Child Left Behind legislation of 2001—have only managed to nibble away at the problem. What policy ideas are even left to try? And can money be redirected to reshape the incentives in the system to lead to better outcomes?

What Works in Education?

We began wrestling with these questions when Ron Huberman, then in his early years serving as the CEO of Chicago Public Schools (and about whom you will read more in Chapter 8) invited us to lunch. As we talked about ideas for curbing youth violence and teen pregnancy in the city, he told us the federal government was considering sending him millions of dollars to improve Chicago's schools. Then he asked a simple question: "If I receive that money, what should I do with it?"

We did not have an answer. Sure, as parents of kids in the public education system ourselves, we could generally recommend spending all that money to increase training and pay for teachers. Maybe some money could go toward an after-school program here or there. Perhaps some could go toward hiring extra tutors and mentors. Some of these options had been tried, and there was evidence to show that some of them worked to improve student outcomes.

But what Huberman was after was a deeper, more holistic solution—one based on solid data that addressed the enormity of the challenges the Chicago Public Schools faced. He wanted to be sure that if he received the money from the federal government, he could uphold his promise to the city to spend it wisely. He wanted to be sure to be able to pin important observable effects to actual policies.

This was music to our ears. We reminded Huberman of how an experiment by Louis Pasteur proved the value of vaccinations. In 1882, Pasteur designated half of a group of fifty sheep as controls and vaccinated the other half. All animals then received a lethal dose of anthrax. Two days after inoculation, all of the twenty-five control sheep were dead, and all of the vaccinated sheep were alive and well, proving Pasteur's theory. Although what Huberman had in mind was less dramatic, he easily recognized that his job was to "inoculate" inner-city kids against the deprivations of violence, ignorance, and poverty.

When studying education, economists begin by thinking about how different "inputs," or influencing factors, combine to make certain "outputs," or results (the jargon term for this is the "education production function"). For example, what inputs are necessary to achieve the desired output of good grades? First, we can think about the various actors involved. The effort of the student herself (one input) is obviously a critical component of the educational process, but the efforts of teachers, school administrators, and parents (other inputs) are also crucial. We also like to think about education by asking questions: *How does the combination of effort on the part of the student, the teacher, and the parent result in better student outcomes such as higher grades? What combination of inputs results in higher test scores, higher graduation rates, and good jobs? And when is increasing student, parent, and teacher effort most effective—during the pre-K years, elementary school, or high school?*

You might think that by now the people who study education would have figured out the answer to these questions. After all, arguments about education have been going on since Aristotle, and America has been formally publicly educating its children for more than one hundred years. Yet the truth is that we have not systematically used field experiments in education to figure out what really works, how well it works, and why it works. In short, we have failed to use the thousands of school districts across the United States as laboratories to create an educational policy that relies on science rather than guesswork and anecdote.

The Microcosm

America is peppered with once prosperous manufacturing towns that have fallen victim to offshoring, unemployment, and, too often, despair. Driving through such towns, you will often see rusted water towers and shuttered factories just down the road from small houses with overgrown gardens and ill-repaired broken windows. Across the railroad tracks, you'll see boarded-up stores and fore-closed homes covered with graffiti. You'll turn off the main road and see two middle-aged men sitting on milk crates, passing the day with the help of whatever is hidden in the brown bags in each of their hands. You can't help but think that in better times, they might have been earning a decent living at good jobs, and maybe bringing roses home to their wives.

Chicago Heights, with a population over 30,000, is a town with neighborhoods like this, and as such, it is a microcosm of the toughest educational problems in the United States. A community located thirty miles south of Chicago, it has an average per capita income well below the poverty line. If you are a child in such a community, chances are you often go to bed hungry and you and your parent or parents—or foster parent, as the case may be—live with an incessant, gnawing, white noise of unpaid-bill stress, with all its attendant furies.

The businessman-turned-superintendent of Chicago Heights District 170, Tom Amadio, manages a system where, he notes, 50 percent of the students are Hispanic and 40 percent are African American. More than 90 percent come from poor families on food stamps; many come from foster homes; and most receive free or reduced-fee lunch. As is the case in other urban schools, roughly 50 percent of the high school students drop out before graduation, many between the ninth and tenth grades.

Amadio is a passionate, straight-talking guy with good business instincts. He may be the only school superintendent in the country who, in a previous life, was a stock trader making a good living. Unlike stereotypical Wall Street traders, though, Amadio cares deeply about the plight of the underprivileged. He rages at the kinds of people who view children from such settings as guaranteed to fail. "These are kids that people assume can't achieve and won't achieve," he says. "You know what I'd like to say to people who want to keep things as they are? 'Stick it up your ass.' Give me the same resources that some of the wealthy districts have. Give my kids a chance to be on par."

When he took over in 2006, Amadio told the school board in no uncertain terms that something radical had to be done in their district to close the achievement gap between poor, inner-city kids and those from wealthier districts. "I told them, 'Listen, our test scores need help,'" he says. "'We need to do something drastic. This is America. Our kids don't have to drop out and grow up to be ditchdiggers. We have our obstacles, but the status quo is unacceptable.'"

Amadio's pleas did not fall on deaf ears. A Chicago Heights orthopedic surgeon, Dr. William Payne of St. James Hospital, felt motivated to help. Dr. Payne has a deep sense of community pride.

"I'd see high school kids in my office, and I'd ask them about their dreams and aspirations," he says. "One student's father worked three jobs to support his family and save up enough money for his son to go to college. The son had decent grades, but his dad still didn't have the means to send him to a good school, so the kid was stuck with a junior college that focuses on remedial education. He was too smart for that, but he didn't have a choice because his dad didn't really know how to go about procuring financial aid or navigating the educational system. Then I started reading about the high dropout rate in our city and wondered what could be done differently."

Dr. Payne reached out to us in the fall of 2007, asking us to help the kids in Chicago Heights; specifically, he wanted to hear our ideas for keeping students in school. He introduced us to some important decision makers in the community and began to forge partnerships with school administration. We began with a singular goal: to improve the graduation rate among Chicago Heights high school students.

Winning the Lottery

One of the reasons we find high dropout rates so puzzling is that dropping out is like throwing away a winning lottery ticket: the data tell us that for each year of school that a student misses, his or her earning power drops by roughly 12 percent. Indeed, the average annual income for a high school dropout in 2009 was $19,540, compared to $27,380 for a high school graduate.[1] Multiply that number by twenty years, and you see an earnings differential of $156,800. That's a real winning lottery ticket—enough to buy a house outright in many parts of the country.

Of course, the decision is a little more complicated than choosing between dropping out and earning enough money to buy a house, in part because the financial reward of an education isn't realized until years later. The gratification of all that hard work is long-delayed. Most of us don't respond well to delayed gratification; we are much more interested in immediate rewards. This is why we procrastinate, fail to save as much money as we should for retirement, eat too much, and exercise too little.

Children have this tendency in spades. Remember when you got sick as a kid, and your parents had to beg and plead with you to swallow tablespoons full of horrible-tasting medicine? You could not really appreciate the future benefit of swallowing the stuff, but you knew well the immediate cost of putting it in your mouth. That's why pharmaceutical companies work hard to make kids' medicine palatable. (Think of bubblegum-flavored children's Tylenol.)

The inability to think about the benefits of future rewards gets worse as children move through adolescence. Teenagers tend to have more of this tendency than others, perhaps because of the immature wiring of their brains.[2] Put differently, teenagers may just be junkies when it comes to immediate gratification. They have no conception of the value of investing in their future. From that perspective, dropping out sometimes seems like a pretty good choice.

Compounding the issue is the fact that many parents do not appreciate the value of teaching their kids noncognitive skills— the importance of investing in their futures, of being patient and trustworthy, and of working well with others. These skills prove invaluable later in life, but most parents underestimate them.

So imagine you are a poor, pimply, hormone-addled teenager whose brain is still under construction. You are living in an inner-city area such as Chicago Heights, walking from sensation to sensation. All you are thinking about is immediate satisfaction: your life in the distant, after-high-school-graduation era is as real to you as the possibility of living on Mars. You want to satisfy your urges *now*.

Is there any way to make a connection between your current state of mind and future rewards?

Do Bribes Work?

Urail King was a fourteen-year-old, black ninth grader at Bloom Trail High School in Chicago Heights. His mom, Theresa, hadn't graduated from high school. Urail was energetic, extroverted, and smart, but school wasn't really his thing, either. Urail's grades hovered between Ds and Cs. He didn't overtly cheat, but he cut corners: instead of reading *To Kill a Mockingbird* cover to cover, he tried to figure out the answers on a quiz by scanning the pages. Urail was right on the borderline. He could choose to make an effort to succeed in school, or he could follow a more negative trajectory.

Another ninth-grade student, Kevin Muncy, was a white kid with short, dark hair and a rhinestone stud in his ear. He loved to skateboard, play video games, and invent things. He was smart and innovative: he impressed girls with a self-made tattoo he'd created with a gadget he'd invented combining an electric toothbrush and a chopped-off guitar string. His mom worked in the bakery section of a grocery store. Kevin preferred to hang out with his friends rather than worry about school. In his classes, he fiddled with a small gaming device under his desk and tried to find fellow students who could help him cheat. Kevin thought he'd like to graduate from high school, but his failing grades weren't going to get him very far. If he didn't graduate, he figured he'd sign up for the military and get his GED while enlisted.

What kinds of incentives would it take to get these two under-achievers to succeed in school? Would paying Urail and Kevin, or their parents, to perform make sense? Before rejecting this idea out of hand, let's consider how we usually get people to do what we want them to do. To get people to recycle more or to buy environmentally friendly cars, we reward them with financial incentives. Could paying students to perform better work, too?

When we took our idea about paying students for performance to the school board of Chicago Heights, it was met with something close to scorn. After all, most grown-ups agree that students should learn for the sake of learning. But the brutal fact is this: millions of kids in public schools just do not see it that way. As we pointed out to the school board, kids should clean up their rooms, but they don't. They should brush their teeth and always obey their parents, but they don't. They should eat fruit instead of cookies, but they don't. And they should like to learn, but often, they don't.

The realism of our argument hit home when a school board member cited research showing that extrinsic incentives, like money, can crowd out intrinsic incentives like enjoying learning and doing well in school. (Sound familiar? He was basically citing some of the psychology and economics research, including our own, we discussed in Chapter 1.) We agreed on the importance of intrinsic incentives and with the spirit of those studies, but we swiftly replied that when there is nothing to crowd out, money talks. We were met with a sigh from the board members who, after all, knew that their district was in dire straits. They grudgingly admitted that they were willing to try anything that stood half a chance of succeeding.

Because monetary incentives in education are so controversial, it's not yet fully known how best to direct them.[3] Our first idea was to shift the incentives to the near term: rather than paying students at the end of the semester or year for good performance, we would pay them closer to the moment of achievement, thus satisfying their desire for immediate gratification. (As we said above, behavioral economists have shown that many people respond much more dramatically to incentives paid earlier rather than later.)

Our second behaviorally based idea was to use a lottery to pay the students. A lottery is a terrific behavioral testing tool, because human beings tend to overweigh low-probability events. For example, the chance of winning a state Powerball lottery is typically lower than one in a million, but people love to play anyway, in part because they believe the odds are better than they really are. (In reality, you're more likely to be struck by lightning than to win a Powerball lottery in most states.) We thought that if we could offer rewards through a lottery, where the prize was large but the chances of winning were small, the rewards would seem more relevant; students might overweigh their chances of winning the lottery, inducing them to try harder.

The final idea was an obvious, whack-on-the-side-of-the-head one that stems from trying to figure out what goes into the education "production function": use incentives to get parents involved, and see how their involvement affects their kids' performance. We figured that paying parents would not only work, but that doing so would tell us more about the most effective ways to increase achievement. Getting parents more involved in helping their children study might help siblings, too. After all, once parents start working with one child, it's only fair to do the same with the others.

We just had one problem, and it was a big one. Pulling off a field experiment to test these ideas would not be easy. And, it would cost large sums of money that we simply didn't have.

The Griffin Gift

Right around this time—in the spring of 2008—we received a serendipitous phone call from a couple of philanthropists, Kenneth and

Anne Griffin. Kenneth Griffin is the founder of Citadel, one of the world's largest hedge funds, and he and his wife were interested in our research. They were looking for help in setting up a charitable foundation, and wondered whether we could possibly meet with them to discuss our work. We had no idea the call would change our lives.

We drove to the Citadel building in downtown Chicago, a gigantic, steel-and-glass tower, with 1.4 million square feet of office space, set right in the economic center of the city. After passing through the marble-walled lobby, we entered the elevator and pressed the button for the thirty-seventh floor. Our ears popped, and we felt a bit nervous. The elevator hushed open, and a nice receptionist ushered us into a tastefully decorated conference room. She offered us coffee, and we waited.

When the Griffins entered the room, our first take was that they looked like one of those gorgeous couples whose nuptial photos you find gracing the pages of the *New York Times*' Sunday Styles section. Kenneth, good-looking and incisive, is a brilliant entrepreneurial type; a product of public schools, he learned all about trading within the confines of his college dorm room. Anne, a French native who speaks five languages, is, like her husband, also a product of a public school system, and her mother was a teacher.

We had little idea what we had gotten ourselves into. Most well-intended, wealthy donors we knew wrote a big check for research and, with a flourish of the pen, said something like "You can talk about your results at my next dinner party." But the Griffins were different.

We launched into some theories of behavioral economics, summarized a bit of our research, and walked through our ideas about what kinds of incentives might work with the Chicago Heights school kids. As we talked, their eyes lit up.

Even though a few hours of the Griffins' time is probably worth tens of thousands of dollars, they spent a long time meticulously working through our experimental ideas, surprising us with their knowledge and insight. "Why do you think people overweigh small probabilities?" they asked us. "Why do you think so many young people don't think graduating matters?" Both Kenneth and Anne grilled us and sharpened our ideas with thoughts of their own. Like us, they wanted whatever interventions we came up with to be scalable, firmly grounded in theory, and cost-effective.

The Griffins soon became our full research partners. They passionately believe in bettering America's public education system, understanding that doing so is the only way to improve people's lives and the economy in general. They wanted to get up to their elbows in interventions that could help urban kids overcome the education gap and raise American educational standards in general.

By the time we left the room, we were convinced of one thing: had they gone the academic route, both Ken and Anne would have been our research equals and then some. We departed with a solid experimental design on our hands, and within twenty-four hours, the Griffins gave us the initial $400,000 we needed to run the experiment.

Before we entered the room that day, Ken and Anne knew how they wanted to change the world; we were fortunate enough to show up in the right place at the right time. Suddenly we understood how Columbus must have felt when Queen Isabella gave him the resources to find the New World. We not only found donors, but two new friends; indeed, our new colleagues would help us tackle one of the most important problems facing America today.

The Voyage to Public Schools

One day, a kind, slim redhead with the gentle demeanor of a good high school counselor called Kevin Muncy into her office. Her name was Sally Sadoff, and at the time she was one of our graduate students administering our experiment.[4] When Kevin came in, Sally smiled broadly at him. "How's it been, starting in a new school?"

"I like it. It's really easy."

"The classes are really easy? Let's see what your report card says." She scanned Kevin's awful grades. "So Kevin," Sally asked kindly, "what do you need to improve on?"

"Everything."

"So you probably want to know what you can get if you meet the new monthly achievement standards—no unexcused absences, no daylong suspensions, and grades of C or higher in all your classes. Right?" She pulled out a folder and handed it to him.

Kevin opened the folder. "Fifty bucks?"

Sally smiled. "And you get $50 every month as long as you keep your grades up!"

"I think a lot of people will start doing their homework then."

"But what about you?"

Kevin began to dream a little. "What could I do with $50 a month? I could pay for my skateboards. Get sponsors and clothes and stuff until I graduate." On hearing about this incentive, Kevin's mom doubled it: if he raised his grades to the monthly standards, he could earn $100 a month.

But there were more incentives, and Sally made a big deal of them. In fact, we pulled out all the stops we could think of. At the end of each month during the eight-month program, the kids all lined up in the school cafeteria for free pizza and the big payout. Each one was called up to a table where Sally and the other researchers looked over their grades and talked with them. If they (or their parents, depending on the experimental treatment) won the cash payout, they walked away grinning—and not just because of the cash.

Even more fun was the big, suspenseful bingo-ball-style lottery. Each month, we drew ten names. If a student who met the standards criteria won, he or she (or their parents, depending on the treatment) would take home the grand prize: $500 in cash (as well as a giant Ed McMahon–style pseudocheck) plus a ride home in a white, chauffeur-driven Hummer stretch limo, complete with comfy leather seats, tiny blue and green interior lights, TV consoles, ice compartments, and all the other trimmings. When Urail King saw the limo, he went wild. "Oh my G-o-d!" he shouted. "This is awesome! Oh yes, yes, you are getting straight As from me! Take me home, Jenkins!"[5]

If the kids didn't meet the monthly standards, Sally and the other researchers would make suggestions for catching up. The researchers even gave the students reminder calls during the month to ask them how they were doing in their classes. And, of course, the parents encouraged the kids and worked with them, too. After all, who would not want their kid to win the grand prize?

So how did the students and their parents respond to all these expensive incentives? Given the wiring of teenage brains ("I want what I want *now*"), was it too much to ask the students to wait a month to receive their rewards?

Our overall results showed interesting gains.[6] We estimated that the program helped about 50 borderline students out of the 400 in the experimental group to meet the ninth-grade achievement standards. Among the students who were on the brink of failing, we figured the program had increased achievement by about 40 percent. Happily, these students continued to outperform their un-incentivized peers after the program ended in their sophomore year. In fact, our estimates suggested that about forty kids who would otherwise have dropped out would receive their diplomas because of our program. (We also found that students' performance increased slightly more if their parents, rather than they, received the reward.)

Given that every additional year of secondary schooling increases lifetime earnings by 12 percent, offering such students an incentive during their freshman year seemed to be a clear, cost-effective intervention. If you also count the fact that the kids spent their time in school, rather than dropping out and hanging around the streets, the program was that much more successful. We had found a way to reach a slice of the kids on the brink—but only a slice.

Reframing Achievement

Tom Amadio was impressed with these results, but he pressed a question on a different front, beyond keeping kids in school: *Could we increase the test scores of his students?* After all, test scores are important door-openers, and are tied to future outcomes like years of education and high-paying jobs. Test scores also determine how much money a school district receives from city and state governments. Unfortunately, at the present time, minority students just cannot seem to catch their white counterparts when it comes to test scores. The racial achievement test gap remains both considerable and stubborn, and many urban schools fail at their mission to close it.

To answer Amadio's challenge, we decided to run another set of field experiments that involved over 7,000 students in a variety of elementary and high school settings in Chicago and Chicago Heights. These tests took place in the schools' computer labs, where students took a standardized test three times a year.[7]

As an introduction to our experimental premise, perhaps you remember the images of two young girls who were gymnasts at the 2008 Summer Olympics. Both were winners. As the girls stood on the podium, each of them was overcome with intense emotion. And no wonder: they had both trained for years for this moment, sacrificing normal lives as teenagers to reach the very apex of gymnastic performance. The photos were taken after they received their respective medals. One was decorated with the silver medal, the other with the bronze. When their photos were published in the press, one was beaming, the other appeared to be holding back tears.

Which do you think won the silver and which the bronze?

We all know that silver is better than bronze, but context is everything. The silver medalist who missed out on the gold was devastated, and her face looked as if she were sucking on a sour lemon. But the bronze medalist who just barely made the podium was clearly ecstatic.[8]

Over the past forty years two psychologists—Daniel Kahneman and Amos Tversky—have revolutionized our understanding of the importance of human emotions like sensitivity to context in everyday choices we make. One of the things these two "fathers" of behavioral economics have shown is that the way humans understand the world has to do with the way we interpret (or "frame") phenomena. Depending on how you frame something when you speak, you influence someone's behavior in various ways. A parent might say to a child, "If you don't eat those peas, you won't grow up big and strong." (That's what behaviorists call "loss framing"—it frames a statement as a loss or punishment.) Alternatively, the parent could phrase the same thing in a more positive light and say, "If you eat your peas, you will grow up big and strong." (That's called "gain framing"—it frames the statement as a benefit or reward.)

———

Imagine you are a thirteen-year-old boy coming into the computer lab to take a standardized test. It's a nice fall day, and you are restless, a little hungry, and all you can think about is that last round of your favorite video game and the pretty girl sitting at the desk behind you. You wish you were anywhere but stuck in this stupid lab to take another stupid test.

In walks the school's assessment coordinator, Mr. Belville, who asks for everyone's attention. (Mr. Belville also happens to be the school's reading coordinator and head of the school's technology department; he is the sort of overqualified and overdedicated administrator that single-handedly makes a school run.) The process of just getting the students to stop talking takes a minute, but finally they quiet down.

"Today," Mr. Belville announces, "you're going to take the next level of the standardized tests that you took back in the spring. But this time we're going to be doing something different. If you do better on today's test than you did the last time you took it, you'll receive a reward of $20."

Your eyebrows shoot up. So do everyone else's. "Awesome!" someone yells. Suddenly everyone starts chattering at once. Mr. Belville immediately quiets the room.

"Now, before we begin the test, I'm going to be handing each of you a $20 bill," he continues. "I want each of you to fill out this receipt confirming you've received the money. On the receipt sheets, I want you to write a little bit about what you plan to do with the cash. You will keep the money in front of you on your desk while you take the test. Remember, you will get to keep the $20 if you improve on the test. But if you don't improve you will lose the $20." He passes around the receipt forms and the $20.

You dutifully fill out the form and think about what you want to do with the $20, which you would like to put toward a new skateboard. You write down your dream on the form, and then place the $20 to the right of the keyboard, just above the mouse. You smile as you look at it. "My wheels," you think. You imagine walking into the skateboard store and plunking down your money.

Mr. Belville returns to the front of the room, interrupting your daydream. "We will begin the test in two minutes. Please sign in on the computer."

You sign in, and the clock advances. You watch the second hand. You can't wait to start.

"Ready? Begin!"

Now, when you've taken these tests in the past, you usually whiz through them because you really don't care about them—you think they are pretty pointless and you leave many questions blank. But this time, with your $20 sitting in front of you, you take your time. Some questions stump you initially, but instead of guessing and moving on, you start to really think about what the best answer might be.

At the end of an hour, Mr. Belville announces that the test session is over. You're the last student still working on the exam. You answer the last question and hit "submit." Almost immediately, your score shows up on the teacher's computer screen. Once the whole class finishes up you can see how well you did compared to last spring's test.

So how did you do?

In this field experiment, we actually divided the schoolkids into one of five groups. As described above, kids in one group received a $20 bill and were told if they did not improve on their previous test score, we would take the money away. This is what we described above as the "loss" group: the kids had the $20, and stood to lose it by not achieving on the test.

Students in the comparison, "gain-framing" group were told that if they improved on their previous test scores we would give them $20 immediately after the test, but they did not receive the $20 beforehand. Because they didn't have the $20 directly in front of them, they stood to gain.

Students in a third group were told that if they improved on their previous test score, we would give each of them $20, but not until a month after the test. A fourth group received a $3 trophy if their scores improved. And as is always the case in our experiments, we had a control group. This group was offered no reward, though we encouraged them to try to improve their scores.

Our incentives had a huge impact. Overall scores improved between 5 and 10 percentile points on a 100-point scale, putting the students on a more even footing with wealthier suburban kids. This was an amazing improvement. Even though the students had no idea an incentive was coming until just before the exam started, they improved remarkably. It showed that an important part of the racial achievement gap was not due to knowledge or ability, but simply to the students' motivation while taking the test.

This result highlighted the importance of understanding what motivates students: though they weren't very interested in taking the test, their scores shot up in the face of financial incentives. (Think of what might have happened had we offered these incentives and also given them time to prepare and study.) The goal of this experiment wasn't to design an incentive scheme to be used in other schools. What we were after was a diagnostic tool that could help us understand whether the score gap was due to differences in knowledge, or differences in effort on the test itself. The answer to this question could help us design relevant interventions to reduce the gap.

That said, the incentives worked differently for the different groups. We discovered that the older students, in particular, responded well to the money, whereas the younger ones liked the trophies we offered instead. Offering a second-, third-, or fourth-grade student a $3 trophy before the test improved her performance by 12 percentile points. These effects were large; indeed, *they were similar to the impact of reducing class size by one-third or considerably improving teacher quality.* This is an important point, as we discussed in Chapter 1. Incentives don't have to come in the form of money. In some situations, and for some people, a trophy (or flowers, chocolate—you name it) can go a long way.

As we expected, giving students the rewards beforehand—and threatening to take them away if their scores didn't improve—boosted scores much more than promising to give them the money later. In fact, the students who were promised to receive $20 a month later did not improve at all. Again, it seemed that framing something as "it's yours to lose" worked better than "it's yours to win, and you will win it later." To understand this, put yourself in a student's shoes. If you are offered the financial reward for improving, you score a lot higher if, before you even take the test, you are thinking about buying those new skateboard wheels. For young children and teens, the world is all about the present; our experiment helped us understand what really motivates them.

Obviously, all we had managed to do here was to convince students to try a little harder. But we were worried. What if incentives lost their effect on behavior over time? That is, we thought we could get students to try hard a few times, but we wondered if, eventually, the incentives would lose their impact on behavior. Alternatively, would kids only try when they were offered an incentive? Would they give up if a $20 bill wasn't at stake?

We often hear concerns from educators, parents, and policy makers that even while financial incentives may produce short-term improvements, children could be hurt in the long run; they might stop putting in any effort without compensation.[9] In fact, we found no evidence of one-time rewards *hurting* test scores in the future. As we expected, the one-time incentives also did not lead to lasting learning gains. The simple short-term experiment did show, however, that the children were more able than one might have previously thought, based on the standard approach to testing.

The next step was, of course, to stretch our behavioral economics interventions even further. What if students were rewarded every week for an entire semester for something like independent reading? So we launched another study that offered students in seven schools $2 (or an equivalently priced nonfinancial incentive) for every book they read over the course of a semester. We kept track of their reading by letting them log onto an online program called Accelerated Reader that has short quizzes for just about every book available to students. The quizzes aren't difficult, but it's hard to score well if you didn't read the book. We decided that if a student scored 80 percent or higher on a quiz for a book, they could receive the rewards, which we gave out each week. As in the test incentive study, we compared giving students the incentive either at the beginning of the week or at the end of the week. We found that the incentives in both cases increased reading by 37 percent, but the extra reading had no impact on test scores.

Can the Same Idea Work with Teachers?

Of course, students don't learn in a vacuum. We needed to find out whether offering incentives to teachers might work, too. After all, it's hard to run a classroom while your students are undisciplined, indifferent, scared, hungry, or absent. And it's harder still to work so hard and face the fact that many of your ninth graders are reading at a fourth-grade level, and that fewer than half of the kids you're trying so hard to teach will graduate.

One of the big criticisms of public education (and other public institutions) is the scarcity of incentive-based pay. In many private-sector companies, the amount you take home in your paycheck is based on your performance. Let's say you graduate with a B.A. in business and want to go into sales. When you get a job, you generally receive a base salary with a bonus incentive. If you perform well for a year, you may receive additional benefits or even a promotion. Other incentives are available, too: if you are part of a sales team and you, as a group, sell more than your expected quota, you get a team bonus. And if your company as a whole does well, you might receive an extra kick in the paycheck.

But if you are a public school teacher (or work for the public sector in general), few of these incentives exist. Three factors determine your pay as a teacher: your level of certification, your postgraduate degrees, and your seniority. That's it. Stick around long enough, you will be paid more, whether you are a star or a slacker.

One of the main reasons why we do not know as much as incentive programs work is because teachers unions are loathe to adopt pay-for-performance schemes. This hit home when we originally took our idea to Ron Huberman. We told him about our ideas to incentivize teachers in Chicago Public Schools. Depending on how well they did, teachers could earn up to $8,000 on top of their salaries. But the teachers unions balked. "No, absolutely not," they told us. "We could not imagine anything like this working." Even when Ron Huberman stepped in to try to persuade them to allow us to run our experiments, they refused.

But we still had Tom Amadio, the maverick in Chicago Heights, in our corner. With his persuasive help, we reached an agreement with the Chicago Heights teachers' union. Fortunately, these teachers were willing to try anything to help their students.

We offered more than 150 Chicago Heights teachers a chance to earn an extra bonus.[10] In one treatment, an individual teacher could strive for the $8,000 bonus; in another one, teachers working in teams of two split the bonus (the idea being that team teaching would allow them to share lesson plans and ideas). We also applied the same gain-versus-loss-framing, carrot-and-stick motivators that we'd used with the students in the computer labs. We wrote checks for $4,000 (the average reward) to some individual teachers before the school year started, with the stipulation that they would have to repay all or some of the money if student performance didn't improve. We also wrote checks for $4,000 each to some of the teachers who were going to work in two-person teams, with the same stipulation. (Given that the average teacher's salary in Chicago Heights is around $64,000,[11] this extra $4,000 was a substantial amount. Imagine yourself getting this extra money in September, and then having to pay it back in June. No pressure, of course.)

Our results showed that when teachers were threatened with losing the rewards they had already received, student achievement in math jumped up about 6 percentile points, and in reading, about 2 percentile points. This type of incentive seemed to work particularly well when teachers worked in teams. Overall, their students' achievement improved between 4 to 6 percentile points.

This result was nothing short of astonishing. To put it in perspective: if the low-income, minority students in Chicago Heights could repeat such percentage-point gains for each year of elementary school, it would be enough to close the entire gap between their achievement and that of wealthier white kids from the suburbs.

Closing the Loop: Incentivizing All Actors

Having figured out how to motivate parents, students, and teachers in isolation, we now wanted to discover what would happen if all three parties—parents, children, and teachers—worked simultaneously to improve student performance. Would their combined efforts lead to improvements in student outcomes such as higher test scores, higher graduation rates, and better job outcomes? Would this kind of cooperation blow their grades through the roof? One might think so, at least on an intuitive basis. But the empirical evidence has been scant.

To learn more, we ran another experiment in Chicago Heights. The test involved elementary school kids who were at risk of failing to meet state standards.[12] We worked with 23 reading and math tutors who in turn met with 581 K-8 students in small groups for 100 days. The five treatment groups included an incentive for the tutor only, an incentive for the student only, an incentive for the parents only, an incentive for both the student and the parents, and an incentive for all three—the student, the parents, and the tutor.

We assessed the students every two months, and if they met all of our achievement standards, we paid a reward of $90 each. In another setup, students, parents, and teachers shared the incentive, receiving $30 each. When we divided the reward between students and parents, they each received $45. We paid the students who met the standards immediately upon completion of their exam.

As was the case in all our other school experiments, the students were excited to participate. But because the study was only open to kids who were failing, other students were disappointed. (We heard anecdotally that some kids were thinking of intentionally doing poorly on their own tests so that they could participate. This information was troubling, but it does say something about the power of incentives to change student behavior.)

We also wanted to provide the parents with a tool for helping their children improve, so at the end of each week, tutors created a homework assignment for students to work on with their parents. After the assessments, parents attended pizza parties we held at the school. We reviewed with each of them their child's performance, paid those who qualified, and made sure they were aware the incentive program was continuing.

We found that when we divided the incentives into three smaller $30 rewards, the improvements were relatively small. Even though everyone was given an incentive to do more, the impact just was not there. However, the $90 payout to one person was quite effective. Interestingly, it didn't really matter whether we rewarded $90 to the students, the tutors, or the parents; as long as one of them was rewarded at the $90 level, the incentive worked well. While it clearly takes a team of people to educate a child, we found that a higher-stakes incentive for just one actor generates the biggest bang for the buck.

And the student results? Test scores shot up between 50 and 100 percent compared to the cases in which nobody received an incentive. If these results seem radical, it's because they are: the incentive was enough to transform the test scores of the average kid in Chicago Heights into the sorts of scores typically only seen in wealthy suburban school districts.

Our explorations into public education have taught us the power of combining field experiments with economic reasoning. We learned that kids really do respond to immediate rewards, and that the threat of taking away that reward is more powerful than paying it later, both for students and for teachers. We also learned that parent participation really helps in teaching kids not only how to read and add, but also how to appreciate noncognitive skills such as patience, and how investment now leads to higher rewards later.

On the downside, we also learned that the behavior of some kids, especially kids in high school—Kevin Muncy, for example—are harder to change. Kevin was already disengaged by the time he entered Bloom Trail High; ultimately he failed all his classes. Urail King, on the other hand, ended up doing better. Borderline kids like Urail were more easily motivated by the cash and the lottery. The improvements we saw in the high schools were promising—

dozens more kids graduated than might have otherwise—but they weren't dramatic. These high school kids just didn't appear to be as easy to motivate as we had hoped.

These insights drive home an important point: even if we offered kids like Kevin a million dollars to solve a hard math problem, he couldn't. Why? Because by the time kids are fourteen years old, they are already tilting one way or the other. They have already missed out on important investments that make it quite difficult to achieve high levels of competency in certain subject areas. They have already been deeply imprinted by their earlier experiences; parents have lost much of their influence and their supply of coercive tools. And if at that point they are only reading at a third-grade level, bringing them up to speed is awfully hard.

If you haven't already learned how to focus on a lesson, solve problems on your own, and stay out of trouble by the time you are in the ninth grade, your odds of success are low. For disengaged kids like Kevin, a more serious intervention is probably more appropriate.

Think of it this way: if we asked you to solve a second-order partial linear differential equation, and told you that we would pay you a million dollars if you solved it, could you? If you haven't been trained to solve this kind of math problem, even a million-dollar incentive will have no effect. If higher-level problem solving isn't already achieved through years of good schooling, applying incentives so late in life won't make a difference.

This does not mean that we give up on those kids; quite the opposite. There is a productive place for everyone in our vibrant world economy. But, clearly, we need to see what will happen if we intervene with younger children. Early childhood education has the chance to give everyone an open door to the highest levels of society.

To find out what we did, turn to the next chapter.

How Can Poor Kids Catch Rich Kids in Just Months?

A Voyage to Preschool

One of the longest-running programs to address systemic poverty in the United States is Head Start, serving millions of young children since it was founded in 1965 as part of President Lyndon Johnson's "war on poverty." Although the original intention of Head Start may have been laudable, the program has proven far less effective in helping disadvantaged four-year-olds get a jump on cognitive and social skills than originally hoped. Several academics have by now dissected the program and have found that it has several deficiencies, chiefly because the teachers are largely undereducated, underpaid mothers, fewer than 30 percent of whom hold bachelor's degrees.[1] Another problem is related to the fact that instead of being run by the Department of Education, Head Start is run by the Department of Housing and Human Services—an agency more involved in making up for the effects of inadequate education than in improving it. We suspect that presented with the totality of the evidence, reasonable people would question whether Head Start provides kids with significant benefits.

This is awfully disappointing, especially when you consider the cost: the price tag for keeping one child in Head Start for a year is about $22,600, whereas day care only costs $9,500. As *Time* columnist Joe Klein has noted in criticizing Head Start, "We can no longer afford to be sloppy about dispensing cash—whether it's subsidies for oil companies or Head Start—to programs that do not produce a return."[2] We could not agree more. The question is: *What would work better?*

After compiling the results of our field experiments discussed in the previous chapter we—along with our colleagues Steven Levitt and Harvard's Roland Fryer—had an honest conversation with Tom Amadio and the Griffins. While we had seen considerable improvements amongst the K-12 students that we touched, we had not hit a home run yet. By the time we reached them in ninth grade, for example, we might be able to help them graduate from high school, but it was unlikely that they would go on to become successful engineers; for that type of impact, our interventions occurred too late.

One idea is to reach children at a very young age, which could potentially give them the leg up they needed early on in the education process. The best way to do this while maintaining the integrity of the scientific process, however, was to build our own experimental schools to learn about the education process—what works, when does it work best, and why.

For academics like us, the entire notion of setting up one's own school to learn about early childhood education is like building a new research laboratory from scratch. While we concluded that this was the most appropriate way to tackle such an important problem,[3] building schools for this purpose presented a new challenge for us. The very first, and perhaps most important, challenge was to come up with resources. We quickly learned that the Chicago Heights school district was hardly getting by. It had few resources to even teach its own pre-K kids, much less expand to serve both its kids and those from the surrounding communities (which was necessary to obtain the sample sizes we required).

Once again, the Griffin Foundation revealed its generosity, this time with a whopping $10 million initiative to work with young kids and their parents. So the Griffin Early Childhood Center (GECC) was born. GECC consists of two preschools in one of the poorest areas of Chicago, and it is the beating heart of one of the largest controlled field experiments in education ever conducted.

The GECC schools are a comprehensive, long-term field experiment to learn what works and why in very young children. By controlling the curricula and everything about the learning experience, we could also conduct several small-scale complementary experiments to better understand why the effects were taking the shape that we observed. The schools would be our learning labs, where we could discover how the "education production function" works for very young children.

The GECC Schools

Imagine two state-of-the-art private preschools. The entrance of each facility is bedecked with colorful signs, trimmed lawns, and flower boxes. The interior, sunshine-yellow walls sport cheerful paintings of houses and flowers. Children's books fill the bookcases, and plastic trays and boxes overflow with toys, games, and art materials. Each school has five classrooms, five teachers, and five assistant teachers—one teacher for every seven or so students.

But this is where the similarities stop. When you dig beneath the surface, you see immediate and radical differences. In one of the two GECC schools, the so-called Tools of the Mind curriculum is based on social skills and structured play. Here preschool children learn to defer gratification. (Chances are that if you can wait for a reward, you will become more focused on the task and perform better overall.) The kids in this school play different roles as they work and stroll through the school "town." In the "bakery" section, a little girl is pretending to sell cupcakes to a little boy who has chosen to be a customer. Another little boy pretends to bake pies and cakes on the play stove. At the "school," one child is a teacher and others are students. At the "doctor's office," a young nurse and doctor visit with another little patient. Later, the children practice playing games in which they see who can stand on one foot like a ballerina, or act like a quiet guard.

In this way, the children develop the noncognitive skills that are so important to successful functioning—learning to socialize, to be patient, to make decisions and follow directions, and to listen. How would learning these skills early on affect their futures? The study will follow them into adulthood to find out.

Nearby, in the other preschool—a partitioned-off area of a larger school—children and their parents enter a similarly colorful, warm atmosphere, but the curriculum is more traditional and academic. In this school, students work on learning their numbers and letters à la *Sesame Street*, and are introduced to basic reading. Small groups of children huddle around the table with their teacher and help each other identify shapes and colors on a big, colorful poster. Several children read to each other in the cozy reading corner, assisted by the teacher, who walks around and helps them. The theme one week comes from children's author Eric Carle, and children's colorful drawings of their own renditions of *The Very Hungry Caterpillar* line the walls.

The students in this particular arm of the experiment proceed through a curriculum called Literacy Express. The study promises to follow the children in both curricula on their paths through adulthood to see whether the preschool program makes a difference in their lives.

Then there is what we call the Parent Academy. In this arrangement, parents attend group meetings twice a month and learn one of the two curricula taught in the preschool. They also receive financial incentives (up to $7,000 per year) based on their attendance and participation, as well as their child's developmental progress. These financial incentives are either short-term or long-term. For example, parents in the "cash" treatment receive their money when the results of the regular assessments come in. Parents in the "college" treatment receive an injection to the child's college account: if their child attends college, they can use their earnings toward tuition and fees. If the child skips college, they forfeit the money. We thought the longer-term incentive would spur parents not only to help their little ones now, but also to encourage them later on as the kids got older.

This ongoing experiment allowed us to test whether we can prompt behavioral change among parents and children. In too many cases, public education is a laissez-faire babysitter. Too many parents send their children off for the day, go to work, come home exhausted, microwave dinner, and eat it with the kids in front of the television. Effectively, many parents leave the navigation of the difficult waters of learning to teachers and the kids' own devices. It's as if they see their job as parents and the job of the schools as separate, like church and state.

We believe they should not be separate. But are we right? What difference would it make in children's lives if education were really a joint process between teachers, parents, and students? To study this question, we needed to include parents and persuade them to take a more active role in their kids' progress.

High Stakes

In the spring of 2010, we set out to accomplish several tasks in an extremely tight timeframe. We had to hire staff and teachers in the same manner in which an urban district would find personnel;

outfit the two preschools with the appropriate equipment, toys, and teaching materials; figure out ways to attract parents and students to the GECC program; and begin our field experiment. Tom Amadio helped us locate the perfect locations, principals, and faculty, and we "auditioned" candidates by watching them teach.

To attract students, we placed bilingual ads in Chicago Heights newspapers, hung flyers in grocery stores, sent out mass mailings, canvassed at student-teacher conferences, and put brochures in churches. In the summer of 2010, more than five hundred parents showed up to the initial meeting, and each received a lottery number. A lucky number would land the child in one of our programs (and possibly determine the trajectory of a child's future), and an unlucky one would find the child in the control group, receiving nothing from our program except for invitations to a few holiday parties.

At the opening of the meeting, we told the assembled parents: "We are tired of sitting around watching our kids get left behind. The Griffin Early Childhood Center is all about receiving a free preschool education that could change your child's life and your own. This is a huge opportunity for you and your children. Thanks very much for attending the lottery tonight. Good luck!"

As the bingo-ball cage began rolling, the parents stared at it anxiously.

"Number 52! Parent Academy!"

"We won!" two voices came from the back. Lolitha and Dwayne McKinney ran with their three boys to the front of the room to sign up their youngest son Gabriel, who was four years old. He was one of 120 lucky winners in the Parent Academy, and they were delighted.

Dwayne and Lolitha both came from rough Chicago neighbor-hoods. Lolitha was lucky enough to gain access to a strict Catholic school education, though Dwayne, like so many young black men, had few resources. He was raised by his working mother and grand-mother in the rough neighborhood of Roseland, where he always felt like he might be a shooting victim. "I couldn't go outside and play until I was ten or eleven," he recalls. He never wanted much out of school; he just wanted to survive.

Today, Dwayne and Lolitha are passionately dedicated to im-proving the lives of their children. In exchange for attending the Parent Academy every other Saturday to discuss parenting tech-niques and learn to teach their children at home, they could earn up to $7,000 per year, depending on how well Gabriel did on his homework, attendance, and performance assessments. "We couldn't have given it a shot unless there were the financial incentives," says Dwayne. "The homework incentive motivated us a lot." Many other parents in the above-mentioned college treatment also felt like they'd won the lottery.

The bingo-ball cage spun again, out dropped number 20, one of the all-day preschools.

"We hit the jackpot!" yelled Tamara, the twenty-year-old single parent of five-year-old Reggie. Tamara valued education, but be-cause she became pregnant and dropped out of high school at the age of fifteen, her own dreams had been derailed. Reggie would join 149 other children in the preschool programs.

A third set of lottery numbers fell into the control group. These parents were disappointed. We tried to console them by saying that it was the luck of the draw, and that they would have another chance the following year. Still, they felt like they had missed out. Indeed, deep inside we believed that they had missed out as well. But we didn't have the resources to intervene in every child's life with our experiment.

The Dangers of Doing Field Experiments

What is precious to one parent is less precious to another, of course. If you are focused on sheer survival, worrying about your child's education will be lower on the list. Getting Gabriel signed up for school was easy because his parents were so enthusiastic and committed. But despite all the enthusiasm we had managed to raise and the disappointments of many parents who missed out, getting all the lottery winners to participate turned out to be a huge challenge.

Of the 150 children who'd won the lottery for the preschools, twenty-two of them seemed to have disappeared three weeks before the programs were scheduled to begin, just as we were frantically putting the finishing touches on the new schools. All the other children's parents had handed in the necessary paperwork. We were worried. Each missing child would lose what we truly believed was the opportunity of a lifetime. And it was likely that the kids who "disappeared" came from the families that most needed educational help. Combining this with the fact that our statistical tests would be more reliable if all these children attended our program, there was only one way to resolve the problem, and that was with boots on the ground.

We called an all-hands-on-deck meeting and told everyone involved in our nascent schools that we had to find these kids, no matter where they were, and get them registered for school no matter what. We had kids to help!

One of our key draftees was our wellness coordinator—the physical education teacher. Jeff, a tall, strapping, strong twenty-four-year-old, was the perfect guy to help us deal with what we knew could be threatening situations in tough neighborhoods. With Jeff, we figured we had the perfect person to reach these at-risk kids. No one in their right mind would mess with Jeff.

Now imagine you are Jeff, a middle-class white kid blessed with a loving family and with friends, interests, and a college education. Raised in Sun Prairie, Wisconsin, a bucolic town near Madison, you have no idea how fortunate you are to have had the background you have. You haven't spent a lot of time in dangerous neighborhoods.

It's a sweltering summer afternoon in Chicago Heights, and you've signed up for this job at an experimental preschool. Your boss (John List, who also happens to be your uncle by marriage) drives you to the address of one of the twenty-two missing children, and hands you a packet of Spanish-language registration papers. "Go up to the door and knock," John says. "When someone answers, tell them you want to sign up Gabriella for school."

You've been warned that this part of Chicago Heights is not a particularly happy place. An awful lot of people who live here are armed and dangerous: you know that even the police sometimes avoid this neighborhood. The mostly minority population is transient: families move often if they can't pay the rent. Many families don't speak English, and children are often left alone, fending for themselves while their parent or parents are at work. Or they're left with an overwhelmed relative or someone who may be strung out on alcohol or drugs. To you, this is a foreign country.

What do you do? Do you cinch up your pants and get out of the car, or do you refuse to go? In this case, you look at John and say, "No way."

After a couple of stare-down minutes, John opens the car door. "Wimp," he snorts as he gets out of the car.

"You're nuts, you know that?" you shout after him as he walks toward the house. You quickly lock the car doors behind him.

John strides up to the door and knocks. No one answers. Then he walks over to a nasty-looking neighbor, a grizzled character straight out of Clint Eastwood's *High Plains Drifter,* peering out from the broken window. "I'm looking for Gabriella," John says. "Can you tell me where she is?" The fellow just stares at him. Your fingers hover over your cell phone, ready to call 9-1-1 in case anything happens. And then a middle-aged woman shows up at the window. "He no speak Engleesh," she says.

"I'm running a school, and Gabriella was chosen to go to it," John says. "I need to get this information to her mother."

"Look in back of house," says the woman. "If a blue car is there, she is home. If not . . ." she shrugs.

Over the next couple of weeks, you and John pay ten visits to this house before you finally see the blue car. John knocks on the door and hands the packet to Gabriella's mother.

One down. Twenty-one to go.

At another house, you also refuse to get out of the car, so John walks up to the door and knocks incessantly. From a distance, you can hear a television blaring the voices of *Dora the Explorer.* Someone must be home. John disappears out of sight as he walks around to the back of this house. Now you wish you'd at least gone with him. Before full-fledged panic sets in, John returns to the front where you watch as he knocks again. "Carmella, come to the door," he says. "I am putting some papers under it. Give these to your mom." He stands there for a long time, and then slowly, slowly, the sheets are pulled from underneath the door.

John tells you later he had to hoist himself up on a ledge to see inside the back window while the neighbors gathered to watch and laugh. "I know Carmella is in there," he told them, "because my kids watch that show too. Why aren't they answering the door?" One of the neighbors told him the girl was probably alone.

Twenty to go.

The next day you drive to where Liliana lives, in the red-brick projects where murders and beatings are not uncommon. As you drive around looking for the right building, you see some big dude following you in his car. You find the right building and park. The guy parks too. You're afraid to leave the car, but even more afraid to stay behind this time. So when John opens the car door, you decide to join him. You both walk up to the apartment and knock. You glance back and see the guy who followed you is standing in the yard now, watching you and John with suspicious, catlike eyes.

The door opens, and dozens of kids answer it, tumbling over each other to see the visitor. Eventually, an old woman with jaundice-yellow eyes comes to the door.

"Is Liliana here?" you ask, feeling the gaze of the fellow who's been following you knifing through your back.

"This is Liliana," says a black girl in her early teens who is wearing a big, bloody bandage around her head. You wonder how this girl got hurt. Did she fall? Was she beaten? The sea of children parts, and a beautiful, wide-eyed three-year-old girl toddles toward the door. You look down at Liliana and then squat so you can look into her eyes. "Do you want to go to school?" you ask.

"Yes," the little girl says definitively. "I want to go to school."

"I signed her up," the teenager with the bandage says proudly. "I'm her sister. She's smart. I want to give her the chance that I never had. She can do it."

You leave the papers with the teen sister, turn around, and walk down a few steps into the yard to find twenty threatening-looking black men staring hard at you and your uncle. "What are you doing here?" one of them asks.

"We're here because Liliana is one of the lucky ones," John says. "She got into a wonderful program. She gets to go to a free school before she goes to public school."

"She don't need nothin'. She got all she needs," someone else says. But they let you and John pass unharmed.

Once you are safely in the car, you send a text to John's wife. "Your husband is completely nuts. You know that?"

How Far Have We Come?

Both of the GECC schools and the parent academy are now up and running; as we noted earlier, our hope is to figure out which key skills children should acquire in early childhood in order to prepare them for later success. The Griffins' ongoing funding also lets us track the educational and career trajectory of the students until the very ends of their lives. Not since the golden era of social experiments of the 1960s and 1970s have economists embarked on a project of this scale.

To see how everyone is doing, we have all the children in the various treatments undergo a series of comprehensive assessments three times a year—once before the start of the program, once midyear (January), and once at the end of the year—in which the kids are tested on academic or cognitive skills (such as vocabulary, basic writing and spelling, basic problem solving, counting, and pattern matching) and executive function skills (or noncognitive skills, such as testing for impulsivity).

We also want to see how well we can prepare very young children from Chicago Heights for kindergarten. As a group, these children have tended to underperform in cognitive development relative to the national average: at pre-assessment, they were, on average, in the thirtieth to thirty-fourth percentile. Would they catch up and close the gap if they completed our experimental program? This question is important, because starting kindergarten as a lower-than-average performer can hinder achievement in grades K-12.

The GECC experiment is still in the early stages, but the results so far have been very promising, despite the unstable and even horrific environments in which many of the children spend their before- and after-school time.[4] By the time Liliana had spent a few months in the program, says her sister, she could look at a book and make up a story; she was mastering verbal skills. Gabriella, Carmella, and Gabriel are all doing well, too.

Overall, the preschool curricula are both working beautifully. Over the first ten months of the program, students in the Literacy Express program have leapt ahead by more than nineteen academic months on their cognitive scores, effectively doubling that of the average preschool-aged child. That is, for every month that has passed, the students have learned almost two months of material. We're proud of these results. Students' cognitive scores have also increased considerably in the Tools of the Mind program. Those children are now testing roughly at the national average for cognitive test scores, and are doing quite well on noncognitive skills such as self-control. Students in the two preschool programs are now doing better than the average child nationwide when tested on both cognitive and noncognitive skills.

In summary: when the right kinds of incentives are applied via the scientific method, poor kids can do just as well as rich kids within ten months.

What about the Parent Academy? Children like Gabriel whose parents are enrolled in this program have shown improvements too, and they are catching up to the national average. But they are not doing as well as the kids enrolled in either of the preschools. Still, the short-term incentives seem to be quite strong: kids who have parents in the cash treatment perform much better than those whose parents are in the college treatment.

One delightful result is that kids with parents in the Parent Academy stayed on track after the program ended. That is, they weren't as susceptible to falling back in the summertime when they weren't in school. So even though the kids in the Parent Academy have not increased their performance by the same margin as those in our preschools, it looks like they could outperform those kids in the long run. This is because adults enrolled in the Parent Academy now have the tools to work with their children, and to continue to work with them long after we have directly touched them. In fact, those parents who were given the long-term, college scholarship incentive invested the most in their kids during the summer.

One unanticipated data pattern showed that the lion's share of gains across all of our programs occurred in the first few months of the program—between September and January of the first year. This result is tantalizing, because it might mean that pre-K education is most beneficial over much shorter time periods than previously believed. Importantly, it opens up the possibility of "kinder-prep" programs that can be completed in the summer months directly before kindergarten—when teachers and school space are readily available. (We are now in the first year of testing this proposition.)

The Griffins' investment in a few years of early education has allowed children who were once consistently at the bottom of the rankings to leapfrog their way past the average. Will these effects persist? Will the impact of parental involvement eventually overtake an investment in early childhood education? Will a kinder-prep program give our kids the extra lift they need to compete in today's global economy? Time will tell and, thanks to the Griffins, we'll be there to find out.

Saving Public Schools

What do the following people have in common—Albert Einstein, Bill Clinton, Martin Luther King Jr., Steve Jobs, Mark Zuckerberg,

Steven Spielberg, Shaquille O'Neal, Michael Jordan, and Oprah Winfrey?

They all went to public schools.

Until the 1840s, only children from wealthy families could receive an education. If that were the case today, most of the US population would probably be illiterate; and most, if not all of the people we just named might have had no work options beyond manual labor. But in the nineteenth century, something wonderful happened: public education in the United States became freely available to all children. Today, 85 percent are literate. If you think about public education in this context, you realize it has really been an amazing success.

But when you discover that kids in poor neighborhoods are graduating at the same low rate as people long ago, you know we can and should do much, much better. Public education is the only way for them to climb out of poverty and up the economic ladder. If it weren't for public schools, many urban kids wouldn't stand a chance. But the unfortunate fact is that such schools barely scratch the surface of what is possible, and they leave millions of children behind to endure wasted lives of grinding poverty.

What have we learned?

For decades, public education has been a source of political platitudes and mired in status-quo thinking. Despite the fact that every presidential candidate coughs up a host of ideas and surrounds himself with dozens of smart advisors who have innovative suggestions for fixing public education, nothing to date has worked. The past few decades of educational reform have shown that innovation for the sake of innovation isn't likely to change America's gap in educational achievement.

But down-at-the-heel Chicago Heights provides hope that there is a way out of this morass. When parents, teachers, and students from preschool to ninth grade are motivated to perform better, they do.

We found that the right incentives, combined with a better behavioral framing of the context, can make a huge difference.

We now understand better how simple incentives work in education, and how, for example, framing incentives in terms of losses boosts performance. Kids respond to bribes, but they respond better to behavioral manipulations; if you give them $20 to perform well on a test and threaten to take it away if their performance isn't up to par, students do much better.

Likewise, when teachers both (a) worked in teams and (b) were threatened with losing a large bonus they had already received, student achievement soared—effectively closing the education gap. Understanding how to reward students, parents, and teachers can raise test scores between 50 and 100 percent—putting the underprivileged kids on the same level as those from rich white neighborhoods.

If it all sounds a bit Pavlovian, it is—but it can work. And if Chicago Heights can close the education gap, then Anytown, America, certainly can too.

The Griffins understand all this, and they put their money to work—doing everything they can to ensure the kids in Chicago Heights get a solid educational platform to stand on. With their help—and, hopefully, with better interventions at the preschool and elementary school levels—we can not only graduate more urban children from high school, but also make learning exciting and fun from the get-go.

So how can we all, as a nation, go further? We must understand that schools are not just about teaching children. They are about teaching ourselves what works. So far, we've paid attention to only one side of this critical equation. We must all realize that our public schools are not just knowledge-pumping (or, at worst, babysitting) institutions dedicated to teaching our children to learn how to become functional citizens. In reality, they are laboratories of learning *for everyone*—researchers, parents, teachers, administration, and students too.

Just imagine how much we could all discover if more people began running and participating in field experiments to discover what works. If everyone who cares about public education ran such experiments, we could save enormous amounts of time, money, and heartache. We would discover which innovations are most promising, and how to apply them, before rolling them out to the entire country. The returns on a thriving K-12 educational system would be enormous for not just our children, but the United States as a whole.

In the following chapters, we'll learn more about how field experiments can help to discover what lies behind other kinds of social inequities.

What Seven Words Can End Modern Discrimination?

I Don't Really Hate You, I Just Like Money

Let's say that after several years of building your career in marketing you took time off and went back to school for your MBA. Now, with your newly minted credential from a top university, you are in the final draw for a top job in marketing at a large multinational corporation. You and two other candidates are to meet the CEO for a final interview. Given all you know about the job and based on your extensive expertise, it seems as if you have a good chance of landing this position.

Dressed in your best suit, you feel confident as you push the elevator button to the twentieth floor. "This is it," you say to yourself.

The elevator door swishes open; you stride up to the assistant's desk and announce yourself. The assistant ushers you in to an enormous office outfitted handsomely with bookcases and silver-framed family photos. The CEO strides over to you, offering a meaty hand. "Take a seat," he says, smiling.

"So," he begins, sitting down and leaning back in his Aeron chair, "you already understand that the job is to market our new product internationally. Your resume is very impressive in this regard. I see you have spent some time working in the Middle East and Europe."

"Yes," you say, feeling encouraged. "I also speak several languages, including Dutch and French."

"Yes, I see that," says the CEO. "It looks like you are eminently qualified. But right now we're going to talk about you. I see that you are married and have two small children. If you have a demanding full-time job, how much time do you think you will need to devote to your family as opposed to your job? This job, after all, entails quite a bit of international travel."

What is your answer to this question? How would you answer it as a husband and father? Or as a wife and mother?

The question and the answer might well depend on your gender. A woman is much more likely to be asked such questions than a man is. And if you are a woman, standing up for family time could well get you painted as "insufficiently committed" to the job—as Uri's wife, Ayelet (the model for this scenario) discovered.[1]

In Chapters 2 and 3, we saw how gender differences work on a deeply socialized basis, and how notions about competition affect women's opportunities. In Chapters 4 and 5, we saw how children from poor neighborhoods suffer from educational inequities.

Now, let's think more broadly about the effects of discrimination beyond gender and poverty: *What about racism, homophobia, and other forms of prejudice? What causes them? Are all forms of discrimination rooted in antipathy toward others, or are other things going on?*

In this and the next chapter, we will walk through a series of field experiments in which we tease out the distinctions. We'll look more closely at discrimination in general: how it affects markets, and how it affects you. We'll show you how field experiments have helped us to sort out various kinds of discrimination in the world. This is important because, while examining raw data in the traditional way can show us *how much* discrimination is occurring in a given market, that approach cannot show us *what kind* of discrimination is at work and what kinds of incentives might underlie it. Understanding the incentives behind discrimination is critical if we, as a society, are going to bring an end to it.

The Faces of Discrimination

Consider the following:

- A black man shopping for a car is quoted a higher price than a white man.
- A salesman ignores a gay couple shopping for a car.
- A disabled person is quoted a higher price for a car repair than an able-bodied person.
- A black man asking for directions on a busy street corner is given the wrong directions, whereas a white woman is given the correct ones.
- A pregnant woman angling for a promotion at work is passed over in favor of a man with her same skills.

If you've been in situations similar to these, you may feel angry, frustrated, or even outraged. But what can and what should we do to eliminate such biases?

A first step is to understand why people discriminate. What incentives are bigots following? Once we know the answer to this question, then we can combat discrimination with our own personal actions and with new laws.

Consider the case of anti-Semitism, which has had a long, ugly history in the world, including in the United States. For example, during the Civil War, Ulysses S. Grant issued an order—rescinded by Abraham Lincoln—expelling Jews from parts of Tennessee, Kentucky, and Mississippi.[2] In the first half of the twentieth century, Jews had trouble getting many jobs. They weren't allowed into the New York Athletic Club or other elite social clubs. Ivy League universities limited the number of Jewish students they accepted. The Ku Klux Klan and the popular radio speeches of the Catholic priest Father Coughlin incited attacks against Jews. The number of Jews allowed into the country was limited; during the Holocaust, America turned away ships bearing refugees from the Nazis. Henry Ford spoke out loudly against the "Jew Threat," and blamed World War I on them. Right-wing ideologues asserted that Jews dominated Franklin Roosevelt's administration.[3]

This kind of discrimination affected not only immigrants and Jews, of course; in many places it has been deeply embedded in cultural history the world over. Think of apartheid in South Africa, of the genocide in Rwanda, of the treatment of indigenous people in Australia and America, and of former slaves (and their descendants) in the United States—the list of humiliations and atrocities is endless.

———

It was into this anti-Semitic environment that a Jewish man named Gary Becker—the man who has arguably done the most to further our understanding of discrimination in modern times—made his entrance.

Gary Becker was born in 1930 in the coal-mining town of Pottsville, Pennsylvania, and was raised in New York City, where his entrepreneurial father Louis owned a successful wholesale and retail music business. Neither of his parents received an education past the eighth grade, and though his house didn't have many books, it was always filled with lively discussion about current events. "My father was an independent spirit and a strong supporter of Roosevelt," Becker explains. "We would talk about politics and social justice issues—rent control, taxation, the treatment of blacks in the south, and how to help the poor."

At the time, New York had the largest Jewish community in the country, but that didn't protect the family from anti-Semitism. They were the targets of racial slurs. Becker's brother, who had obtained a degree in chemical engineering from MIT, tried to land career positions in chemical firms but could not get promoted, so he founded his own firm. Although discrimination sometimes kept Jews from getting ahead, says Becker, "my father often said that if you worked hard you could overcome it."

Becker worked hard enough in school to be admitted to Princeton, thinking he would study mathematics. But he also had a strong interest in contributing to society. He happened to take an economics course his freshman year, and he got hooked. He developed the wild and crazy idea of somehow combining economics with his interest in social problems. After graduation, he went on to the University of Chicago, where he became a student of Milton Friedman, who saw in Becker a glimpse of genius.

Becker began studying the economics of discrimination. "I had a feeling discrimination wasn't one, simple thing," he recalls. "It's manifested in many ways, including earnings and employment. For example, if an employer was prejudiced against black workers, what did that mean for the black workers compared to equally skilled whites?"

Becker saw a way of identifying the prejudices of workers, employers, customers, and all kinds of other groups and putting them through the blender of economic analysis. In a sense, what Becker did was to identify the incentives that make people discriminate. "But I had to work in the dark," he remembers. "There was no work on this, despite the importance of the problem." His economics professors were so skeptical about his thesis that they required a sociologist to serve on his Ph.D. committee, but the sociologist wasn't at all interested in what Becker was doing.

Of course, Becker's work *was* all about economics; economists just didn't know it yet. His notion of combining economics and sociology wasn't a small step in the tradition of economic thinking—it was a whole new direction. His work showed what happens to markets and economic interactions when people discriminate. For instance, what happens in the labor market if a company prefers to hire one person rather than another (say, it hires women for certain kind of jobs, but not for others)? If you can develop good answers to this question, you can probably understand an important factor in what drives an economy. Yet economists didn't seem to have such answers in the context of discrimination.

Despite the skeptics, Becker had enough support from Friedman and others that he didn't completely lose his faith, and after receiving his Ph.D. he landed a job teaching at Columbia University. In 1957, at the age of twenty-seven, he published a book based on his thesis, called *The Economics of Discrimination*, in which he described what he called "taste for discrimination"—prejudice that springs from hatred or "animus" toward others. This kind of discrimination shows up when one person avoids or acts against another "just because" they don't like that person's race, religion, or sexual preference.

The incentives that Becker studied were not just money. Hating someone could be a strong motivation to discriminate against him. According to Becker's theory, people who bear this kind of animus don't just hate the "other," but they would also willingly surrender money—profits, wages, or income—to cater to their prejudice. For example, a white man who harbors animus toward blacks would rather work for $8 per hour alongside a fellow white man than for $10 per hour alongside a black man. In this case, the "animus incentive" overcomes the monetary one.

Still, when he first traveled around the world presenting his work on *The Economics of Discrimination*, a common objection from other economists was that "this is not economics." Basically, their argument against Becker went like this: "It's not that this work isn't interesting or important; it's just that you should leave it to psychologists and sociologists." But things began to change with the advent of the civil rights movement of the 1960s. Soon, people were fiercely interested in the topic of discrimination and economics, and Becker's was the only serious book out there.

"Suddenly, influential people began reading it, and the whole thing snowballed," he recalls. The book was reprinted in a second updated edition in 1971 and is considered a classic because it forever changed the way we understand discrimination. By the time the Nobel Committee gave Becker the Nobel Prize in Economics in 1992, its members specifically praised *The Economics of Discrimination*. "Gary Becker's analysis has often been controversial and hence, at the outset, met with skepticism and even distrust," the Nobel Committee noted in its press release announcing the prize. "Despite this, he was not discouraged, but persevered in developing his research, gradually gaining increasing acceptance among economists for his ideas and methods."[4]

Prejudice Is Shrinking

Obviously, animus-based discrimination is still virulent. Sometimes, it breaks out into the open, as anyone who has ever listened to "hate radio" shock jocks can attest. Whites and blacks still don't necessarily get along in all parts of the world. And gays are still the objects of bullying, beatings, and bullets.

Despite all this, we have come a long, long way. If the average American had gone into a coma in 1957 and woken up today, he would no doubt be amazed at the changes in social attitudes. Culturally speaking, life is not the same as it once was; people's social proclivities and preferences have evolved. For example, there is no longer the widespread assumption that women are inferior to men or that their lives should be only focused on husbands, children, and home life. Nor are those women who work outside the home relegated to so-called pink collar professions such as teaching or nursing. Approximately 39 percent of Harvard's MBA class of 2013 was comprised of women, the highest percentage ever; and in 2011, women surpassed men in the number of master's degrees awarded.[5] In fact, plenty of employers now fight over the opportunity to hire qualified women, and they happily pay for maternity leave in order to keep women at the firm after they get pregnant.

Additionally, innate animosity of whites toward blacks appears to be dropping overall.[6] According to a USA Today/Gallup poll conducted in 2011, the public accepts interracial marriage more than ever. The poll showed that 43 percent of Americans think it is good for society; 44 percent say that such marriages make no difference. More than a third of those surveyed said that a relative of theirs is married to someone of a different race, and nearly two-thirds said it would be fine if a family member decided to marry someone of a different race or ethnicity.[7]

Many African Americans are no longer marginalized when it comes to public policy; policy makers are now focused on shrinking the educational achievement gap between white and minority children. Americans even elected a black president twice. In short, we are no longer living in the twentieth century, which is a good thing when it comes to ending animus.

Economic Discrimination: A Rising Problem

While this cultural evolution of the incentive to discriminate based on hate is good news, another variety of discrimination is on the rise today, and it shows up in a very different form than the animus of Becker's youth. Economists call this different kind of prejudice "economic" discrimination,[8] and though it is more subtle than bigotry, homophobia, or sexism, it is increasingly widespread, multifaceted, difficult to parse, and often quite nefarious. And it's based entirely on financial self-interest and "looking out for number one." Animus is about self-interest, too, though the hater is not interested in money but rather in satisfying his desire to harm others.

You are probably already aware of economic discrimination because it shows up in your bills. If you are a smoker, your medical insurance may cost you more because, economically speaking, you run a higher risk of contracting diseases that cost a lot to treat. If your credit rating isn't stellar, banks will charge you more for loans because you present a comparatively higher risk of defaulting on them.

Another very straightforward example is car insurance. If you are a male driver, you pay as much as 20 percent more for car insurance than a woman does for identical coverage. You might wonder if this unequal treatment is illegal, because civil rights laws clearly state that discriminating on the basis of arbitrary characteristics such as race and gender is illegal. On average, however, women have fewer driving accidents than men. The costs of insuring women are therefore less than for insuring men, so the courts have ruled that charging women lower—or men higher—rates is legal.

In this case, society seems to accept that discrimination based on differences in the *cost* to provide the service (such as insurance) is okay. But there are movements abroad to curb such economic discrimination. For example, the European Union is debating banning economic discrimination for car insurance. If it is banned, car insurance companies say men can expect their rates to fall by about 10 percent. (Of course, if such bans occur, women can expect their insurance rates to increase; the insurance companies won't lose.)

Economic discrimination also springs from the beliefs that people have information—correct or not—about others' economic situations. For various reasons, people and companies may believe that they have incentives to discriminate between individuals in order to make more money. For example, a contractor might charge 20 percent more than his going rate to repair the roof of a fabulous house of a millionaire CEO because he thinks the owner can pay more than people with more modest homes. A company might be thinking that in order to meet its stockholders' profit expectations, it must increase the prices some consumers pay. This type of discrimination is not based on animus. It is based on a cold, hard, monetary incentive.

None of this apparent inequity is particularly pleasant if you are the person being targeted for higher prices, but it doesn't mean the contractor who is charging you more bears animus toward you. It's because he's looking out for his bottom line. From his (or the insurance company's) incentive-driven point of view, economic discrimination is a way of making more money. It's as simple as that.

On the surface, economic discrimination in our transaction-based economy may seem perfectly acceptable, but it can be very nasty, especially because the victims often don't know it is happening to them. Economic discrimination is even expanding because of the Internet, along with the wealth of data that is collected on each of us. Consider the overwhelming amount of personal information collected about us daily by the Internet firms. Companies can easily slice and dice data to figure out who is a "preferred" customer and who isn't—and so they put these data to good use by engaging in economic discrimination to enhance their bottom line.

As an example, consider the case of Robert Cole, a sixty-five-year-old resident of Ferguson, Missouri, who likes to do research online. To help out a friend with diabetes, Cole searched websites for information about the disease, and passed the information to his friend. Not long afterwards, Cole began to notice that he was receiving direct-mail and online advertisements for diabetes testing supplies. Who had gotten hold of Cole's identity and personal information? How were the search terms that he put into Google being tracked, analyzed, and used? "Am I in somebody's database as a diabetic? Because I'm not. I don't even know how to correct that," he told a reporter.[9]

This is scary stuff. What happens if the electronic fingerprint you leave behind—the detailed information about your purchasing history, the websites you last visited, and your financial status—are used against you?

In fact, most Internet sites use search information in ways consumers don't understand. Automated bots sweep the Web for consumer information, and websites use cookies and browser fingerprinting to follow users, while third-party data brokers sell users' projected online behaviors in real time. Every time you shop online, or even search, you leave an electronic fingerprint that allows businesses to collect detailed information about your purchasing history, the websites you last visited, and your financial status. Many websites use this information, in turn, to set prices. Companies use the information out there to understand your incentives and act on it to enhance their profits.[10]

An online company that engages in such economic discrimination may be able to analyze your financial status by looking at your purchases over time, and decide that you are able to pay more than the next person. If you happen to be better off than others, or are willing to search less than others, you will likely be the victim of economic discrimination.

But, you may ask, what is really wrong with this kind of discrimination? After all, in the real world, customers often pay different prices. Anyone who has bought an airline ticket, booked a hotel room, or rented a car has faced such economic discrimination. Companies vary prices between customers all the time, trying to figure out what incentives to offer customers to buy their products. If you are a well-heeled businesswoman who needs to fly from Chicago to San Francisco for a quick one-day meeting, you may care less about the price than if you are a teenager on a tight budget. Why shouldn't the airline charge you, the businesswoman, more?

The problem with the online world is that customers don't know they are the objects (or victims) of discriminatory behavior because they can't see the differing prices. The person who walks into a car dealership in a costly suit and gets offered the most expensive car on the lot likely knows what's going on, and that the sticker price serves as a starting point for further negotiation. But the same person, buying a plane ticket online, may not realize her high wages and lifestyle are translating into pricier plane tickets—and she is powerless to do anything about the discrimination.

A website's pricing is based on a computer algorithm—one that contains information about shopping history, home address (having sorted "desirable" from "undesirable" zip codes), spending patterns, credit card accounts, and more. And such programs are incredibly adept at recognizing and taking advantage of even subtle differences among people. Even if the customer knows the website has offered the same ticket to another consumer for a lower price, she cannot necessarily use this information to haggle over the price; the website simply doesn't let her purchase the ticket at the lower price.

You might say, "So what? If a rich person can afford to pay more, maybe she should." But think about it: in the brick-and-mortar world, when women, minorities, and people in wheelchairs are quoted higher prices than others, it seems wrong. While economic discrimination is a gray area under the civil rights laws, most people believe that this type of behavior is unfair.

Like animus, economic discrimination also occurs in all kinds of everyday situations—when people ask for directions on the street, when they go shopping (whether online or in the "real" world), when they apply for jobs, when they get their cars repaired, and so on. But deciding what is and isn't bigotry is often difficult. And awareness of this difficulty is important, because until we understand what really motivates people when they discriminate, policy makers cannot begin to protect people from injustice.

So how do we sort out animus-based prejudice from economic discrimination? We took to the streets to find out.[11]

Dress for Success

Jan, a fifty-year-old white mother of teenagers, had graying hair, gold-rimmed glasses, and a nose red with cold. She wore a navy wool coat warmed by a beige muffler, and she was our secret agent. We paid her to ask random people on the street for directions to Chicago's well-known Willis Tower (formerly known as the Sears Tower). The first person she asked was a middle-aged white woman. She told Jan that the tower entrance was a short distance away. "Walk down two blocks to Michigan Avenue, cross the street, and walk down a block to Van Buren, and the entrance will be on your right," she said obligingly. Jan thanked her for the directions and walked on. Were the directions correct?

Our next secret agent was Tyrone, a twenty-year-old black man wearing a hoodie and low-slung, baggy jeans. Tyrone politely stopped another middle-aged white woman and asked for directions. Without stopping, she responded, "Um, I don't know." When Tyrone asked for directions from a businessman in his thirties, the respondent gave him a long look—and then the wrong directions.

In our experiment, we wanted to find out what kinds of reactions people of different ages, genders, and races would receive when they asked for directions. Does discrimination affect people's willingness to help? How would a passerby react when a gentle middle-aged white lady asked for directions to the tower? How might he or she respond to a young black man? A young white woman? A young white man? An older black man? And so on.

We asked people of different ages, genders and races to help us, as you can see in the chart below. What did our experiments reveal? How often did each "secret agent" receive a helpful response? How long did it take, on average, before the helper moved on?

The numbers in the chart tell an interesting story: if you are looking for directions and happen to be a female, chances are you'll receive the help you need, especially if you are young. If you're an older black

"SECRET AGENT"	PERCENTAGE OF "HELPING" RESPONDENTS	SECONDS OF INTERACTION
20-year-old black female	60%	20 seconds
50-year-old black female	63%	20 seconds
20-year-old black male	31%	13 seconds
50-year-old black male	61%	20 seconds
20-year-old white female	75%	24 seconds
50-year-old white female	63%	18 seconds
20-year-old white male	52%	16 seconds
50-year-old white male	59%	20 seconds

male, you'll receive slightly more help than you will if you are an older white male. But if you are a young black male, you should probably carry a GPS. Young black males were less likely to receive help than young women of either race (who received the most help), middle-aged people (male or female) of either race and young white men.

You might assume that people who didn't stop to help the young black man were indulging in racism, and in some cases, you'd be right. However, the data showed that older black men and women, and young black women, received helpful directions, so animus against black people in general can't explain the data. If you are generally willing to help black people find their way, but you perceive this particular young black man as somehow threatening, we would consider that economic discrimination.

The incentive to ignore Tyrone was not based on hatred—rather, it was based on fear and the desire for self-preservation. Fear of Tyrone could be rooted in a fear of criminality, as unfortunately, criminal rates are higher among young black males than other groups. By the same logic, we're guessing that if we had put a young white male who had a shaved head, jackboots, and a swastika tattoo on the same street corner, passersby would have walked away from him with all speed.

To check this conclusion, we decided to insert an economic signal into the mix. We sent Tyrone and other young black men like him out again, but this time they were dressed in business suits. If the response to them sprang from animus, we surmised, the young men would continue to receive poor treatment. On the other hand, their attire might signal to passersby that they were "safe," and so they would be given good directions.

Indeed, this time, the young black men were treated quite well and received the same quality information the young women had received. The conclusion is then clear, even if we don't like it. If you are white, the way you dress is less important than if you are black. If you are a young black man, one way to reduce discrimination against you is to dress up.

This finding is obviously controversial. When an unarmed young black teenager named Trayvon Martin was shot and killed in a gated Florida community in 2012 by a half-white, half-Hispanic neighborhood watch captain named George Zimmerman, Martin was wearing a hoodie—something Fox TV commentator Geraldo Rivera believed contributed to the young man's death. "I am urging the parents of black and Latino youngsters particularly to not let their children go out wearing hoodies," Rivera said on *Fox & Friends*. "I think the hoodie is as much responsible for Trayvon Martin's death as George Zimmerman was."[12]

Rivera's comment drew—rightly, in our opinion—outraged protests from those who believed that the talk-show host was blaming the victim. He appeared to be suggesting that dark-skinned individuals who choose to wear hoodies can easily be perceived by others as "gangstas" and a threat to society. But *did* the combination of Martin's race and choice of clothes contribute to his death? Rivera seemed to be saying as much. And, unfortunately, our study on the streets of Chicago seemed to show that clothing did, in fact, make a big difference in the way the young black men were treated.

Here's what Martin's father noted when Rivera apologized to him: "Let me just add one thing with the wearing of the hoodie. I don't think America knows that, in fact, at the time of the incident when he initially made the call, it was raining. So Trayvon had every right to have on his hood. He was protecting himself from the rain. So if . . . walking in the rain with your hoodie on is a crime, then I guess the world is doing something wrong."

Allow us to put this into a broader perspective. A hundred years ago, horrible events like Trayvon Martin's shooting would hardly have made local news in the "white man's world" of the Jim Crow South. But fifty years ago, in 1963, the shooting of the activist

Medgar Evers lit a fire under the civil rights movement, bringing people of all colors together in a fight for justice for all. Today, the shooting of a single unarmed teenager raises another firestorm, as it should, and it once more brings people of all races together to call for justice. And it shows how our more tolerant society—something so many have fought and died for—can easily shift in the reverse direction.

On the basis of our experiment on the streets of Chicago, we would argue that animus and racism have, for the most part, evolved into economic discrimination, which is much more subtle. But sometimes, animus and racism can combine with economic discrimination in ways that have terrible consequences.

Joe the Wheelchair Man

So far, our field experiments have teased out one distinction between economic discrimination and animus: the former is based on "looking out for number one," while the latter is based on hatred of the "other." But we wanted to push our demonstration further. We decided to look at another kind of differential treatment, this time against disabled people.

Imagine you are confined to a wheelchair. You've lost the use of both your legs, due to an early childhood disease. It's 6:30 A.M. and −20°F on a January day in Chicago. You—let's call you "Joe"—live on the seventh floor of an apartment building in downtown Chicago. You press the off button on your alarm clock and then, working patiently and using your arms, you push your covers off, pull the underwear and pants you have put at the foot of the bed over your hips, and, finally, your socks onto your feet. This effort tires you out, so you wait a few minutes to recover your strength. Then, rocking your hips from side to side, you roll yourself out of bed, letting your legs drop to the floor.

With a mighty effort, you hoist yourself onto your powered wheelchair. After you inhale a quick breakfast (orange juice, coffee from the auto-timed pot, and a muffin), you wheel yourself out of your apartment and take the elevator to the ground floor. The walkway and parking lot have been cleared of snow, but they are frosted with slippery ice. Tentatively, you maneuver your wheelchair toward your dented, specially equipped van.

Using buttons on your keychain, you command the side doors of the van to open and present you with a small lift. After maneuvering your wheelchair onto the lift and into the van, you swivel it into the driver's spot and insert your key. Taking careful grasp of the hand controls, you maneuver the van out of the parking spot, through the lot, and onto the street.

After a fifteen-minute drive, you pull into "Guy's Auto Body," one of the shops you have found with a designated handicapped parking space. You lower the lift on your van and try to push your way through the uncleared snow and onto the wheelchair ramp. The ice forces you to struggle, but you press on. Eventually you make your way to the top of the ramp and tap on the door of the repair shop.

If this sequence of events is painstaking to read, think about what it's like for millions of disabled people who expend much more energy taking care of daily tasks than able-bodied people can possibly imagine.

Only a handful of studies have looked into discrimination against the disabled—which is a little surprising, given the fact that as the number of elderly people rises around the world, so does the number of people with disabilities. Joe, of course, was our secret agent. For him, every errand is a battle. Even after he struggles to get his van to the repair shop, he faces the challenge of getting a ride home, because many taxis can't accommodate wheelchairs.

How many price quotes do you think Joe would get for repairing his car? Would he drive from one shop to another, looking for the best deal? Or would he be forced to settle on the first quote for the sake of much-needed convenience?

When you go to an auto repair shop, you usually don't know what the work will cost (unless you're getting some routine work done, such as an oil change or a smog check). The people at the shop base their estimates on the level of work needed, as well as their own discretion. For this field study, we asked several men between the ages of twenty-nine and forty-five to act as our secret agents. Half of these men were like Joe—they used wheelchairs and drove specially equipped vehicles. We sent all of them to get price quotes to fix different cars. In half the cases, the disabled men drove into the body shop asking for a quote. In the other half, the able-bodied men did the same thing with the exact same vehicles.

On average, the disabled men received price quotes that were 30 percent higher than the able-bodied men. Ouch. But why?

For an answer, put yourself in the shoes of the person behind the counter in the mechanic shop. You see Joe wheeling into the office. The dialogue goes something like this:

> You: Hello! Cold out there this morning!
> Joe: (grunts) Right. My van needs some work. It's out there (pointing). Can you give me an estimate?
> You: (eyeing Joe) Well, we're pretty busy, but I'll ask them to take a look as soon as they can.
> Joe: That's okay. I'll wait.

While Joe rolls his chair into the waiting area, you are making a mental calculation. You feel sorry for him, understanding that it must have taken quite an effort to get to your shop. Joe clearly needs a break. On the other hand, what are the chances Joe would go to all this trouble to drive to another repair shop for an estimate?

Half an hour later, the repair folks call you with a time and cost estimate about the work. You tell Joe it will cost $1,415. That's 30 percent more than you would charge an able-bodied person. In fact, doing a similar exercise dozens of times with our testers visiting mechanics reveals the data pattern we discussed above: *the disabled, on average, receive price quotes about 30 percent higher than the nondisabled.*

Are you, the mechanic, reacting to incentives, or do you just dislike helping, and serving, disabled people? Our intuition was that the mechanic recognized that he had a captive customer. Joe had to go to a lot of trouble to get his van repaired, so the mechanic decided to charge him more because he assumed that Joe wouldn't go through the hassle of collecting another price quote. In other words, the mechanic thought he could charge more and get away with it when he was dealing with a disabled person.

To test our intuition, we sent an entirely new group of testers out for price quotes. This time, we had both the disabled and abled testers mention seven simple words:

"I am getting three price quotes today."

Guess what happened?

This time around, both the disabled and the abled testers received *identical* offers. So the case was closed. The mechanics were making a simple economic calculation. By propping up their sales in this way, they were engaging in classic, blatantly unfair, economic discrimination by taking advantage of the customer's disability. The mechanics were reacting to the incentives they were facing—in this case, the opportunity to make more money.

———

As we have tried to show, economic discrimination is based on simple calculations. For various reasons, people and companies may believe that they have incentives to discriminate between individuals. Amazon.com may think that it should increase the fee some customers pay in order to meet shareholders' profit expectations. Insurance companies may increase premiums for smokers because they view it as fair for people who take health risks to pay for those risks. Mechanics may overcharge disabled drivers to stay afloat. And the reason that Uri's wife was not hired had nothing to do with dislike of women: it had everything to do with the expectations regarding her on-the-job availability. This type of discrimination is not based on animus. It is based on economic incentives. To combat it, the person who is targeted for unfair treatment needs to signal that he or she is like those people who are not being discriminated against.

In the next chapter, we'll dig deeper into the issue of animus and economic discrimination by visiting new markets, and close with some reflections on addressing discrimination as a society.

Be Careful What You Choose, It May Be Used Against You!

The Hidden Motives Behind Discrimination

When we think of how far Western civilization has come since the early twentieth century, we can't help but be impressed. If our grandfathers were born today, it's unlikely that they would have encountered anything like the widespread animus of their youth. It is, indeed, heartening to see animus on the wane. But we are a long, long way from having an equitable society, and the rise of economic discrimination is certainly muddying the waters. In some cases, economic discrimination makes it easier for animus to hide in its folds.

Why? Because while most of us would agree that animus is bad, we're likely to disagree about whether some forms of economic discrimination are acceptable. Some kinds of economic discrimination may seem justifiable, others less so. Some types of economic discrimination are offensive; some are not. Some deserve legal censure;

others do not. Some are based on incontrovertible facts; some are based on cultural stereotypes and beliefs. And as we have tried to suggest, sorting out what is acceptable from what isn't is often tricky.

Let's return for a moment to our example of a hypothetical roofing contractor from the previous chapter. If he happened to be facing stiff competition in the marketplace, and he was running into severe money problems, he might feel justified in charging his CEO client more for his work. In such a case, we might feel more lenient toward him because, after all, his motive would not be based on simple greed, but on pure survival. But if he charged more because he was saving up for a yacht, we might feel differently.

Many of us feel that if a person like this roofer discriminates to avoid a financial or other kind of loss, that's okay. But if the person discriminates just to enhance his bottom line, we think he's a greedy profiteer. When you sit back and think about it, however, "loss" and "gain" are simply two different ways of framing, as we showed in the education chapters. Any gain can be framed as a loss—and vice versa, if one is creative.

In other cases, economic discrimination may have to do with the very sensible-seeming motive of reducing risk. One might think that charging smokers more for their health insurance makes sense,[1] and that it also makes sense to charge men more for auto insurance, or that rental car companies have every right not to rent cars to drivers under twenty-five years of age. Though such blanket policies may seem unfair to safe male drivers and excellent younger ones, the insurance company argues that they are necessary in order to control costs. Likewise, obese people whose employers cover insurance may have to pay higher health insurance premiums than other employees. And some airlines, such as Air France and Southwest Airlines, charge for two seats rather than one if the passenger in question is too big to get into a seat with the armrests down.

For an obese person, it could be humiliating to have to be confronted with this situation at the ticket counter. When Kenlie Tiggeman tried to buy a ticket at a Southwest Airlines counter, she was asked several questions: "I was asked what size clothes, and how much I weigh. I gave answers in front of a gate full of people, some of whom were snickering," Tiggeman said.[2] While Southwest's policy may make economic sense from the company's standpoint, an obese person could easily view it as animus-based.

Let's say you are a hiring manager at a construction company, and you're looking for a foreman. Does it make sense for you to refuse to interview women for the job on the basis of your belief that a man would be more qualified?[3] After all, limiting the candidate field to those who have a good chance of fitting in with the rest of your crew saves you and such applicants time, effort, and money. That's a perfectly good argument for economic discrimination, but it's also blatantly sexist. Would you simply decline to interview female applicants, just as employers ignored John when he went on the academic job market in 1995?

Consider another kind of discrimination—that against gays. Although this issue has become more topical as American society has evolved, anti-gay discrimination has a long and storied history. Societies have criminalized homosexuality for centuries, as Leonardo da Vinci found out when he was arrested for sleeping with a male prostitute. The Nazis rounded up gays, castrated them, and used them as slave laborers and as fodder for Dr. Mengele's nefarious medical experiments. Between 1933 and 1945, German police arrested approximately 100,000 men just for being homosexual.[4]

Today, despite the persistence of angry screeds against gays by a shrinking minority, and though many states have made it illegal for homosexuals to marry, homosexuality is no longer considered a crime in the United States. But which kind of discrimination against gay people is more prevalent in markets: *Is it the animus-based kind that drives hate crimes and social isolation? Or is it the economic kind? Or some combination of these?*

In our continuing quest to get to the bottom of discrimination, we decided to look at the behavior of people in a benign, neutral, everyday kind of market environment—a car sales lot. Car sales are some of the most common and important transactions in the economy for most individuals, as roughly sixteen million cars are sold annually in the United States. In addition, the stakes are high, but the transactions are relatively short, making them the perfect place to run field experiments in which the participants don't know that they are being observed.

Would You Sell a Car to Those Guys?

Compare the following scenarios:

Scenario A:

It's a sunny autumn morning at a Toyota dealership in Chicago, and the new Corollas are just in. Bernard, the salesman, looks forward to earning some handsome commissions that day.

Around 10 A.M., two young men walk in. They head straight to the shiny, dark-blue Corolla CE sedan in the center of the floor. "Tom," says one to the other, "didn't I tell you? Isn't this car just the most beautiful thing? Check out that color!"

"You're right, Joe," says Tom, peering in the window at the grey leather seats and taking note of the sunroof. "I think this will be perfect."

As the two men investigate the car, Bernard approaches them. "You guys like that car, I see," he says. "Check this out." He shows them the heated seats and other features, and then invites them to enjoy a cup of coffee while they discuss the virtues of the car.

Scenario B:

On the same spring morning, Jerry and Jim walk into the Honda dealership down the street. As they enter the dealership, they hold hands in an open display of affection. They walk over to the new Honda Civic CE in the center of the floor.

"You know, Jer," says Jim, inspecting the sticker listing the car's facts, figures, and price. "This is really just the right car for us. It's compact, it gets great mileage, and these things run forever."

"No kidding," says his partner, opening the passenger side door and sniffing happily. "And don't you just love that new car smell?"

The dealer, George, watches the couple purr over the car for a minute, picks up a brochure, and then approaches them. "Looks like you really like this car," he says coolly. "It's brand new on the market. It's a pretty good deal at that price. Here's a brochure. I'll be right back."

In this experiment, we worked with our colleague Michael Price in assigning pairs of men to pose as our secret agents: straight men acting as friends, straight men playing loving partners, gay men acting as friends, and gay men portraying partners. Each of these pairs visited various car dealerships to negotiate the purchase of a new car. Every "couple" bargained at different randomly determined dealerships, and every dealership was approached twice. We observed not only what kinds of offers the various "couples" received, but also how often they were offered niceties like a test drive and a cup of coffee.

Our results showed that the people acting as gay partners got shabbier treatment. Many dealerships rejected offers from buyers they perceived as gay, while accepting *identical* offers from our straight buyers. More than 75 percent of the time, dealers quoted the gay couples higher initial prices; when the gay couples extended counter offers, they were much more likely to be rejected and the salespeople ended the negotiations.

Still, these results weren't consistent across the board. In some dealerships, the gay couples received the same polite treatment as the straight couples. They were offered cups of coffee, test drives, and other amenities.

As it turned out, treatment of the gay couples depended heavily *on the race of the salesperson.* We found that minority salespeople (either African American or Hispanic) were much more likely to discriminate against the gay couple than their majority (white) colleagues. When a gay couple inquired, minority salespeople made initial offers that were about $1,233 higher on average than majority salespeople made. In fact, minority salespeople seemed to want to limit their contact with the gay customers, not offering test drives or the opportunity to purchase a less expensive car—implying they were so put off by the couples that they were willing to forgo a nice commission in exchange for not having to deal with them. (This does not mean that *all* minority salespeople acted in this way; just that a majority did.)

One would perhaps think minorities might be more tolerant of differences among people, but we found the opposite held true. They were more likely to forgo the incentives to sell the car when the buyers were posing as partners. One possibility for this finding is that minorities are more likely to self-identify as religious, and many religions view homosexuality as wrong. Religious people, according to some research evidence, are more likely to believe that sexual orientation is a *choice* rather than genetically determined. According to a 2007 survey conducted by the Pew Research Center's Forum on Religion and Public Life, black Americans "are markedly more religious on a variety of measures than the U.S. population as a whole."[5] (This suggestion is related to a line of research, including our own, showing that individuals hold more prejudice toward those who they feel have a "choice" in conditions such as obesity and homosexuality—conditions the prejudiced people believe are controllable.)

Would we discover the same sort of discrimination when it came to race—something that is clearly not a person's choice?

Let's Make a Deal

Once again, we sent several men out shopping for cars, but this time they weren't posing as friends or partners; they were operating on their own with instructions from us. All were middle-aged; half were black and half were white. To get an idea of the settings, compare the following two scenarios, taking note of the differences:

With a base price of $55,000, the 2012 BMW 335i is expensive, but it is a beauty. A gorgeous burgundy-red convertible with alloy double-spoke wheels and black leather seats, it is a real work of automotive art.

The salesman, an athletic-looking young man named Richard, smiles at Jim. "Pretty little thing, isn't it? Care to take it for a drive?"

"Sure," says Jim coolly, trying to hide his excitement. This is going to be fun.

While Richard fetches the key, Jim thinks about the bells and whistles that would add to the price tag—heated seats, active steering, alloy wheels, maybe high-end headlights, which his wife would appreciate on those dark, rainy winter nights.

Richard comes back with the key, and Jim takes the wheel. As the convertible pulls out of the parking lot and heads toward the highway, Richard takes the measure of his customer. A white man in his late forties, Jim wears khakis and a green parka over a plaid woolen shirt.

"How long have you been looking around for a car?" Richard asks.

"For a while now," Jim says, grinning. "I've been thinking about an anniversary present for my wife. She always dreamed of one of these."

"I can just imagine her face when she comes out the door and sees this in your driveway," says Richard. As they drive, Richard asks Jim some polite questions about his wife and family.

After the test drive, Richard offers Jim a cup of coffee and a comfortable seat in his cubicle. Jim says he's ready to make a deal. After long negotiation, one emerges: Jim will pay $60,925 for the car.

Now imagine the exact same scenario in the exact same conditions. The only difference this time is that Jim is a black man.

Here's the question: How much does Richard ask the black man to pay for the car? More? The same? Less?

We found that, when shopping for high-end cars, black men were given final offers that were approximately $800 higher than the quotes white men received.

Is this the same kind of discrimination as we saw in the gay experiment above? Why did the dealers treat the African American customers looking at the expensive cars comparatively poorly? Why were they less likely to offer them a test drive or coffee? To find out, we ran another set of experiments.

Bob thinks the new Toyota Corolla is a good looking car. The asking price is $16,995. Bob wants to secure a trade-in on his 2007 Pathfinder, which the Kelly Blue Book has listed at $10,000, minus a few dings. He just wants to get rid of the Pathfinder, so he's ready to give it up for less than he could sell it for by himself.

As he inspects the shiny wheels, the salesman sidles up to him.

"Nice car," says Bob. "Can I take it out for a test drive?"

"Of course. This is the only one we have left on the lot," says the salesman. "My name's Tony." The salesman warmly extends his hand, which Bob shakes. "I'll be right back, and you can take her for a spin."

When Tony returns with the key and pops open the doors, Bob sinks into the driver's seat, appreciating the feel of the soft, gray leather and that new-car smell.

As he pulls out of the dealership parking lot, Tony tries to figure out what kind of customer he has on the line. Bob is a black man who looks to be a little north of forty. He wears jeans and a non-descript blue parka over a red flannel shirt.

"So, how long have you been looking around for a car?" Tony asks.

"For a while now," said Bob. "We're in need of an upgrade, and I wanted to get a new car this time, not another used one."

After the test drive, Bob says he's ready to make a deal. After a long negotiation, a deal emerges: Bob will pay $400 above the price ($19,295) minus $8,000 for the Pathfinder.

———

Now, imagine the exact same scenario in the exact same conditions. The only difference this time is that Bob is a white man.

Here's the question: which man gets a better deal?

In this case, neither—they both get the *same* deal. We found no difference in price quotes across testers when bargaining over *lower-end* models like the Toyota. The fact that the price quotes from dealers for low-end cars were the same regardless of the customer's race suggested that the dealers were exercising economic discrimination in their pursuit of profits. That is, the dealers discriminate when they think that the prospective buyer's race in-dicates that he might be less likely to buy the expensive car. They don't discriminate when they think that the buyers, regardless of race, are just as likely to buy the less expensive car.

To explain: we conjectured that the dealers may have thought the white men were more likely to buy the pricier cars, so they took the extra time to engage in a little sweet talk, offering them coffee, and so on—as Richard did with Jim. In this case, the dealers simply reacted to the incentives they were facing. They were also willing to negotiate more with the white buyers, believing that the process was going to lead to a deal.

In other words, if you are a bigot, you will consistently act like a bigot. But if you discriminate only when you think it boosts your profits, you are engaging in economic discrimination. Such discrim-ination may very well be unethical and unfair, and in the case of the BMW car dealers, you are treating some people poorly based on their race. But it's still not animus.

Discrimination and Public Policy

Remember the Archie Bunker remark to Sammy Davis Jr. we men-tioned in the Introduction: "Your bein' colored, now, I know you had no choice in that. But whatever made you turn Jew?"[6]

As we suggested above, our research points to an interesting con-clusion: based on everything we have studied, we've found that animus most often rears its ugly head *when the discriminator believes the person they are judging has a choice in the matter.*[7] For example, on seeing a person who is obese, some of us attribute that person's size to a lack of self-control. If we look at a person who is openly gay, some of us attribute that characteristic to choice. But people can't do much about their race or gender (unless they are transgender, of course).

These findings are consistent with what psychologists have denoted as attribution theory—that is, we make inferences about other people in an effort to explain causes or events to ourselves. We attribute causes of obesity, homosexuality, criminality, and so on based on these inferences, when in fact we know nothing at all about the individual in question. And the better we know someone else, the less likely we are to attribute stereotypes to them.

So now let's revisit the issue on the importance of knowing the underlying motivation for why people discriminate. What difference does this knowledge make? After all, either way, people are behaving in an unfair, discriminatory way.

Our answer is simple: we cannot begin to craft serious legislation to address discrimination until we understand its sources. The fact that animus, although dangerous, is waning, whereas economic discrimination is rising is important information for the policy maker. And although policy on discrimination continues to change, we know little about the relationship between policy interventions and the two types of discrimination.

For years, the US government has been codifying and erecting rules that forbid animus-based discrimination. Affirmative Action is arguably the most often-used public policy to fight discrimination. The term *Affirmative Action* entered public discussion in the United States in the early 1960s; it refers to regulations aimed at reducing bias against and compensating groups that were historically discriminated against on the basis of religion, race, or gender. This genre of policy is not restricted to the United States. For example, post apartheid South Africa adopted a policy of "Broad-Based Black Economic Empowerment," which introduced the minimum representation of black employees companies had to meet.

In a sense, Affirmative Action is the opposite of Jim Crow, apartheid, and other terrible policies that historically discriminated against various minorities and kept them from desired jobs.

The supporters of Affirmative Action proposed reversing the effect of such harmful policies by increasing the participation of underrepresented groups in desired professions. This reversal certainly made sense in the 1960s and 1970s, when animus against minorities was strong.

But today we have, as a society, moved on to more subtle forms of discrimination. One of the problems with Affirmative Action, some opponents say, is that although the goal of promoting equality in societies is fine, such policies are no longer necessary given the advances women and minorities have made in the last fifty years.

An example of the problems associated with Affirmative Action policies has to do with the wrong inferences people may make regarding the success of a targeted minority. Think, for example, of a very intelligent and hard-working African American woman who graduates from a top law school. In the absence of an Affirmative Action policy, people would attribute her success to her strong skill set. But in the presence of Affirmative Action policy, people may attribute her success to government intervention. They would think she graduated due to favoritism, not so much because of her hard work and skill.

As a reaction to these types of objections, in some states Affirmative Action is no longer legal. For example, Proposition 209 in California now bars preferential treatment of women and minorities in public school admissions, government hiring, and contracting.

If a graduate admissions team at a university doesn't admit a talented black woman because, all else being equal, it simply doesn't like her race and gender, then a "reverse discrimination" policy such as Affirmative Action is probably a good solution. But if the reason for not admitting her is based on economic discrimination—for example, if the admission team believes that she can't succeed—then Affirmative Action is not the right way to help her. The discrimination is based on the university's "economic like" calculation: they want the best students to graduate, and they believe that she's less likely to perform. In this case, the solution is to change the cost-benefit analysis these committees follow. For example, if you are the candidate, you should try to signal that you can actually make it in the graduate program by earning good grades in more difficult undergraduate coursework. This is a different prescription than in cases where the discrimination is based on hate.

Our research suggests the old policy-making tools to combat modern-day discrimination in the labor market, such as hiring quotas and Affirmative Action are antiquated and misguided because they don't deal with the real problems of discrimination today. Rather, they deal with the wrong type of discrimination, not the one that is prevalent and growing—modern-day economic discrimination.

Shop 'til You Drop

The riddle that we proposed in the previous chapter: "What words can end modern discrimination?" have a simple solution:

"I am getting three price quotes today."

As we learned in the experiment involving handicapped drivers, this works when the person offering the service or product is engaging in economic discrimination. Just for fun, next time you're shopping in a venue that allows haggling, tell the salesperson "I'm getting three price quotes today." Using this simple sentence, you might have completely changed the salesperson's perception about the incentives she faces. Instead of trying to make a huge profit out of selling something to you, she will back up and give you a reasonable price, since she would understand that otherwise the competition could offer you something better.

Consider the following example. A few years back, while Uri was teaching a negotiation class in Singapore, he needed to buy a new lens for his Nikon camera. He went to a shopping area with lots of camera stores, most of which offered great deals. On entering the first shop, Uri asked the salesman for "a good lens for this Nikon camera."

The salesman explained what the options were and explained the details for each, then directed him to a lens he thought was the best. He wanted $790 for it. When Uri walked out, the salesman followed, asking how much Uri was willing to pay.

Now knowing more about the specific lens he needed, Uri could shop in earnest. Entering several other shops, he learned exactly why he wanted this particular lens. The more he learned about what he wanted, the better offers he received. In the end, he walked into the last shop, asked for "Nikon Nikkor AF-S 55–300mm f/4.5–5.6 ED VR High Power Zoom Lens, DX," and bought the lens for $328. No negotiation was needed.

What happened? The first guy wanted to charge $790 because he saw that Uri was clueless. The last salesman understood that Uri knew what he was doing, so he gave him a much lower price. The bad treatment from the first salesman had nothing to do with his disliking Uri: he simply categorized Uri as an uninformed customer and tried to get the most money out of him.

The moral of this story is simple: If you want to reduce economic discrimination when shopping, make sure that you are armed with enough information about going rates and product information to counter it. When you do, and you signal this to the other side, you dramatically change the salesperson's incentives to discriminate.

If we could wave a magic wand over policy makers so that they would put our findings to work, they would focus less on animus, and more on policies that help those subjected to economic discrimination. To do this, they would need to run more field experiments to tease out the various forms of economic discrimination in their markets of interest. Based on this research, they could then do a better job of ensuring that workers have equal access to jobs. They could work to see that consumers have equal access to products. When buyers try to get a home loan, they should be able to signal their credit-worthiness on a level playing field. And lawmakers could ensure that as more commerce goes online, prices are fair and transparent for everyone.

Our friend at the University of Chicago, Richard Thaler, had a good idea how to implement this. In his column in the *New York Times* called "Show Us the Data. (It's Ours, After All.)," he wrote, "Companies are accumulating vast amounts of information about your likes and dislikes. But they are doing this not only because you're interesting. The more they know, the more money they can make."[8] This may still be fine—why shouldn't they collect information and make money out of it? What isn't fine is for companies to abuse consumers by using this information. Thaler's solution is for Congress to pass a law requiring the companies to give you access to these data. Once you get them, you can see what's working against you, and you can find a product or service that better fits your needs. If the companies have to share your data with you, they will have a much harder time using it against you. Thaler argues that these companies are making our choices so complicated that we cannot be educated consumers without their data.

Thaler's solution is a good start. But if you really want to stop such discrimination, you need to not only have access to your data, but also understand how these companies are making use of them.

Ultimately, a deeper understanding of the workings of discrimination cannot help but make the world a better place. As Gary Becker noted in his 1992 Nobel banquet speech, "Economics surely does not provide a romantic vision of life. But the widespread poverty, misery, and crises in many parts of the world, much of it unnecessary, are strong reminders that understanding economic and social laws can make an enormous contribution to the welfare of people." We hope that you now have a better understanding of discrimination, and how incentives are critically linked to prejudicial behavior.

In the next chapter, we'll explain other ways in which public policy efforts to improve society can be more intelligently applied.

How Can We Save Ourselves from Ourselves?

Using Field Experiments to Inform Life and Death Situations

It's a late-September afternoon in 2009, and the students of Fenger High School on Chicago's South Side are crossing a vacant concrete lot on the way home from school. Some live in the Altgeld Gardens housing project. Others live in a part of Chicago's rough Roseland neighborhood (a.k.a. "The Ville.") Some of the students from these two different areas have developed fierce antipathies toward each other, though the groups are more like cliques than gangs.

As the teenagers cross the lot, a fight breaks out. Kids from the two groups, as well as other student passersby, get caught up in the scrum. Someone pulls out a cell phone and starts recording a video of fifteen to twenty kids going at each other. There are no clear sides, and the altercation seems to be no different than the hormone-induced brawls that occur at high schools all over America. Around a minute into the video, someone discovers a couple of two-by-fours lying in the empty lot. Eugene Riley, sporting a red motorcycle jacket, takes one of the big pieces of wood from a pal and swings it like a baseball bat into the back of sixteen-year-old honor student Derrion Albert's head.

"Dannnggg!" someone exclaims. Screaming and shouting, the kids start running—some toward the shouting, others away from it. Derrion tries to get to his feet but he is punched and kicked as someone shouts, "Oh my god, you guys!" Derrion attempts to protect his head.

The camera pans away from the empty lot and back to the street. A shirtless man in his early thirties faces down a much younger adversary who threatens to hit him with a two-by-four. The older man has arms like tree trunks. The kid does a quick calculation and decides to just throw the wood at the man and run for it. The camera pans back toward the lot. Derrion is still on the ground, defenseless, staring blankly at the camera. His attackers renew their beatings for ten more seconds and then run away. The cameraman and others run up to Derrion. Someone says, "Get up, son." His friends pick him up and bring him into a community center adjacent to the empty lot. His friends scream his name, desperate for him to respond. Two minutes into the video, you finally hear a siren.[1] Derrion died hours later.

The brutal death of Derrion, replayed thousands of times on YouTube, was one more awful example of the violence that continues to threaten inner-city youth, along with high rates of drug use, unemployment, teenage pregnancy, school dropout, and obesity. For decades now, policy makers have tried nearly everything to address these problems, but even when crime rates drop, it's never been clear which policies help and which ones are just a waste of money.

Desperate to try new things, policy makers such as then-Chicago Mayor Richard Daley and Ron Huberman turned to us. "Why don't we know what works?" Ron asked us. Our answer was simple: we have not experimented enough in this area to understand what works and why.

There is, however, an antecedent for such large-scale social experiments that Ron had in mind for us to do. Many took place in the 1960s, especially from 1963 to 1968 when President Lyndon Baines Johnson was president. During the LBJ era, social scientists sought answers to questions like "What is the ideal way to provide health insurance?"[2] The studies that resulted were incredibly influential, but when federal support for them dried up, researchers were much more likely to turn to their computers and their labs, leaving big social experiments behind. Only recently have academics again teamed up *en force* with policy makers to test the impact of large-scale policy interventions on behavior.

———

It didn't take long for the three-minute video of Derrion's murder to reach the public. It aired on news stations in Chicago; the video was embedded in just about every online news story related to the killing. Voyeurism? Sure. But the video helped identify the perpetrators, and prosecutors won convictions in five cases. The defendants were slapped with sentences ranging from seven to thirty years in prison. Even with good behavior, Eugene Riley is likely to spend the majority of his life behind bars. Five convictions are also a major cost to society. In Illinois, the per-person cost of incarceration hovers around $40,000 a year, and it is estimated that the cost of a homicide to society is well over a million dollars in medical costs, investigations, legal fees, and incarcerations.

How can we spend our taxpayer dollars to most effectively lower teen gun violence?

The Data Driller

Ron Huberman has served as one of the most brilliant public servants in Chicago (or perhaps anywhere). A handsome, deep-voiced, openly gay ex-cop, Huberman was born in Tel Aviv in 1971, the second son of two Holocaust survivors who went to Israel as tiny children after most of their own families had perished. His parents moved him and his older brother to Oak Ridge, Tennessee, when Huberman was five years old. His mother, a onetime concert pianist and linguist, went to work for the local high school, where she taught foreign languages. His father, a brilliant and prolific cell biologist, accepted a job working for the government doing cancer research. "My dad had tons of offers to work for pharmaceutical companies," Huberman recalls, "but he chose to do medical research for the government, earning less than he would have otherwise because he felt that he could make a difference for people. I think his decision led me to have my own sense of public service and a desire to give back."

In elementary and middle school, Huberman was not a very serious student, but he did manage to get good grades in high school and entered the University of Wisconsin, where he studied English and psychology. After he graduated, he went to the police academy, became a cop in 1995, and went to work on Chicago's graveyard shift. Being on the police force, he recalls, gave him a front-row seat to observe what works and what doesn't in a big, violence-prone city.

Murders in Chicago had been steadily rising over the years; the 1990s proved to be one of the worst decades for homicides in the city. In 1992, there were 943 murders in a city of fewer than three million people, resulting in a murder rate of 34 per 100,000. In 1999, 6,000 people in the city of Chicago got shot. Of those, 1,000 died. Answering calls about shootings in public housing projects, Huberman says, "taught me about the degree to which people simply become resigned to horror. There wasn't a night when someone wasn't shot or killed. The community's sense of moral outrage disappeared beneath a kind of fatigue as the shootings went on and on."

———

Having seen too many young people die, Huberman felt that there must be a smarter way for the police to do things. He began asking himself what levers might be strengthened and pulled to make the police force more effective. The police could not do anything much to change things on their own; they were mostly responding to crime rather than preventing it. So Huberman decided to go back to school during the daylight hours and pursue master's degrees in two wildly different—some might even say opposing—disciplines: social work and business.

Shortly thereafter, Huberman was promoted up the ranks to the level of assistant deputy superintendent of police. One of his first postgraduate projects was to bring the police force into the information age by developing the equivalent of an electronic medical records system. "Before this system, everything was done on paper," he recalls. "If an assault occurred, the witness would say, 'The guy had a tattoo of a bunny on his shoulder.' The investigator would then have to go into the basement and spend hour after hour looking through hundreds of pink paper forms looking for descriptions of assaults, and try to find one or two that mentioned a bunny tattoo. It took forever to get enough information on enough suspects to form a lineup or to identify crime patterns."

The force didn't have the millions of dollars it would take to turn this mess into a real-time electronic database, so Huberman went hat in hand to the giant software firm Oracle and persuaded them to develop it, telling them that they could go on and sell the system to other police forces around the country. Oracle took the bait and put in $10 million to do the work. Huberman gave them the information they needed to build it; a matching grant campaign pulled in the rest of the money.

The Citizen and Law Enforcement Analysis and Reporting System (a.k.a. CLEAR) has changed the equation on crime in Chicago. Today, when an assault occurs, the victim tells the policeman that the guy had a bunny tattoo on his shoulder, and tapping into his electronic device, the cop can identify likely offenders on the spot. Commanders can also strategically deploy officers to hot spots where crime is likely to occur. CLEAR has allowed police commanders to test their hypotheses on a regular basis. Are crime reductions, for example, better achieved through drug-related arrests, or gang-related arrests? The data show which police officers are most effective in reducing crime, and officers are promoted on the basis of that data. Today we believe that, partly due to this system, shootings in Chicago are down by two-thirds from the time CLEAR went live in 1999.

Cultivating Calm

After setting up CLEAR, Huberman quickly implemented similar systems in other large, complex, culturally complicated city government organizations. Following September 11, 2001, the day when all the big cities in the country were placed on high alert, Mayor Richard Daley decided to put Huberman in charge of a variety of big systems management challenges in very short order. When he appointed Huberman, Mayor Daley said, "I have utmost faith in him. I can go to sleep at night, and just close my eyes. I don't have to worry about Ron Huberman."

Huberman became like Chicago's own version of Superman, attacking one big, thorny problem after another and saving the day in each case. Huberman started with emergency management. His job: to coordinate agencies protecting the city from terror attacks, public health crises, and natural disasters—and figure out a way to handle the more than 21,000 calls to 911 every day. He created an integrated command center to coordinate all of the city's resources during crises—a system that then US Homeland Security Secretary Michael Chertoff called "revolutionary." Next, in 2005, Huberman went to work as Mayor Daley's chief of staff, where he was put in charge of rooting out city corruption and bringing accountability to city government. Then Huberman overhauled the Chicago Transit Authority, where he vastly improved ridership experience and re-negotiated collective bargaining agreements for all twenty-one of the Transit Authority's unions. In his spare time, he launched the largest ex-offender hiring program in the country.

All these systems relied on the same statistic-tracking, data-drilling methodology that characterized CLEAR. In each case, Huberman put together teams of like-minded, cross-disciplinary people in various departments. Together, they created detailed, measurement-oriented statistical tracking systems that often pulled in data beyond traditional government sources, and that laid out clear performance goals for people in every area of city government.

In 2009, not long after Derrion Albert's murder and Arne Duncan, then the head of Chicago Public Schools, went to work for President Obama as secretary of education, Huberman took over Duncan's job as CEO. Shortly after assuming the job, Huberman began attacking the problem of teen shootings. With the help of federal stimulus money, Huberman launched a program called Culture of Calm. The program targeted a handful of high-risk Chicago schools and threw every single intervention they could think of at them. Researchers scrutinized everything that put kids at risk of violence, from the way students were disciplined to the design of the entryways. Teachers put in more effort with at-risk students.

Additional school counselors were hired. Once the at-risk children received the attention they needed, the cultures of the schools began to change. But to really alter the landscape, something more was needed.

Enter Kanye West, the famous rapper and record producer. If anyone is a motivator for urban black kids, he is. A handsome, daring, outspoken, square-jawed black man who favors a leather skirt and a hoodie when performing, West has collected awards aplenty for his five solo albums, all of which have gone platinum; he's also one of the best-selling digital artists of all time.[3]

Talking with Huberman about an incentive featuring West, we decided that an intimate concert with the superstar (who would give the concert *pro bono*) would really get the attention of the kids in the thirty-two most violent schools. So we offered the prize of a private concert to the school that would most profoundly change its culture for the better. Every school had its own Culture of Calm committee, and the competition among the schools was fierce.

Farragut High School, the winner of the prize, underwent a huge transformation as a result of the Culture of Calm program. Located on Chicago's southwest side, the school's population is roughly 70 percent Hispanic and 30 percent African American. Before the Culture of Calm program began, the hallways were filled with kids behaving aggressively toward each other—pushing and shoving, throwing insults and sometimes punches. The only adults visible were roving security guards who literally pushed kids through the doors of their classes when the bells rang.

Farragut High students started by forming a Culture of Calm committee comprised of student leaders—not just the class president and student council, but "influential" kids who played football and so on. It was this committee's job to decide the basic rules, and they also agreed to two big, overarching requirements: a marked improvement in school attendance and a reduction of violence-based incidents not just in school, but outside school as well.

Motivated by the competition for the prize, the kids went to work applying peer pressure. The incentive worked like magic. While all the schools in the Culture of Calm program showed dramatic reductions in violence and a boost in attendance, Farragut reported that incidents of misconduct dropped by a whopping 40 percent.

Of course, the concert, held in Farragut's gym in June 2010, was fabulous. West brought along two other adored performers—Lupe Fiasco, who performed his hit song "Superstar," followed by another superstar, Common, who performed "Universal Mind Control." Then came West, and the students went wild. For them, it was an unforgettable night.

But as it turned out, the concert incentive isn't what really turned things around. The opportunity to see West, in fact, merely legitimized what the kids already wanted: a safe place to learn. "They cared about seeing him, but even more importantly, they felt free to stand up to say 'We want a safe school,'" Huberman says. To that end, the students succeeded beyond their wildest dreams. At all of the thirty-two schools in the program, the culture at the schools has remained calm. Teachers are in the hallways; kids don't pick fights. And violent incidents such as shootings have dropped by 30 percent.

So was this Huberman's only solution? As it turns out, this was just the tip of the iceberg.

Operation Chicago Public Schools Secret Service

A month after Derrion Albert was murdered, Huberman sat at a table in a school auditorium confronting a roomful of angry parents and teachers. They had come to tell him off for wanting to spend a

whopping $60 million on a two-year experimental program to re-
duce school violence, while the rest of the budget was being slashed
to the bone. Some teachers had lost their jobs; others faced over-
sized classrooms. And parents of students who weren't in danger
didn't understand why so much money would be diverted toward an
untested idea for helping the "bad" kids turn their lives around.

Huberman challenged the assembly. "Which is more important—
reducing class size or saving lives?" he asked. In a typical year, he
pointed out, more than 250 students were shot and, on average, 30
of these shootings were fatal. As a former cop, he'd personally witnessed too many tragedies, and they'd gotten to him. Besides, he
argued, kids in dangerous schools could not focus on academics
anyway because they had something much larger, such as the possibility of being murdered, on their minds. After a shooting, attendance
dropped to 50 percent. "If you are a logical, motivated kid, and a
shooting occurs near your school, do you risk your life or risk falling
behind in your classes?" Huberman asked. "And if you are a teacher
at one of these schools, and half your kids don't show up, do you
reteach when the frightened kids come back, and slow everyone
else down? What does it take to break out of this cycle?"

Huberman got his way, though plenty of parents continued to
question his wisdom—arguing that the academic programs were
being shortchanged. Perhaps the boldest aspect of Huberman's plan
was a program that would identify the kids who were most at risk—
the ones who were the most likely to be involved in a shooting crime.
The program would match an at-risk student with a highly paid
advocate who, in Huberman's words, would "act as mentor, advocate, and engaged adult who could serve as a parent figure to the
youths." To get the project started, Huberman asked us this question: *Out of 700 schools and 400,000-plus students, how do we
figure out who is most likely to be part of a shooting crime?* He figured
if that question could be answered, then the system could inter-

vene effectively. Without that information, the system would fail with certainty, he concluded.

So we set to work. First, our research team looked at retrospective data covering 500 shootings between September 2007 and October 2009. We wanted to see if we could decipher which factors put kids most at risk.[4] What did we find?

The first factor may seem blindingly obvious: it's being male. Race also plays a strong role, with Hispanics and African Americans pretty much running the same risk, but at a level much higher than Caucasians. And then there were the behavioral issues (school misconduct, past shootings, test scores, progress toward graduation, suspensions, incarceration history, and so on). Of these, the strongest predictor was having spent time in a juvenile detention center. This group had victimization rates more than ten times higher than that of a Caucasian student and six times higher than the typical African American or Hispanic male.

We also found that serious misconduct, absences, juvenile detention, and being over-age (that is, being held back a grade) were particularly detrimental for African American males, and suspensions and absences were strong predictors for Hispanics. For example, a seventeen-year-old freshman in high school was at considerably more risk than a fifteen-year-old freshman. Additionally, we learned that shooting crimes typically happened in the hours before or after school—a factor that explained why many kids who did well in other classes flunked first and last periods. They didn't show up because they were scared of the gangs that congregated at those hours.

As it turned out, our filters were fairly accurate, especially considering a shooting event usually only happens with a small number of kids. Out of all the students in Chicago Public Schools, we found that roughly 10,000 out of 410,000 (or 2.5 percent) of students were at serious risk of gun violence. Most of these at-risk students attended one of thirty-two schools in rough neighborhoods, were Hispanic or African American, and tended to live in poverty. Out of 410,000 kids, 1,200 students fit the model for very high risk. They needed intervention, and fast.

Now that we'd identified the most-at-risk students, the next step was to pair them with mentors through a program called Youth Advocate Programs, Inc. (YAP). One of YAP's mentors is Chris Sutton, a forty-year-old, African American, married father of two, who owns a car wash and holds a bachelor's degree in marketing. Sutton describes his dangerous job in five short words: "I keep my clients alive."

YAP pays Sutton between $12 and $30 per hour for each of his five clients/students, so he earns between $60 and $150 per hour in total. The pay is certainly good—yes, it "pays enough" to incentivize him—but it's a dangerous, twenty-four-hours-a-day job, and he says that the money isn't his chief motivator. Sutton really wants to help at-risk kids; he knows that if they were left alone on the streets, they would surely die. So he drops his young clients off at school in the morning and picks them up in the afternoon—the two times when school violence is at its peak. He takes them to work, and then to dinner and home in the evenings. He's on call the rest of the time.

One of Sutton's most recent ultra-high-risk clients was an impulsive young black man named Darren who pretty much fit all our criteria for shooting victimhood. Darren's parents are addicts who've spent time in prison. "If you are surrounded by people who are always doing the wrong thing, you have to be ten times stronger to do the right thing," Sutton observes. All of Darren's friends dropped out of high school, and because Darren has so often been in trouble, he has missed a lot of school, making him older than his peers. He was on probation for bringing a loaded gun to school. He lives with a foster parent in Englewood, a very dangerous section of Chicago where drive-by shootings are a daily occurrence. "It's like the OK Corral over there," says Sutton.

Darren is bright and hardworking, and he holds a city job, cleaning gutters and parks, that he procured through YAP. Unfortunately, he has a habit of gambling his paychecks away, and it's been a struggle for him to understand that all his impulsive actions have consequences. Because Darren is highly suspicious of institutions and adults, Sutton has had to walk a fine line to earn his trust. "You have to go undercover with kids like him," Sutton says. "You have to dress like they do, listen to the same music, and listen deeply. You collect intelligence about the really bad kids, and alert the school principals to them so we can get them into YAP, too."

While the program indeed saves lives, mentoring is very risky work. One day, Darren and other YAP kids with Sutton happened to cross the wrong line. Darren got into an argument with another kid, and then a gang member from a rival group entered the fray. Soon the bullets were flying. Darren and another student were hit. Sutton reclined his seat in the car, called 911, and prayed.

The good news is that Darren survived the shooting. He has managed to graduate high school. To his own astonishment, he even pulled a B in music, and tells Sutton he couldn't have done it without the help YAP provides. And Darren is still holding down a job with the city. "If kids like Darren can hang in there and get through high school, they will be prepared to hold a full-time job—provided they can secure one—after they graduate," Sutton says. "We can't take tests for them, but we can provide safe transportation, study help, and guidance. And eventually we can pull off the training wheels."

The YAP program is certainly expensive—averaging $15,000 per student—but it's nothing compared to the cost of incarceration, and for those it helps it does seem to stick. So far, while on most of the outcomes that we measured, the YAP kids are not different from the control group kids, none of the successful YAP kids have gotten into serious trouble after graduation; most of them, including Darren, have shown a dramatic improvement in behavior.

Nevertheless, YAP can't save all the at-risk kids in Chicago, and money is always tight, particularly for experimental programs. Even if they are lucky enough to qualify for YAP, many children, facing tremendous odds in their lives, simply give up and drop out. We need to continue to learn what works for these kids.

The Silent Killer: Obesity

Schoolkids—not just in Chicago, but all across the country—face another big threat: the danger of obesity, the rate of which has nearly tripled since 1980. According to the Centers for Disease Control and Prevention, 17 percent of children aged two to nineteen and one in seven low-income preschool-aged children are now obese. Obviously, these kids are spending too much time on the couch and not enough time exercising. And they are eating too much high-fat, processed food—not just at home, but also at school.

We call obesity the "silent killer" because most people do not understand just how deep the problem runs. A 1999 study that appeared in the *Journal of the American Medical Association* concluded that 280,000 to 325,000 US adults die each year due to obesity. That is one person every few minutes, or nearly forty deaths an hour. This rate of death exceeds many other well-known killers, such as drunk-driving fatalities and breast cancer.

Most adults barely remember—or have repressed—what the "lunch ladies" in hairnets and white smocks served them in the school cafeteria. There were "burgers" made of a quizzically brown meatlike substance pressed between white bread buns. Pigs-in-a-blanket made mostly of bread, with a tiny hot dog hidden within. Stale French fries. Bagged lettuce, which passed for a vegetable offering, doused in ranch dressing. Instant mashed potatoes spooned over with an unidentifiable gravy, pocked with cubed giblets. The kind of stuff that you wouldn't feed your dog, but too many American parents, or the government, pay for their kids to eat it anyway.

One night in March 2010, millions of TV watchers tuned in to watch Jamie Oliver, the famous British chef, go on a rampage in a school cafeteria in the town of Huntington, West Virginia, dubbed the unhealthiest city in America (because half the adults are obese). His goal was to improve what the town puts in its collective mouth. Oliver said he didn't like what he was seeing. Pizza for breakfast, followed by a lunch of chicken nuggets?

The lunch ladies were, not surprisingly, defensive. Why was Oliver picking on them and not their boss? "Those things are set up on a monthly basis by a nutritional analysis on the meals," said one lady, pointing to the label on a container of frozen chicken nuggets that Oliver had yanked from their very disappointing freezer. "The first ingredient is white meat chicken."

But as Oliver moved down the list of ingredients it was hard to find another pronounceable name. The majority of the list was unrecognizable chemicals designed to improve the freezer-hardiness, cohesiveness, springiness, chewiness, and gumminess of the chicken-like substance, including things like sodium benzoate, tertiary butylhydroquinone, and dimethylpolysiloxane. Oliver held a nugget up. "Would you eat that?" he asked the ladies. "Yes," one of them replied. "It's good!"

The US School Nutrition Association took umbrage at Oliver's charges and issued a countervailing press release, arguing that a 2009 survey of more than 1,200 school districts across the country "found that nearly every school district offers students fresh fruits and vegetables, low-fat dairy products, whole grains and salad bars or pre-packaged salads. Most schools still bake items from scratch in their kitchens, and school districts are offering more vegetarian meals and locally sourced foods. School nutrition programs have reformulated kid favorites to make them healthy, like pizza prepared with whole wheat flour, low-fat cheese and low-sodium sauce."[5]

Obviously, something between the lunch ladies in Huntington, the School Nutrition Association, and Oliver got lost in translation. But to its credit, the US federal government is, in fact (slowly, painfully), trying to improve matters to the tune of around $1 billion in annual spending. In 2011, the US Department of Agriculture (USDA) overhauled its school nutritional guidelines for the first time in fifteen years. But in November of that same year, Congress pushed back on the USDA's healthier school lunch standards by limiting some of the USDA's aggressively pro-health policies (prompting late-night comedians to poke fun at the idea that the tomato sauce on pizza and French fries are still to be considered vegetables). In spite of this setback, a spokesperson for the School Nutrition Association says that they expect most schools to continue to follow the USDA guidelines for healthier lunches.

Despite all the good intentions, here is the big problem: most kids still prefer French fries and pizza to spinach and apples. While many schools have tried to introduce healthy options, such as fruit instead of desserts, kids tend not to choose them—and even if they do choose them, they don't end up eating them. Some parents try very hard to instill a love for broccoli and brown rice in their kids, only to find themselves defeated by the influence of grocery store checkout lines and well-meaning but uninformed relatives, friends, and neighbors.

Aside from the fact that their taste buds have been spoiled, kids face another problem, of course: they have no long-term perspective, as we discussed in Chapter 4. Popeye ate his spinach, but if you tell a child "eat your veggies because it's good for you, and it will make you grow up big and strong," you'll be met with a blank stare. Children aren't thinking about their future health (or future anything, with the possible exception of their birthdays).

In Chapter 1, we talked about using incentives to make people exercise more, showing that paying students to visit the gym for a month made a change in their habits. Could the same kind of incentive work here? *What does it take to get kids to choose fruit over cookies?* To find out, we worked with the Chicago Food Depository to set up a study involving 1,000 schoolchildren in the Chicago area, where we worked with after-school meal programs to see what could entice children to choose healthy food. In our experiment, we first told kids in one group, "Today we have some extra desserts. Would you like a cookie or these dried apricots?" Predictably, 90 percent of the children went for the cookies.

Next, the children received some nutritional education, in which they were taught the importance of eating healthy fruits and vegetables and got to do fun things like drawing their own colorful food pyramids. After the program, we offered the children the same choice—cookies or fruit? To our (predictable) chagrin, the nutritional program didn't make a dent in their preferences. The kids still went for the cookies.

So we tried yet another treatment in which we told a different group of children, "You can have either a cookie or fruit. If you choose the fruit, you get a prize!" (The prizes were a small rubber ducky in fruit colors, a wristband, a pen imprinted with the words "eat strong to be strong," or a fruit keychain.) This time, 80 percent of the kids ate the fruit, compared to just 10 percent when there was no prize offered. We were also delighted by what happened when we combined the educational program with the prizes. When we came back a week later, 38 percent of the kids were still choosing and eating the fruit—demonstrating that some of the kids were beginning to accrue some longer-term good habits.[6]

A slightly different approach produced an even more positive result. We moved back a few steps to think about what happens in grocery stores. "Packaging and placement is something every grocery store does," Ron Huberman observes. "Why not apply that to institutional food?" (It's true: if you put the healthy food in a brightly lit, attractive, easily accessible place, and put the less healthy stuff in the aisles, more people will move to the "healthy" areas.)[7]

We started by eliminating the bad choices and replacing them with healthier ones, but—and this is important—we didn't stop there. One innovation was to replace the chips at the front of the lunch line with bags of sliced apples. This did the trick, Huberman thinks, because the packaged apple slices were less daunting than choosing a gigantic apple with skin that gets stuck in braces, and because we made the chips harder to get. The chips and cookies were put in a place where the kids had to ask the lunch lady to get them. Who wants to ask the grouchy lunch lady for anything? Effectively, we changed the cost of consumption. As Huberman says: "Make it hard for them to ask for the cookie and make it easy for them to grab the sliced apple." Duh.

The net-net? Once again, it's all about adaptation—combining nutritional education with healthy choices and making sure those choices are much more appealing than the less healthy ones will make the difference.

Nudges Versus Nuisances to Save Lives

A week before Thanksgiving in 2012, John's father-in-law, seventy-three-year-old Gary Einerson, lay in a hospital bed in the Intensive Care Unit of the University of Wisconsin's hospital, while the

Grim Reaper patiently waited for him to breathe his last. Once an athletic, six-foot-two-inch, 200-pound college basketball player, he was known as a no-nonsense high school principal who got things done at Deforest High School, just outside of Madison. Awaiting a liver transplant, Gary had shrunk to just 138 pounds. The doctors said that if they failed to secure a matching liver within a few days, Gary would not survive. But he was fortunate: a liver, possibly from a nineteen-year-old boy killed in a car accident near Madison, arrived just in time. The transplant was successful, and Gary went home on Thanksgiving Day. The oldest organ recipient in the hospital's history, Gary is today gaining weight and doing well.

According to the US government website organdonor.gov, eighteen people die every day while waiting for an organ; a single organ donor can save up to eight lives. You have doubtlessly heard the heart-wrenching pitches about the need for organ donors. The pitches go something like this:

> My cousin Janice, a mother of two small children, discovered that she needed a new kidney. Twice a week, she had to endure kidney dialysis. Of course, she put herself on an organ waiting list right away. If she didn't get a new kidney, she would die. Twice over the period of a year, she received a phone call saying that a kidney from an organ donor was available. But these kidneys were not a good match for her, so she had to keep waiting and waiting, becoming sicker and sicker in the process. One day, she received another call. This time, the kidney was a good match. A woman had died in a car accident, and she was an organ donor. That generous woman's kidney saved Janice's life.

Given the need for organs, policy makers in some US states and around the world have made it easier to locate donors.[8] When you go to conduct some official business, such as getting your driver's license renewed, you can "opt in" (meaning that you give explicit consent to be a donor) or "opt out" (if you don't refuse, you're going to be a donor by default). Strong evidence suggests default opt-out policies increase donor consent rates. For example, countries with opt-out policies, such as Austria, have higher donor rates—as high as 99 percent, while countries with opt-in policies, such as Germany, see donor rates of roughly 12 percent.[9]

This kind of default opt-out system is a perfect example of what our colleague, University of Chicago behavioral economist Richard Thaler, calls a "nudge." A nudge is, very simply, a way of making tiny shifts that change people's behavior for the better without their being aware of it. In their book *Nudge*, which Thaler coauthored with Harvard law professor Cass Sunstein, the authors take note of policy changes that have subtly coerced people to make smarter choices, like making it easier for kids to choose fruit or salad rather than cookies or chips.

Although an opt-out system has worked quite effectively in various settings (and it sounds like a great way to get lifesaving organs to people who need them), the problem with signing people up in such a manner is that some find it deceitful. Objectors might think that if they are going to be kind enough to give away their precious kidneys following a fatal accident, it might be polite to at least ask them beforehand to make an explicit rather than an implicit promise.

In 2007, we teamed up with Dean Karlan of Yale University to see whether it would be possible to increase donor rates even if we were explicit about it.[10] In our case, we decided to see what we could do to raise donations of corneas, which are in short supply. We worked with a nonprofit called Donate Life, whose mission is to increase organ donation, and ran an experiment that pitted nudges against a different approach—"nuisances."

As it happened, the state of Illinois had recently introduced a new system of donor registration. People who had been previously registered as organ donors needed to reregister as a result of a change in the law. So we ran a test in which our research assistants talked to more than 400 households in various neighborhoods around Chicago. The students told people that because of a new driver registry, they unfortunately might not be registered anymore. Then the students popped the big question: "Would you like to receive information on signing up as an organ donor?" If they chose to opt in to receiving information, they filled in a form with their name, address, gender, date of birth, and so on. Of those we asked, 24 percent signed up, giving us our baseline group.

But what if we changed the default option and households had to opt out in order to *not* receive any information? In another treatment, people who didn't want the information had to fill out the same form with their names, addresses, and so on if they wanted to opt out. This time, 31 percent of the people we asked signed up. It looked like changing the default was enough of an incentive to get more people to participate.

In yet another test, we made the signup form much shorter. In fact, all people had to do was write down their names to receive information from Donate Life. This time, 32 percent of people signed up to receive the information. This result showed that we could still get more donors this way than we could by directly asking them to opt in.

The results showed that reducing nuisances—and saving people time and hassle—worked slightly better than nudges, which means we do not necessarily need to use default to achieve the same level of success when signing people up. We can be explicit and still achieve better sign-up rates.

These results have potentially important implications beyond donating organs. For instance, Americans don't save enough for retirement. To increase peoples' savings rates, many argue that the default trick can work well. Our results suggest that simply lowering nuisances and explaining savings rules, clearly and simply, might do a similar trick. Likewise, reducing nuisances in helping make the right choice of health plan can go a long way toward getting them enrolled. (Of course, we'd need to do more field experiments to see whether such incentives could work.)

A Threat to Us All: Global Warming

Global warming poses one of the biggest threats to humans. Hurricane Sandy, which devastated large swaths of New York, New Jersey, Pennsylvania, and other areas, was just an appetizer for what looks like a full and endless meal of climate-related disasters coming our way. According to the National Climate Assessment released in January 2013, "certain types of weather events have become more frequent and/or intense including heat waves, heavy downpours and in some regions floods and drought. Sea level is rising, oceans are becoming more acidic, and glaciers and Arctic sea ice are melting."[11] The experts are more or less in agreement that the future will bring hotter, drier summers; wetter and more devastating storms; shut down power and transportation; and wreak havoc on food and water supplies.

To fight this scenario, inventors around the world are working hard to develop new technologies that can help to mitigate the global warming problem. But it's sometimes difficult to get people to adopt those technologies. How can field experiments help?

In search of an answer, we conducted a field experiment that revolved around lightbulbs. Currently, only about 11 percent of potential sockets in houses have compact fluorescent bulbs, or CFLs. Protecting the environment, of course, has a lot to do with the small changes we all make in our lives. In fact, if every household in the United States would replace just one incandescent lightbulb, we would prevent nine billion pounds of greenhouse gas emissions per year, equivalent to those from about 800,000 cars., and save $600 million in energy costs.[12]

To that end, President George W. Bush signed the Energy Independence and Security Act in 2007. The Act stipulated, among other things, that old-fashioned incandescent lightbulbs had to go away because they were energy-inefficient. Unfortunately, their replacements—compact fluorescent bulbs, or CFLs—were no great shakes. They flickered. Their light felt coldly institutional. Performance was iffy. They didn't work well in the cold. They contained mercury, making them difficult to dispose of and a problem if they broke. Resenting the new bulbs, a lot of people went on buying sprees to hoard the old ones.

The quality of CFLs has improved a lot since 2007, but many people are still holding a grudge against them, and some in Congress want to outlaw them. So what would it take to get people to get over their prejudices and switch to CFLs? As it turns out, this is a more complex process than one might think, because it involves a combination of peer pressure and pricing.

One big, persuasive tool in changing behavior is applying "social norms"—that is, subtle keep-up-with-the-Joneses cues that get people to follow others. Social norm cues are everywhere. When all the other parents arrive on time to pick up their kids from day care, that's a social norm cue. When you see a commercial on television telling you that "7 out of 10 customers agree" that a certain kind of cereal, toothpaste, car, or any other item is a good one, that's a cue. And when you go into a hotel bathroom and see a sign that says "73 percent of the guests who have stayed in this room have reused their towels," that's another cue.[13]

Another thing that persuades people to try something new is, of course, good old-fashioned money. To find out what combination of money and social pressure would work to get people to switch bulbs, we worked with David Herberich and Michael Price on a large field experiment in which student solicitors—our secret agents—went knocking on nearly 9,000 households in the suburbs of Chicago.[14]

The people who answered their doors were offered up to two packages of CFLs to purchase. The bulbs cost between $3.75 and $7.15, but we set our baseline price at $5.00 a pack. We also tried selling them at $1.00 a pack—about the same price as a pack of old-fashioned bulbs. Additionally, the students plied various households with social pressure, saying, for instance, "Did you know that 70 percent of US households own at least one CFL?" or, if we wanted to really apply the social pressure thumbscrews, they said, "Did you know that 70 percent of the households we surveyed *in this area* own at least one CFL?"

We found that there are two ways to induce people to buy CFLs. One way is to lower the price. Most people think that the government should subsidize CFLs so that they cost as much as traditional bulbs. Unfortunately, that's not going to happen when government budgets are shrinking. Our results, not surprisingly, show that this approach could work. A second way to get people to buy CFLs is to tell them that their neighbors use them. Reminding people of what their neighbors were doing worked in a way that was roughly equivalent to a 70 percent drop in price on the $5.00 pack. Importantly, when we came back and offered the CFLs at a low price, we found that people kept buying them.

So here's the big takeaway: if you want people to adopt new behaviors, the best tool is a one-two punch of social norms and pricing, which work as complements and build on each other. Start with peer pressure: people really want to keep up with the Joneses, so let them know what the Joneses have done. This will get them into the market, so that they buy their very first pack of CFLs. Then, once they are owners, peer pressure really does not work that well. At this point, you need to offer the product at a lower price. They will then buy greater numbers of CFLs.

In this way, the combination of social norms and prices can do the trick in convincing people to buy green products. More broadly, when we have green technologies that promise to help the environment, the government (or businesses) should make their first steps into the market with social norms. After reaping the benefits of the social pressure, further social pressure will not work. That is when prices enter the picture.

It's not often that academic economists studying endemic problems like poverty, homelessness, drug abuse, and crime get the opportunity to go beyond analyzing what has happened in the past, and instead get involved in generating models that could be implemented as public policy. So when we get an opportunity to work with people like Ron Huberman, who asked us how to properly design incentives in order to help solve many of society's biggest problems, we get pretty excited. And we'd definitely like to see many, many more experiments happen.

Public officials typically focus on programs that have the biggest *average* impact. In reality, though, some programs work very well for some and not at all for others. What if we applied a scalpel to social problems instead of a hammer? Data from our experiments make it clear that no one rehabilitation program will help everyone. It may be that tailored programs like YAP, rather than applying a one-size-fits-all solution, may be more helpful in bringing at-risk people like the gangstas of Chicago around.

For example, what if the programs like the Culture of Calm could be scaled down, but be applied in a more targeted manner? For example, some students may respond strongest to social incentives like a Kanye West concert. Others may need financial incentives. The idea would be to do more than just identify some students as at-risk, but to run a battery of tests that would allow us to diagnose more fundamental reasons for behavioral problems and to prescribe interventions based on that diagnosis. That is, tailor the policy to the individual. For example, how can you reduce AIDS transmission, teenage pregnancy, pollution, and high school dropout rates?

Of course, running big field experiments takes time, energy, and courage. In belt-tightening times, it's hard to think about spending money to conduct field experiments before applying social policies. But this is the wrong way to think about it: only by conducting research do we know what works, so that we can save money in the long run. And many experiments can be done virtually cost free. As Ron Huberman knows, it is possible to use research to improve outcomes for all of us—from children and the poor to planetary health.

What Really Makes People Give to Charity?

Don't Appeal to People's Hearts;
Appeal to Their Vanity

When you see a homeless person in the street, or the disfigured face of a child on the cover of an envelope, or a Salvation Army volunteer ringing a bell during the holiday season, chances are you will be moved to open your pocketbook. And if you are like most Americans, you probably give time or money to worthy causes all around the world every year.

In fact, Americans tend to be a pretty generous bunch. Nine out of ten people in the United States donate time or money to at least one charitable cause every year. Charitable giving by individuals in the United States is now more than $300 billion dollars a year—about the size of Greece's entire GDP. Add in charitable contributions by companies and foundations, and that number jumps much higher.[1]

In total, we're talking about a gigantic amount of money. Over the past forty years, charitable foundations have popped up all over the place. Although this trend has certainly relieved the strain on the US federal government to provide such public goods as aid to the poor, one question remains largely unanswered: *Why, exactly, do we give?*

Most people would say they give because they want to help others. But is such altruism the only reason for people's generosity? Our research reveals it is not. In fact, our multiple field experiments with several different charitable causes—which involved communications with over a million people—show compelling evidence that (brace yourself) our psychological reasons for donating are often more selfish than most of us would care to admit.

One obviously selfish reason for donating is the tax benefit we get from doing so. The US government effectively subsidizes our donations to causes that range from church auctions to saving the whales. Of course, even in the absence of tax relief, people still spend their hard-earned cash to help a cause; we usually don't ask for a receipt from the homeless person.

So if we give for reasons other than pure generosity or tax benefits, what are those reasons? From a fundraising point of view, this is an important question. Surely people who raise money for charities need to know the underlying motivations for giving, why donors remain committed to the cause, and why funders might stop writing checks. Nonprofits also need to know how to increase donations, particularly in a time of massive cutbacks for services at the local, state, and federal levels. Additionally, the US government would probably be interested in finding out whether the billions of dollars citizens write off annually from their tax returns makes real economic sense. If the government were to cut back on tax breaks for charitable gifts, would people stop giving?

Like every type of organization, nonprofits rely on their own peculiar blend of conventional wisdom. In our travels, we have learned that people in every walk of life tend to follow the received wisdom of previous decision makers, or rely on "gut feelings" rather than verifiable data to make their decisions. In the charity world, for example, soliciting donations has been pretty much a matter of tradition and trial and error. When setting up the next pledge drive, fundraisers rely on past practices based more on anecdote than science.

But regardless of whether you run a charity, a corporation, an auto shop, or a startup business, operating on conventional wisdom is usually a silly thing to do, particularly when your stakeholders (your employees, the people you serve, and the people who support you with their dollars) count on you to intelligently manage things. In this and the following chapter, we slide the charity sector under the microscope and put some standard ways of doing things to the test.[2]

But our findings don't just apply to charities. As you will see, they have wider implications for any organization.

Planting Seeds

The origins of our research in philanthropy date back to 1997, when John was a wet-behind-the-ears assistant professor from the University of Central Florida (UCF). At that time, John was spending most of his time testing economic theory, slowly making his way up the research hierarchy using field experiments in the only market he really knew well: sports card collecting.[3]

One day, John was approached by Tom Keon, the dean of the business school at UCF. Keon wanted UCF to become a top research institution. The only way to do that, Keon was convinced, was for each academic department in the business school to choose one niche area in which to specialize. After the department made its choice, he would funnel gobs and gobs of resources into that area.[4]

With a background in environmental and experimental economics, John decided that one of his niche areas should win the "contest." After months of bickering and lobbying, the faculty voted nearly unanimously in favor of environmental economics, with experimental economics serving as a strong complement. It was a big day for John and his colleagues, who celebrated with beer and pizza.

Soon after the vote came in, Tom Keon delivered the winner's spoils. "John, congratulations; your area has won. I have decided to make this really work, we need to start a Center for Environmental Policy Analysis" (CEPA, as it was later called). "And you are going to be in charge of that."

John quaked in his loafers.[5]

"Of course, you're going to have to go out and raise money for it," the dean explained. "The school will give you $5,000 in seed money. You're going to have to figure out how to use it to raise a lot more."

John had never studied the public sector, and he didn't know the first thing about fundraising beyond occasionally responding to some of the heart-wrenching pleas he regularly received in his mailbox at home. So he decided to do a little research into tactics for using seed money for a fledgling nonprofit. He read everything he could find on the subject, but absolutely no quantitative research existed about how much money was required to start a campaign. Indeed, he found little rigorous research of any sort. So he had to do his own research. What were the assumptions upon which this world of fundraising was built? He decided to talk to the fundraising experts at some of the largest charities in the world.

One afternoon he found himself chatting with a dapper, silver-haired gentleman in a tweed jacket who worked for a large animal-protection foundation. The conversation went something like this:

JOHN: The dean gave me $5,000 in seed money. How much more will we need to start a capital campaign?

HIM: Ah. There's a silver bullet for this!

JOHN: Really?

HIM: Yes (leaning forward). You need 33 percent of your goal. So if you're trying to raise $15,000, you need $5,000. 33 percent is the magic potion.

JOHN: Wow. That's great, thanks! But how do you know it's 33 percent? Why not 50 percent or 10 percent?

HIM: Because I've been in this business for a long, long time, and that's how it's done. It's exactly 33 percent. If you start the campaign with more or less than that, the campaign will not raise as much money.

JOHN: But how do you *know* that's the case? What's the evidence for that? I haven't been able to find any research on this . . .

HIM: (a little exasperated) I know because I learned it from my former boss, who was in fundraising for a long time himself. This is what we always do. Trust me.

JOHN: (equally exasperated) But how did *he* know?

You can see where this conversation was going. This well-meaning guy hadn't given much serious thought of his own to raising more money. He knew much more about putting together a charitable gala than about fundraising innovation. But there John was, just a few weeks into his foray as a part-time charitable fundraiser, and he already seemed to have reached the depths of what some of the most accomplished folks in the business knew about seed money.

There is something "off" about charity, John thought. But people like the dapper gentleman were smart; what was missing? John concluded that they had not used economic field experiments to scientifically study the underpinnings for why people give. Their vibrant sector was driven by anecdotes, not science. This was disappointing but, for a young researcher, it represented a unique opportunity. Here was a sector that could importantly be influenced, and tremendously helped, by field experiments. In John's mind, the end game would be a scientific revolution that dramatically changed the manner in which the charitable sector conducted its business.

———

Before getting into how seed money works, let's try a little thought experiment just for fun. The following ideas are common in the fundraising world, and they are typical of the assumptions people make every day. (Some of them have been proven to work well—the others, not so much. In the course of the next two chapters, you'll discover which gimmicks in each group have been shown to be the most effective, and why.)

Group A:
- 1:1 matching grants ("If you call now, an anonymous donor will match your donation dollar-for-dollar—doubling your donation!")
- 2:1 matching grants ("tripling your donation!")
- 3:1 matching grants ("quadrupling your donation!")

Group B:
- Lotteries ("If you donate, we'll enter your name in a lottery.")
- Refund and rebate offers ("If we don't raise $20,000, you'll get your donation back!")
- Tontines ("The more you donate, the bigger the prize you stand to win!")

Group C:
- Door-to-door solicitations
- Direct-mail campaigns with a picture of a suffering animal or child and an outer envelope that says, "Your donation can save a life today!"
- "We have $5,000 in seed money. Help us raise $25,000!"

The more we looked into it, the more we realized that everyone had an opinion about what worked and what didn't. But there was little scientific evidence pointing to *why* people give money to charity, or why they respond to marketing schemes like these in general. Think about it: how often do marketing and sales people use tactics like this to coax prospective customers to part with their money? In fact, the whole economics of charity looked like a promising field of inquiry, because the implications, as you will see, apply broadly to just about every walk of life.

Follow the Leader

The first thing the research center needed was some new computers. Six, to be exact, and the $5,000 wasn't going to cut it. So late one night, we got to talking with our friends and fellow economists James Andreoni and David Lucking-Reiley, and together we concocted a plan to develop our first test of charitable fundraising practices.[6]

We split the full capital campaign for the research center into several smaller campaigns to fund the six computers the center needed, and each campaign served as a separate experimental treatment. We sent several versions of the same solicitation letter to the homes of 3,000 central Floridians, explaining that the new Center for Environmental Policy Analysis (CEPA) at the University of

Central Florida would examine local, state, and global environmental issues such as air and water pollution, endangered species protection, and biodiversity enhancement. Would they contribute some money to buy computers for the researchers?

In asking people to consider making a contribution toward the purchase of a $3,000 computer, we suggested different seed level amounts in a variety of treatments. In one letter, we said we'd already obtained 10 percent of the cost, so we asked for money to cover the remaining $2,700. In another letter, we said we'd raised 33 percent of the cost, so we asked for help in garnering $2,000 more. Another letter stated we'd raised 67 percent of the cost, so we hoped donors would chip in an additional $1,000. Some letters said that if we didn't raise the money for the computers, the money would be used to cover CEPA's operating expenses. Another treatment said that if we didn't raise the money, we would refund the donation. All these different letters were accompanied by the usual "thank you," a contribution form, and a postage-paid envelope. We sent the letters out and waited.

As the responses trickled in, we discovered that the received wisdom in the industry was correct, but only partially. Seed money does work to attract other donors. But the 33 percent number some of the experts had given us was completely wrong. As it turned out, giving increased when we told people we had 33 percent of the funds already raised, but it increased even more if we told them we had already raised 67 percent of the goal. At lower seed levels (say, 10 percent), the contributions dropped off.

It looked like the good people in the charity industry had been leaving free money on the table by focusing so intently on the 33 percent seed-money figure. Still, their combined intuition may not have been completely wrong. You see, seed-money levels convey competing pieces of information to prospective donors. On the one hand, you would think that the closer a charity comes to achieving a fundraising goal, the less a donor would feel she has to give to help reach the goal—she can "free ride" on the donations of others.

But on the other hand, donors are busy people. They don't have time to investigate every detail of every charity, so they may look for signals from other donors. Saying you have raised a lot of seed money from an anonymous donor conveys that an "insider" has done her homework and has given a large gift.

People like to play follow-the-leader this way. Indeed, our research found this follow-the-leader component is important to donors—so important that it completely overwhelms the free-rider effect. How far one can push this argument is still an open empirical question. For example, if we announced that we had already raised 99.9 percent of what was required, we suspect donors would not have given much. But that's just our hunch.

Putting this follow-the-leader effect into action isn't easy, though. We told some letter recipients that if we failed to raise all the money, we would send them their donation check back. You would think a rebate would boost giving, because there's no free-rider problem and it has a follow-the-leader enticement. But when we crunched the numbers, we found that offering a rebate didn't change giving at all.

Just to make sure we could be more certain of our results, we took our idea to the Sierra Club of Canada, a long-standing organization with a donor base and a history of running three to four mass-mailing solicitation campaigns a year. The British Columbia chapter of the club was willing to let us in. So along with our colleague Daniel Rondeau, we ran another experiment asking 3,000 households to help the Sierra Club expand educational offerings to K-12 students in the area.[7] We told half the letter recipients (the control group) the fundraising goal was $5,000; we told the other half that $2,500 of the $5,000 had already been raised. Did planting the seed work this time around?

You bet it did. We raised a total of $1,375 from the control group, and $1,620—an 18 percent increase—from the seed group. Seed money, again, worked in the direction of the prediction.

The net-net of all of this? Many nonprofits appear to be terrified of announcing higher seed levels, because they worry about the free-rider effect. We think that these organizations simply don't understand that donors want to play follow the leader. In fact, the follow-the-leader effect is so powerful that it overrides the free-rider effect.[8]

The Snickers Equation

While some folks on the fringes of the right wing see National Public Radio (NPR) as one of the places where liberals gather to launch socialist plots, it actually is a pretty good organization and, for many, even a vital part of the day. As NPR likes to point out during its pledge drives, it gives you not only great national and international news coverage, but also fun shows such as *A Prairie Home Companion* and *Wait Wait . . . Don't Tell Me!*

Still, if you're a commuter who likes to listen to the soothing voices of the station's local hosts, you probably know the worst weeks to be out on the road are during NPR's seasonal pledge drive. Each day of pledge week, the otherwise gracious hosts transform themselves into anxious pleaders who use a number of different ploys to increase giving. One of the favorite schemes of these fundraisers is to say, "If you donate $100 now, you can double your donation with a matching grant from a generous donor!"

Such a pitch makes perfect sense, economically speaking. Normally when you contribute to a charity, every dollar you give translates into just one dollar for the cause. But when you're told that if you pay $100, the charity will actually get a gift of $200, you might think you're being offered a two-for-one special, and that's exactly what fundraisers want you to think.

Think of it this way: if you can get either one Snickers bar for $1 or two for $1, you'll go for the two-for-one deal. This is Economics 101. And if this tactic works for grocery stores, it should work for fundraisers, right? The intuition is so strong in the fundraising community that the fundraising bible warns that one should: "never underestimate the power of a challenge gift" and that "obviously, a 1:1 match—every dollar that the donor gives is matched by another dollar—is more appealing than a 1:2 challenge. . . . and a richer challenge (2:1) greatly adds to the match's attractiveness."[9] Are matching grants really the equivalent of a two-for-one special that we find in grocery stores and shopping malls? Or, put another way, do matching grants really work the same way discount sales do in the consumer world? After all, big donors have relied on this idea for years. For example, an anonymous donor recently gave Drake University $75 million and stipulated that the school should leverage that money by offering three-to-one and two-to-one matching grants to solicit more money from donors. In other words, the donor told Drake to multiply the gigantic sum of money by using the Snickers bar idea, on steroids.

But do matching grants like this really work? To find out, we again joined forces with Yale University's Dean Karlan, a left-of-center economics professor who was also interested in investigating the question of what makes people give.[10] Following George W. Bush's 2004 presidential election, Dean wrote to a particular liberal nonprofit organization he admired, saying that we wanted to run an experiment with 50,000 of its supporters.[11]

The nonprofit was glad to have our help with their fundraising drive, so it accepted our offer of help. Working with their people, we designed an experimental fundraising campaign. One letter (the control) simply asked for contributions and didn't mention a match. The other letters looked like different versions of the following:

> Matching Grant
> NOW IS THE TIME TO GIVE!
> Troubled by the continuing erosion of our Constitutional rights, a concerned member has offered a matching grant . . . to encourage you to contribute at this time. To avoid losing the fight to defend our rights, this member has announced a [$1, $2, $3] match for every dollar you give. So for every $1 you give, we will actually receive [$2, $3, $4]. Let's not lose this match—please give today![12]

We randomly divided people into four groups: three match levels and one control group. People in Group 1 received a 1:1 match invitation telling them that for every $1 they gave, the organization would receive $2. Those who received the 2:1 match letter were told the organization would receive $3 for every $1 they donated, and so on.[13]

Then we sent out the letters and waited. The expected part was that the match worked: when all the responses had come in and we looked at the data, we found that those people who received a match offer were roughly 20 percent more likely to send in money. That is, we increased our response rate by 20 percent by just having a match in place. So it definitely looked like the promise of a matching grant worked, and worked well.

But, then the surprise came: the *size* of the match did not matter at all. A 3:1 matching grant offer was no more effective than a 1:1 challenge. And the 2:1 challenge did about the same as the 3:1 and 1:1 challenges. In light of the strong anecdotal evidence that higher match levels are better than lower match levels, this evidence from thousands of observations was shocking.

We found something else, too. The match worked much more effectively in "red" or conservative-leaning states than "blue" or left-leaning states (remember that the nonprofit was a liberal one). Why might that be the case?

The short answer is that birds of a feather stick together. Let's say you are a liberal in the so-called People's Republics of Massachusetts or Vermont where your senators and congressmen agree with you. You receive a letter from a progressive organization asking you for money. You are more than willing to hand money over, with or without a signal of the quality. Regardless of the organization's credentials, you decide to help. "Everyone around me is sending in money, so I will too," you reason. To you, the left-wing organization soliciting left-wing prospective contributors for money in blue states, there isn't a lot of need for a quality endorsement.[14]

But birds who aren't of a feather shriek louder. The match served a different, and important, signal to liberals in red states. If you are a leftie living in Mississippi, Tennessee, or Arizona—or a conservative in California, Oregon, or Vermont—you feel outnumbered. You rage against the machine, but you are not so sure that the charitable organization is high quality. Lo and behold, someone comes along and says "Join my fight; your friends out there in (enter your red or blue state here_____) are fighting hard and giving a lot to the cause." Given that you spend considerable time feeling at odds with the ruling powers (or your neighbors), you will be more responsive when you know that your contribution supports a good cause. It's like being on the side of the idealistic students and the starving paupers in *Les Misérables* or John Gult from *Atlas Shrugged*, if you're persuaded otherwise—there's a sense of pride and glory in what you are doing.

A theory from social psychology lends itself well to this reasoning. As the theory goes, individuals from a minority group have a stronger sense of *social* identity. Accordingly, the social cue of the matching grant acted as a catalyst to trigger people's "peer identity." Thus, the "signal" generated by the leadership gift is likely quite effective in engaging those in the minority political group.

Now, if people give because giving to charity is the right thing to do or believe in the charity's purpose, what do the politics of their state have to do with their giving behavior? Our research was beginning to hint at something: charitable giving is more connected to ego-identification than we might think. This notion of charitable egotism has a name: the "warm glow" theory, made famous by our friend James Andreoni.

The warm glow comes from feeling good when we donate; helping the local elementary school, supporting the food bank, saving the rainforest, or protecting harbor seal pups raises our self-esteem. Surely, a component of altruism motivates giving, but a warm glow (a.k.a. "impure altruism") is also a motivator. New York City mayor and billionaire Michael Bloomberg put it eloquently: "We're put here on this earth to share and to help each other. And nothing I will ever do—or you or anybody else that's generous—will give you as much pleasure as you get when you look in the mirror just before you turn off the light and say, 'Hey, you know, I'm making a difference.'"[15]

In the end, matching grants aren't at all analogous to offering two or even three Snickers bars for the price of one. Our experiments led us to the conclusion that donors do not behave like customers at a fruit counter. Donors want to know their gifts are an example of doing the right thing. They are wary of being duped. But every day people also give because they like feeling that warm glow.

So what does this finding imply for all the hosts of public radio, the dapper gentleman from that animal-protection organization, nonprofits, marketers, and businesses in general? Our advice to them: stop relying on hand-me-down formulas or assuming that selling donations works like selling Snickers bars. Matches do work—remember, any match looks better than no match at all—but our research shows that a one-to-one match works just as well as a two-to-one or three-to-one match.

Above all, it's important to appeal directly to people's appetites for the warm glow by showing them how good they will feel after donating. When charities (and marketers) recognize that feature of human motivation, they'll be able to come up with a hundred new and interesting ways to get Mr. and Ms. Citizen to open their wallets.[16]

The Beauty Effect

On a chilly Saturday afternoon in December 2005, Jeanne, a bright, energetic junior at East Carolina University (ECU), trotted up the walk of a suburban home in Pitt County, North Carolina. Jeanne was equipped with a professionally embroidered shirt emblazoned with the name "ECU Natural Hazards Mitigation Research Center." She wore a badge with her picture, name, and solicitation permit number. She also carried a clipboard and several brochures. She knocked, and a middle-aged man opened the door.

"Yes?" he said, eyeing her.

"Hi," she said, smiling brightly. "My name is Jeanne. I'm an ECU student visiting Pitt County households today on behalf of the newly formed ECU Natural Hazards Mitigation Research Center."

Jeanne went on to explain the center was dedicated to providing support and coordination in the event of natural disasters such as hurricanes, tornadoes, and flooding—events not unfamiliar to the area.

The man nodded. Jeanne widened her smile. "To raise funds, we are conducting a charitable raffle. The winner will receive a $1,000 prepaid MasterCard. For every dollar you contribute, you will receive one raffle ticket. The odds of winning this raffle are based on your contribution and the total contributions received from other Pitt County households. The winner will be drawn at noon at the center on December 17 and will be notified and the results posted on the center's website. All proceeds will fund the Hazards Center, which is a nonprofit organization. Would you like to make a contribution today?"

Of course, the man who opened the door had no idea Jeanne was a double agent. Yes, she was trying to raise money for the center. But she was also part of a bigger field experiment involving dozens of college students like her who were trained and paid to knock on the doors of 5,000 households in Pitt County. Some of the students just asked for money, but the others, like Jeanne, added the raffle bait. All of them were part of our study to see whether the raffle would increase donations to the center.

Interestingly, we found that the lottery treatment (which we called "the lottery effect") raised roughly 50 percent more in gross proceeds than the request for donations alone. We found that more people participated in the lotteries; roughly twice as many people opted to donate compared to the treatment where we simply asked for donations. Lotteries provide fundraisers with a tool to generate "warm lists," or a larger pool of active donors to draw from in future fundraising drives. In this spirit, lotteries give the fundraiser a "double dividend"—a chance to earn more funds immediately, as well as establishing a large warm list.[17]

We also discovered something else that was very predictable: the more attractive the solicitor, the bigger the donation received. We call this "the beauty effect." To obtain measures of physical attractiveness, we took digital photos of each solicitor during the initial interview to prepare an identification badge.[18] We then allocated the photographs into files that contained the pictures of three other solicitors. The files were printed in color and independently evaluated by 152 different observers (undergraduate students from the University of Maryland–College Park).

The observers rated solicitors like Jeanne on a scale of 1 to 10 for attractiveness. Jeanne was rated high at 8, and she raised about 50 percent more than an equally qualified woman who rated a 6. Perhaps not surprisingly, the women raised the most money when a male answered the door. Jimmy was also scaled to be much more attractive than Stan, and he raised more money than Stan; but women raised more than the men did.

What was interesting to us was not that there was a beauty effect—it was the size of the beauty effect. We found that the "beauty" effect was about as large as the "lottery effect." That is, just by changing the solicitor's attractiveness from a 6 to an 8, we could increase donations by as much as adding the lottery.

Beauty aside, does a raffle ticket really lead to any long-run meaningful change in giving? Years after this first field experiment, we revisited the solicited households with another.[19] We found that people who were initially attracted by the lottery continued to give at a much higher rate. However, the guys wowed by Jeanne's beauty the first time didn't continue to give unless another, equally attractive solicitor came to their door.

It came as no shock to us that the beauty effect did not lead to a lifetime of donations—after all, a visit a long time ago from a pretty face per se is no reason to continue to support a cause. We found, however, that people who gave because of the *raffle* continued to give for years to come. This is a lot like what we found in setups in which the participants felt the charity was invested in the outcome (more on this in a moment). The raffle, like an initial seed-money investment, signals that the charity is "giving something to get something." It also signals that the charity is a durable organization.

Murders, Opt-Outs, and Other Temptations

In a February 2011 episode of *The Daily Show with Jon Stewart*, Stewart, playing the straight man, asks the show's resident expert on everything, John Hodgman, to offer a solution to the big, tough problem of balancing the US budget. After suggesting we reduce the Pentagon (the building) from an overinflated five-sided building to a four-sided rhomboid, Hodgman suggests we raise revenue in an unconventional way. "If you really want to fill the nation's coffers, you know what you have to do is—legalize it," he says. (The audience, hearing the intimation of legalizing marijuana, laughs and applauds.) The rest of the conversation goes like this:

> HODGMAN: You know what I'm talking about. Legalizing murder . . .
>
> STEWART: You are talking about legalizing *murder?*
>
> HODGMAN: Murder. All I am saying is, let's put our free market Darwinian theories to the test. Let the weak perish and let the strong take their lives. So long as they can pay the bigamy tax.
>
> STEWART: What about Social Security and Medicare?
>
> HODGMAN: That's half of our budget right there. And what? Dedicated to taking care of the oldies and sickies instead of the youngies and sexies like us? . . . The point is it's not fair.
>
> STEWART: You are saying get rid of the old and the infirm?
>
> HODGMAN: No, no, don't get rid of them. I'm saying let's make Social Security *fun*. Make it a competition. Winner take all.
>
> STEWART: You don't mean . . .
>
> HODGMAN: Yes, John. A *tontine.* A gentleman's agreement in which the last living participant collects all of the Social Security money.

STEWART: But if murder is legal, then what it does is incentivize people to kill each other to win the pot! . . .[20]

The best model of such ridiculous arguments is Jonathan Swift's "A Modest Proposal for Preventing the Poor People in Ireland from Being a Burden to Their Parents or Country, and for Making Them Beneficial to the Public," in which the author argues that poor Irish parents should sell their children as food for rich gentlemen and ladies. But tontines are actually a time-honored way to make money, and they are more than a gentleman's agreement.

Basically, a tontine is an interesting mixture of group annuity, group life insurance, and a lottery, and it isn't just the stuff of mysteries or comedies. Tontines have a fascinating place in economic history, and they played a major role in raising public funds in Europe during the seventeenth and eighteenth centuries. Tontines get their name from one Lorenzo Tonti, a Neapolitan of little distinction until his sponsor, Cardinal Mazarin of France (who was responsible for the country's financial health), supported his position in the court of the French king in the 1650s.

In this capacity, Tonti proposed a form of life-contingent annuity with survivorship benefits whereby subscribers, who were placed into different age classes, would make a one-time payment of 300 livres to the government. Each year, the government would make a payment to each group equaling 5 percent of the total capital contributed by that group. These payments would be distributed among the surviving group members based on each participant's share of the total group contributions. The government's debt obligation would cease with the death of the last member of the group.

Based on their success in France, tontines spread. Governments used them to finance wars and municipal projects, such as the oldest standing bridge in London (the Richmond Bridge). Built in 1777, the bridge garnered its funding from shares priced at a then–hefty

£100 each. Investors were promised an annual return based on the income from toll crossings. When one shareholder died, the surviving members received a share of the leftovers (which is why tontines seem custom made for murder mysteries and are banned in the United States).[21]

Tontines have a fascinating place in fiction as well. Agatha Christie used them as the underpinning for several novel plots, including *Murder on the Orient Express*. More recently, in an episode of *The Simpsons*, Abe Simpson and Mister Burns discover they served together in World War II, and their squad came to possess priceless German paintings that would go to the last surviving member of the squad. *The Wrong Box*, a wonderful old film starring Peter Cook, Dudley Moore, Ralph Richardson, John Mills, and many other comics, is based on an old Robert Louis Stevenson story in which nephews of a tontine's last surviving member fight over the fortune.

Because we knew, based on our earlier research, that lotteries help increase charitable donations, we wondered whether tontines might do the same thing. That is: *Rather than using tontines as a mechanism to finance government debt or provide a lifetime annuity for subscribers, could charitable organizations use them to elicit more donations? How would a tontine-like mechanism work in comparison to the other charitable ploys we'd examined?*

First, think about our charitable lottery. For every dollar you give, you earn a raffle ticket; each raffle ticket represents a chance of winning the prize. So the more you give, the higher your odds of winning the prize. No matter how much money is raised, the prize doesn't change; but, the chance of winning the raffle prize decreases as others give more, because the total number of raffle tickets increases.

If you think for a moment, however, it's unclear why charities would focus on lotteries when reversing this structure might be ideal. A charitable tontine would work by giving each donor a fixed probability of winning a prize, with the size of the prize proportional to the amount donated.

For example, let's say you walk into your county fair and discover that people at a booth are raising money for the American Cancer Society with the help of a charitable tontine. The nice volunteer tells you that no matter how much you give, you'll have a 25 percent chance of winning a prize, but the more you give, the better the prize. Then she shows you the various tiers of prizes for which you'll be competing. If you give less than $20, you'll be eligible for a few small trinkets, such as a bookmark and a water bottle. For between $20 and $50, you're eligible to win a bottle of fancy wine. For $50, you might win a shopping spree; for $100, a weekend vacation at a resort; and for $200, you get a shot at a new Lexus. You begin to think of your donation as an investment opportunity.

To test whether tontines might work this way, we joined Andreas Lange and Michael Price to devise a laboratory game played by students of the University of Maryland. The game was contrived, but financially very real. The students' decisions had actual financial stakes, perhaps made deliciously salient by the conversion of tokens to cash.

Here's how the game went: each student was clustered with other students. At the start of each round, each of the students got 100 tokens. They could either give those tokens to the public good (a charity in this case) or keep them. If they kept them, they would get a few cents for every token they kept. If they donated them, one of two things happened. In one condition, each token donated to the public good grew in value. So if you donated five tokens, they would grow in public value to six tokens. (This arrangement roughly reflects what happens when you donate to a charity. For example, when you donate blood to the Red Cross, your own blood isn't worth much to you, but it's really valuable to someone else.

The increase in the value of each token in the public good was supposed to reflect this effect.)

In the other condition, everyone in a cluster benefitted from each donation. Even if you donated nothing to the public good, you could still enjoy the fruits of others' donations. (Similarly, when Bill Gates gives billions of dollars to charities, he makes the world better off, but we don't have to pay anything to enjoy the fruits of his generosity.) After being assigned to a cluster, the students had a simple decision to make: how much should they keep and how much should they give to the public good? But then we added an extra wrinkle: we entered them into either a lottery or a tontine.

We found that tontines outperformed lotteries in two very important instances. First, in cases where people have very different tastes, tontines raise much more money than lotteries. When people really diverge in their preferences for what is being offered, tontines can be a very good tool to get the people who like it to give more. Second, when people are really risk averse—say, they don't like to gamble or place much of their money at risk—the tontine is a good tool to raise money. Since both of these features— people are different and people are risk averse—represent the world today, the tontine is a viable tool for fundraisers.

The results of our experiments also suggested people are much more likely to donate when they're invested in the game. This finding makes sense—after all, if you feel the charity is trustworthy (remember the follow-the-leader effect?), and if you stand a chance of "winning" with it now or in the future, you are more likely to respond to its appeals.

———

All told, our research suggests that giving is less about doing something good for others and more about doing something good for oneself. "This is less depressing than it may sound," wrote David Leonhardt, who summarized our results in the *New York Times Magazine* as follows:

> For one thing, the charities are still getting the money, no matter what the donors' motives are, and many of them are putting it to good use. For another, the warm-glow theory means that philanthropy can be more than a zero-sum game. If giving were strictly rational, the announcement of a big donation might lead other people to give less to the cause; they might figure it no longer needs their money as much. Thanks to the warm glow, though, Warren Buffett's $31 billion gift to the Gates Foundation won't cause other people to think that they no longer need to help fight dysentery. If anything, Buffett's gift might make them more likely to make a donation. They can then have the sense that they're joining forces with someone else—with Warren Buffett, no less—and becoming part of a larger cause.[22]

This is a key point, and one that cannot be understated: while human behavior might seem irrational, everything changes once you understand what motivates people to act. Once you understand people's motivations, you realize that their behavior is, from their point of view, quite rational. We are all just trying to satisfy different wants and needs, but these don't fit into traditional, boxed-up assumptions, fixed ideas and hand-me-down recipes and traditional ways of doing things.

As we observed in Chapter 1, for example, people imagine that a gym membership will inspire them to work out far more often than it really does. So they purchase the monthly membership in hopes that will be the case. They may end up not working out as often as they planned, but they had a rational reason for signing up in the first place.

Returning to our experiment on matching gifts, then, it makes sense that having a match in place works, but that higher match levels work no better than smaller ones. As an example, consider what some economists claim is a major national problem: we do not save enough for our retirements. How do most of us save? Usually our employers match what we place in a 401k retirement savings plan. As our colleagues Richard Thaler and Cass Sunstein point out, people who put money into their 401ks contribute *exactly* the same amount that triggers the match. If an employer matches the first 5 percent of salary 1:1, then people will save exactly 5 percent of their salary. But if an employer matches the first 5 percent of salary 1:2 (the employer contributes $0.50 for each $1.00 that you save), then people *still* save exactly 5 percent of their salary.

This might have seemed puzzling at first, but it is directly in line with our findings. So, can we leverage this behavioral insight to make the world a better place? If we are convinced that people need to save more, here is what we can do. Companies that currently match the first 5 percent of salary 1:1 should simply say, "We have decided to change our retirement plan. We will now match the first 10 percent of salary 1:2."

What will happen? Let's say you are someone who currently earns $50,000 per year. Under the old regime, you will personally save $2,500 and your employer will match with $2,500, for a total savings of $5,000. Under the new scheme, you will save $5,000 and the employer will match with $2,500, for a total savings of $7,500. By simply changing the rules, the employer has raised your savings and it does not cost the company an additional penny. Assuming the US government supported such a change to 401k rules, a simple policy solution could be put in place, and you and millions of others would save much more.

In the end, giving to charity is nothing like purchasing a Snickers bar; it's more about doing the right thing and joining a fight, and feeling good about what you give. In this way, giving to charity is just as much about your personal proclivities as it is about the effect of your gift. If you are a silver-haired CEO of a philanthropic organization, then, you must understand that donors respond to triggers that are different from the ones you have traditionally applied, or your charity will not reach its potential.

In the next chapter, we'll explore strategies that a specific charity used to raise money and learn more about the ways people respond to one special "trigger."

What Can Cleft Palates and Opt-Out Boxes Teach Us About People's Reasons for Giving to Charity?

The Remarkable Phenomenon of Reciprocity

Smile if you recognize this face:

If you don't know her, you should. Her name is Pinki Sonkar, and she's the star of a 2008 Academy Award–winning documentary called *Smile Pinki*.

Pinki was born in the poor rural village of Mirzapur, India. She spent her days sitting in the corner of her house. She dared not go outside because people would point and stare at her.

She wasn't even allowed to go to school. She felt hurt and angry and wanted to know why she was different from others. Her father was certain she would never be able to marry and said she would be better off dead. One day, she met a kind social worker named Pankaj who, in turn, introduced her to a doctor named Subodh Kumar Singh.

Do you recognize her now?

Pinki's was no uncommon malady. Approximately 35,000 Indian children are born with cleft lips and palates every year, and millions around the world suffer as Pinki did. Their parents, who can't afford surgery, often leave them in ditches on the side of a road, feeling as if a curse has fallen on them, and the children who aren't abandoned are kept hidden away in shame. Eating and breathing is difficult for them. If they survive, children with clefts are shunned by their peers at school and by their communities.

The faces of children with cleft lips are ubiquitous, thanks to Smile Train's ads in newspapers, magazines, and, of course, the award-winning film. The ads have generated millions of dollars in donations for the charity, which offers free surgeries to children in developing countries around the world who suffer from this common, easily corrected birth defect, one never seen in the United States because it is corrected shortly after birth.

Today, Pinki is a hometown celebrity. She has many friends, and she likes to wear lip gloss.[1] And she is one of 100,000 kids around the world who get their cleft palates fixed for free annually because of some out-of-the-box experimental thinking on the part of one Brian Mullaney, the cofounder of Smile Train and WonderWork.org.

In the previous chapter, we learned that people are motivated by many things—their own human desire for a "warm glow" feeling, among others. Here, we'll show how a unique field experiment using direct mail, and based on principles that apply equally well in business, made a huge difference for Pinki and millions like her by appealing, once more, to a fundamental human desire.

A Sister's Curse, a Brother's Gift

Brian Mullaney is one of those curly haired, blue-eyed, fighting-Irish guys you meet in an airport bar during a long layover. The light in his eyes shines with intelligence, candor, and a dancing, catch-me-if-you-can entrepreneurial spirit. He has a friendly, distinguished, Harvard-by-way-of-Ohio way of speaking that is simultaneously incisive and casual. You sit down at the bar, and he asks you your name, where you are off to, and what you do for a living. Soon you find yourself buying him a Guinness, passing him a business card, and saying, "So what about you?" Then, shoulder to shoulder, you listen to his story.

Mullaney, who was born in 1959 in Dayton, Ohio, is the second-oldest of five children in a strict Catholic family, the son of a line of lawyers on his father's side. His paternal grandmother, Beatrice, was one of the first women to graduate from Boston University Law School in the 1920s, and she became the first female judge in Massachusetts. His father, Joseph, graduated from Harvard Law School after spending some time in the ROTC; he rose to become a government and corporate attorney, and eventually a vice chairman of Gillette. His stay-at-home mom, Rosemary, was a product of Stonehill College and Brandeis University.

The Mullaneys were a tight-knit, happy family until tragedy struck when Brian was eleven. His adored, beautiful little sister Maura contracted a high fever and was diagnosed with an autoimmune condition called Stevens-Johnson syndrome, which resulted in a bloody rash that spread and blistered, eventually causing the top layer of the skin on her face to die and peel away in sheets.

Within weeks of the fever, Maura went from being a healthy, pretty eight-year-old to what Brian Mullaney describes as a "ninety-year-old shell" bound to a wheelchair. Though she was blind and in constant pain, she bravely tried to return to school. But the other children teased and taunted her. Brian protected her as best he could, but he deeply resented the fact that Maura was ostracized on the basis of her looks. She died at the age of ten. Brian was only thirteen, and yet he keenly felt the injustice of the treatment Maura received from those who did not understand her suffering.

After what happened to Maura, Brian transformed from a pious, well-behaved altar boy to a rebellious, indignant, out-of-control teenager who cared only about basketball and hanging out with his friends. By the time he was in the ninth grade, he was flunking out. His parents yanked him out of public school and marched him to a private, jacket-and-tie boys' school where kids who got *bad* grades were teased. So he turned himself around and wound up going to Harvard, where he majored in business economics and began sharpening a healthy disrespect for status-quo thinking. He started by producing editorial cartoons for the Harvard *Crimson*.

The cartoons, some of which poked at hypocrisy, got him in trouble. In one cartoon, which he produced when the openly gay Massachusetts representative Barney Frank was first running for office in 1980, Brian ribbed the Catholic Church, whose priests were telling parishioners not to vote for Frank. The cartoon showed two men leaving church after confession, where the priest has told them to atone for their sins. One says to another, "I didn't mind the

20 Hail Marys for cheating on my wife, but the 50 Our Fathers for voting for Barney Frank was a little too much." "The Catholics on campus hated me for that," Brian says.

But things got much worse when he made fun of the policies of Harvard's nascent Third World Center. The center, which was going to be dedicated to serving the needs of minority students, stipulated that no white people could serve on its board because Harvard already had too many Caucasians. In his cartoon, Brian—who hated racism of any kind, including the reverse sort—drew a picture of a castle with a sign that said "No Whites Allowed" on it, and a caricature of the then president of Harvard, Derek Bok, handing bags of money to a black man and a Chinese man on the steps. The caption showed Bok saying, "Go away, Honkey. It's President Bok, and I'm here with your funding!" The black students went wild, labeled Brian a racist, and stormed the editorial offices of the *Crimson*. The editor hid under his desk, and Brian was forced to hire personal protection and a defense attorney. "It was horrible," he recalls.

One day, Brian got the bright idea of earning some money for himself as an ad man. He donned a suit and tie, and approached businesses around Boston, telling them he could produce advertisements, jingles, and posters for them. He did pretty well for himself in this field, and after graduation, landed a job at Young & Rubicam as a copywriter, much to the dismay of his parents. "They asked me, 'Why did we spend all that money sending you to Harvard and then you go into an industry where you don't even need a college degree?'" Brian recalls.

At Young & Rubicam, Brian learned just how far inside the box people in the ad industry could be. "We would produce hundreds of good ideas, and then the agency tested everything in focus groups," he recalls. "But they refused to go with any of the good ideas that came from the testing sessions because the ideas didn't have anything to do with the client's corporate strategy. Instead the agency went with boring, ill-conceived commercials that had everything to do with strategy and nothing to do with selling potato chips or Jell-O," which happened to be what they were selling.

Brian needed a better place to sell his creative ideas, so he took a job at J. Walter Thompson, where he made million-dollar beer commercials. "I'd go into the board room of Miller where a bunch of old white guys in suits made all the decisions. I'd play the youth card and tell them, 'I'm the only guy in this room who was in a bar at one in the morning,'" Brian says. "I was winging it with my ideas. I didn't go in with PowerPoints and a lot of data. I just spoke with a lot of passion. Eventually I got to be good at making presentations to rich people."

Brian walked around Madison Avenue, resplendent in Armani suits and Gucci loafers. He thrived in the *Mad Men*—esque world of cocktail lounges and beauty everywhere—beautiful ads, beautiful products, and beautiful people. But he grew restless working for other people, so he started his own advertising firm. His talent for selling ideas paid off when he cofounded Schell/Mullaney in 1990. The firm served clients in the media and high-technology businesses, such as Dow Jones, Computer Associates, and Ziff-Davis.

On the outside, Brian was a smart, competitive businessman who swam with the Madison Avenue sharks. On the inside, he was walking around with the memory of what had happened to his little sister. In 1996, he and his partner sold the firm for $15 million dollars, and at the age of thirty-six, Brian was "done. It was an unbelievable amount of money," he says. "Suddenly I realized I had the freedom to do what I really wanted."

Brian was too entrepreneurial to follow the typical conquests of the newly rich. He didn't try to sail around the world or earn his PGA card. He was the type of guy who loved to innovate, to push the envelope. Maura's memory drove him to want to help children, so he went on a medical mission to China. There he witnessed the social isolation children with cleft palates suffer and how easily their lives could be transformed with a simple surgical procedure. So, in 1998, he partnered with Computer Associates founder Charles Wang to found Smile Train.

Not bad for a Madison Avenue adman.

The Business of Smiling

People such as Brian who are founders of charities are driven by passion, but making a charity a real success requires acute business sense. "Most charities are very inefficiently run by do-gooders," Brian insists. "No matter how inefficient or incompetent you are, it is almost impossible for a charity to go out of business. As long as you have a set of PowerPoint slides with pictures that can make people cry, you can raise enough to stay in business."

Smile Train is unique among charities because Brian set it up like a business. In the same way Brian innovated as an adman, he destroyed the curve when it came to both raising money and doing good works. Basically, he turned the old missionary-style do-gooder model on its head. Instead of sending Western doctors to perform cleft surgeries, Smile Train developed state-of-the-art 3D technology to educate doctors in developing countries in cleft palate surgery (Brian calls this the "teach a man to fish" model.)

Smile Train is also unique because it conducts field experiments to see which kinds of donor incentives work best. For example, says Brian, Smile Train ran a lot of tests to see which would work better: a "before" and "after" photo of a child, or simply the "before" photo? As an adman, Brian knew the standard formula was to show both the before and after photos. "After all, it was a famous advertising edict that people want to see the 'before-the-wash' and 'after-the-wash' shots, as they do in Proctor and Gamble detergent ads," he says. "But when we ran the test, we found when we only ran the 'before' photos, the response rates went up 17 percent. Why? The picture of the kid with the cleft palate haunts you." The implication, he says, is that the photo of the child in need made the plea for money personal. Donors felt they *had* to help the kid with no upper lip.

Smile Train also conducted several field experiments to discover what kinds of photos could get the donation envelope opened. They tested responses to forty-nine different envelopes emblazoned with pictures of black, brown, Asian, and white boys and girls of various ages and wearing different expressions—some smiling, some frowning, some staring, some crying. As Smile Train discovered, faces are powerful attractants, and certain kinds of faces draw more donor money than others.

In December 2008, Smile Train tested twenty-one of these different photos on the outer envelope of another direct-mail package assortment. The winning photo attracted 62 percent more donors than the one that donors liked least. Smile Train discovered that the photo of the sad-looking Caucasian child (who was Afghani) drew the most response. Why? Brian conjectured that white donors—who comprised the majority of the donor pool—preferred to help someone who looked like them.[2]

The "Once and Done" Option

By the time we got to know Brian, he had honed in on several unique ways to raise money, which were guided by his unswerving use of field experiments. He would send potential donors letters that would "invite" them to donate, or to "save the life of a child." The messaging in the letters would reflect the learnings from years of field experimentation on direct mail that drove Smile Train's annual donations up to nearly $100 million per annum.

Brian was intrigued by our ideas about behavioral economics and charity. He wondered if we could help Smile Train outperform the best direct-mail letters that he had personally spent years developing and refining. We decided to set out by starting with Smile Train's best-performing letter and working to improve it. Though we didn't know it at the time, we had begun a path toward one of the most interesting, large-scale field experiments we had ever run.[3]

Back in April 2008, we started with a test. We sent letters to 150,000 households. The control group received a standard Smile Train solicitation asking for a donation. We had no special text or slogan on the outer envelope. The experimental group received letters sealed in an outer envelope that read, "Make one gift now and we'll never ask for another donation again." The letter told prospective donors they could exercise this right by checking a box on the reply card that said, "This will be my only gift. Please send me a tax receipt and do not ask for another donation." Donors were given one more option; they could also elect to receive "limited mailings" (which could prove to be a boon for Smile Train in postage savings).

This mechanism might seem a little crazy. Many fundraising experts, manuals, and guides would mock the very idea, because one of the most important tenets in fundraising circles is to develop a so-called donor pyramid.

In a donor pyramid, the base includes dedicated donors who will give to your cause again and again. When you find such donors, why on earth would you tell them "thanks for helping our cause this one time! Now, we will never contact you again"?

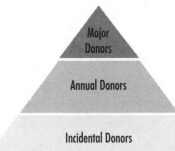

A visual representation of the types of donors a typical charity has and how numerous they are.

In the months after the first test in which the mailing was sent out, the donations started to trickle in. And all signs pointed to one thing: our experiment had been a gigantic success. In response to the letters sent out in April, the standard letter raised $13,234 from 193 donors, whereas the "once and done" letter raised $22,728 from 362 donors. In total, the experimental treatment raised much more money and engaged many more donors than the standard letter did. Interestingly, only 39 percent of donors checked the opt-out box.

The "once and done" campaign was so successful that we decided to step back and use it in other field experiments. In total, we sent mail solicitations in five waves to more than 800,000 individuals between April 2008 and September 2009.

Again, we found a dramatic increase in giving under the "once and done" campaign. The "once and done" letters generated a response rate nearly twice as large as the standard letter. It also brought in slightly larger gifts (on average, $56 versus $50). Consequently, the "once and done" campaign raised more than twice as much initial revenue as the standard letter ($152,928 versus $71,566), yielding a remarkable $0.37 per letter mailed.

Of course, if subsequent donations were lower in the "once and done" group, then the conventional wisdom would have been correct. That is, we should not have been urging people to "bug off." Interestingly, what we found was that the subsequent revenue raised turned out to be nearly identical across the "once and done" and the standard letters.

Combining the revenue from both initial and subsequent donations, "once and done" generated a total of $260,783 compared to $178,609 for the control mailings—an increase of 46 percent. In addition, because of the restrictions on future mailings dictated by checkbox responses, Smile Train also saved mailing costs because they were not continually sending to an uninterested donor.

Just having such a successful drive is important, but we wanted to dig into why "once and done" letters work so well. What was going on?

Reciprocity: The Key to Customer Satisfaction

After analyzing the hundreds of thousands of observations across the various field experiments, we found that *switching the power from the charity to the donor* was the game changer. By giving recipients the chance to opt out, Smile Train basically offered donors a *gift*. It relieved them from having to say no to future solicitations. Instead of merely asking for money, the charity basically said, "You scratch our back, we'll scratch yours."

Traditional economics assumes that, acting in their own best interest, many people will just smile and toss away the direct-mail appeal. Yet, not all of us are selfish. Some of us, even some economists, are nice people who really do want to return a kindness with a kindness.[4] Knowing this, appealing to people's sense of reciprocity can work. Nonprofits, especially, like to send preprinted address labels, maps of the world, or calendars, hoping to get a donation in return.

More generally, our result highlights hidden returns associated with incentives that are overlooked if one maintains a standard economic model. For instance, our interpretation also means that the psychological message that is conveyed by incentives—whether they are perceived as kind or as hostile—has important behavioral effects. Intentions matter: if you are a company that cares about customers, then it's important to know that customers really appreciate being asked their opinions, and they love being asked if they want to opt out.

Our explorations in the world of charity have big implications. In policy circles, people want to know the answer to this question:

If we get rid of the tax write-offs for charity, what happens to all the charities that hold society together? What happens to government grants? Before detailing the effects of such proposed changes, we need to understand why people give to charities in the first place.

———————

Here's another thing that Brian, adman-turned-philanthropist, can teach us about business. If he understands anything, it is scale. Smile Train now conducts roughly 100,000 surgeries a year, and that number is going down—not because Smile Train can't help more children, but because the charity's services have caught up with the world's needs. Children with clefts no longer have to wait for the help they deserve. Brian didn't want to stop with fixing clefts, however; he wanted to go after even bigger problems. Having come away with what works to drive charitable donations, he parted company with Smile Train and founded a new operation called WonderWork.org.

This new charity attacks five easily fixable problems poor children around the world face: blindness, club feet, burns, hydrocephaly ("water on the brain"), and holes in the heart. Inexpensive surgeries can address each of these. Take blindness, for example. More than forty million blind people populate the world. Of these, says Brian, "half could regain their eyesight with a ten-minute outpatient surgery that costs a hundred bucks."

WonderWork.org, which *Time* named in 2011 as "one of 10 ideas that change the world,"[5] has a unique organizational structure no charity has ever tried. "We are going to build a General Motors of Compassion with different charity brands that tackle single causes," says Brian. "Just like GM has Chevrolet and Cadillac, we will have a blindness brand, a club foot brand, a burns brand, a hydrocephalic brand, and a hole-in-the-heart brand. By managing five causes under one roof, we reduce overhead and administrative costs for each cause by 80 percent. That gives us huge advantages. If we are successful in creating five new Smile Trains, we can create 100."

While Smile Train has made great use of "once and done" campaigns so has WonderWork.org. One of WonderWork.org's "brands," Burn Rescue, has also used it to great effect.

After extensive testing in a 2012 mailing of over four million pieces using the "once and done" campaign, WonderWork.org expects to bring in over 350,000 donors and raise around $15 million with this offer in 2013.

Even better, Brian hopes to double the revenue per donor because contributors will have more than one cause from which to choose. The new structure doesn't let donors lapse, because it "cross-sells"—something unheard of in the nonprofit sector. "Charities hate the word 'selling'!" Brian says. "*But I love it.*"

Obviously, not too many people in the charity world are like Brian. He is an entrepreneur. Most of the bigwigs in the nonprofit world are still terrified of changing business as usual—which isn't to accuse them of negligence, just status-quo bias. Their hearts are in the right place. Many probably got involved in nonprofit work because of a deep belief in trying to do as much good as they possibly can in the world. Acknowledging that donors might not share that belief, or be as altruistic as charities would like to believe, might feel like conceding defeat.

Still, it's increasingly obvious that charities are the frontline providers of many kinds of important public services and goods. As federal and state governments cut back on funding, resources for aiding children, seniors, the poor, the environment, and the arts all lose. Organizations such as the Sierra Club, Amnesty International, the Red Cross, and all the great nonprofits that do everything from feeding, housing, and educating the needy to providing us with great arts and entertainment need someone to step up for their cause. Scientific reasoning can help.

The Foundation for Long-Term Success

Having dug deeper into the economics of charity, we have uncovered solid, quantifiable evidence on how incentives work to attract new donors and customers; more importantly, this evidence lays the foundation for long-term success. We now know that seed money, humbly proportioned matching grants, raffle tickets, sad-eyed Caucasian children with cleft palates, and a pretty woman on a fellow's doorstep can all help raise money. Our evidence shows that social pressure accounts for a sizeable proportion of the motivation to give. We believe tontine-like schemes might work to open people's pocketbooks. And we've discovered that giving people the right to opt out not only increases giving now, but lays the groundwork for efficient campaigns later as well.

In the end, we suspect that even though everyday givers focus on that warm, glowing feeling, larger donors—those who give millions of dollars a year—are more influenced by changes in the tax code. If you think about it, this makes sense. Come tax time, the federal government allows you to deduct dollars you give from your reported income if you itemize your deductions. For those itemizers in the 35 percent tax bracket, this allowance effectively drops the price of giving a dollar down to about something like 65 cents. Not a bad incentive to give.[6]

We all assume that people give because doing so helps others. But the truth, as we have seen in our field experiments again and again, is that many people give more out of self-interest. Sadly, charities haven't understood this just yet. To get people to open their wallets, charities have applied certain tricks of the trade—announcements of having raised 33 percent of seed money, 3:1 matching grants, direct-mail appeals, and so on—relying on tradition and formulas. In so doing, they have left money on the table.

In a wide variety of experiments—from Smile Train campaigns to the Sierra Club, from the University of Central Florida to neighborhood streets around the country, we found that certain long-held assumptions about charitable giving don't hold much water. Frankly, we were not surprised to discover that men give more when beautiful women ask them. But we were surprised to learn that Smile Train donors more frequently open an envelope when the kid on it looks like them. In the words of the inimitable Carly Simon, we are (all) "so vain." In the end, we need to feel that we have some skin in the charitable game.

Our conclusion is simple: charities, by necessity, will need to stop relying on hand-me-down formulas and begin experimenting more; if they do not, they will lose to their competition.

We hope that the field experiments described in these chapters offer a set of new ideas, prescriptions, and lessons that can help organizations to take that first step (or at least call us to make that first step!). As the sector advances, field experiments will serve as a tool that revolutionizes it, and field experiments will become the rule in the nonprofit world, rather than the exception.

Next, we will visit another set of managers in need: those who lead for-profit companies.

Why Is Today's Business Manager an Endangered Species?

Creating a Culture of Experimentation at Your Business

It's a sweet, blue-sky September day in New York City. The year is 1965. The taxi driver drops a man at the corner of 1st and 64th. He steps into the new art-nouveau restaurant. Checking himself out in a greeting mirror, he finds he looks super-sharp in his Brooks Brothers suit, black necktie, and starched white shirt. A hint of Old Spice drifts from the pulse in his neck.

He greets the three marketing guys from Westinghouse like best friends while the hostess, outfitted in stilettos and a bottom-hugging pencil skirt, nods and smiles coyly at him. She guides the party to a linen-and-crystal-adorned table beneath a gorgeous, multicolored Tiffany-glass ceiling. He and his guests sit down and scan the menu while the waiter takes the first round of drink orders.

"Hello, Roger," he says familiarly. "I'll have the usual. Dry martini with triple olives. What's your soup today?"

"Our soup is a freshly made, creamy Maine lobster bisque, sir. Delicious!"

"No, I'll pass," he says. "I had the lobster yesterday. I'll take the pâté en croute to start, followed by the wild boar, and the lemon custard pie with coffee for dessert."

Just one lunch in the day of the life of another Madison Avenue businessman, albeit nearly fifty years ago. What does the rest of his workweek look like? A short week, thanks to all those three-martini lunches that last for hours. More client meetings in the fanciest restaurants and clubs in New York City. More bourbon-laced office meetings. And, of course, the hanky-panky.

This is the kind of weird world depicted in the TV series *Mad Men* (and, no, it isn't a huge exaggeration of the then-reality). The setting makes for great drama, hence the thirteen (and counting) Emmy awards. But from the perspective of the curmudgeonly economist, the series begs the question: *What on earth were the businesses that hired fancy-schmancy, Don Draperesque advertising guys thinking?* They were certainly creative, but how did they know that what they suggested worked?

Today, top executives might not always make big, important decisions about products, prices, and ad campaigns at booze-filled lunches, but too often they make such decisions based on little more than hunches. We think that businesses that don't experiment—and that fail to show, through hard data, that their ideas can actually work before the company takes action—are wasting their money. Not only that, but these executives are clearly placing themselves on an endangered species list.

Netflix: A Case in Point

Netflix, the movie delivery service, is the poster child for the need for experimentation in business. Because its product and client base is second to none, it was able to avoid bankruptcy following a series of breathtakingly, entirely avoidable, bad moves it made in 2011.

Netflix was founded in 1997 on the basis of a great question: *Would people pay a monthly subscription to have DVDs delivered to their doors (without late fees) instead of having to tromp down to the local video store (which made a lot of money on late fees)?* The market responded with a resounding "yes." The feisty little Silicon Valley company delivered movies people wanted, delivered them fast, and in general did a fantastic job of playing David to the Goliath of video chains such as Blockbuster.

Later, Netflix also started offering streaming online videos, though the selection was far more limited, so that customers could watch films two different ways. In so doing, it effectively disrupted brick-and-mortar video rental outfits, including the giant Blockbuster, which was forced to shutter many of its stores. With twenty-five million happy subscribers, Netflix was a darling of the stock market, too: it was trading at nearly $300 a share by July 2011.

But then, the company did something strange: it told its customers in a lengthy, rather confusing email that it was breaking up its bundled mail and streaming service into two separate services. Customers already paid $9.99, $12.99 or $14.99 a month to rent one, two, or three DVDs at a time, respectively, depending on their plan, and a limited number of streaming videos. But now, the company said, it would charge all customers $7.99 a month for one-at-a-time movies by mail and another $7.99 a month for streaming service, effectively raising its previous prices by 60 percent.

Customers vociferously disapproved of the move, likening it to a "brain fart" on the part of management. Posting a comment on the Netflix site, one fellow named Greg (signing himself as an "ex-customer") wrote the following:

Dear Netflix,

To say the least, I am shocked and appalled at your recent behavior. It seems like yesterday we were the best of friends. You informed me with your poignant documentaries; I always laughed at your corny B horror flicks. For four years you've been the gracious receptacle of my hard earned money, but alas, your current actions have forced me to reevaluate our relationship. Your nominal price increase, while unexpected, does not deter my loyalty. However, your mouthpiece Jessie Becker's presentation of this upcharge—as an added choice for my own benefit—insults my intelligence and reveals the breadth of your arrogance. Had I been treated like an adult and informed of these changes in a straightforward, honest manner, perhaps we could rekindle our spark. Unfortunately, this course of action is no longer available; your condescending and manipulative tone has irreparably ruined our relationship.[1]

Netflix got so many complaints that it had to hire extra customer service employees. The company's stock plunged 51 percent. Then, in September of 2011, CEO Reed Hastings apologized to customers and announced that Netflix was going to try to correct the situation. How? By splitting the company into two operations: one, called Qwikster, would be the mail-delivery business, run by a new CEO; the other would be the online streaming service, called Netflix.

This announcement made customers even angrier. Now, subscribers to both streaming video and DVDs would see two separate charges on their credit card statements and have to log on to two different websites. The stock dropped another 7.4 percent.

Realizing they'd made things even worse, "The Netflix Team" sent out the following email to customers in October 2011:

Dear [Customer's Name Here],
It is clear that for many of our members two websites would make

things more difficult, so we are going to keep Netflix as one place to go for streaming and DVDs. This means no change: one website, one account, one password . . . in other words, no Qwikster.

Netflix thought that some customers would leave; but they were shocked that close to a million customers would drop Netflix. By this time, Netflix was being universally slammed as a badly managed company. Even *Saturday Night Live* wound up making fun of it.[2]

To see just how costly it was not to experiment, take a look at Netflix's stock price, pre– and post–mess-up in 2011:

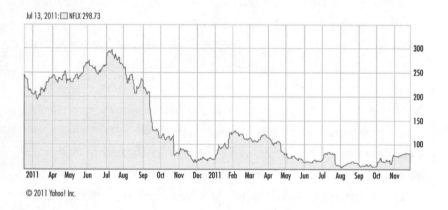

Jul 13, 2011: ☐ NFLX 298.73

© 2011 Yahoo! Inc.

We tell you this story because the company could have avoided the loss of billions of dollars and the damage to its brand if it had run some simple field experiments. Rather than coming up with a national scheme to thrust upon customers, and instead of relying on rough-hewn ideas (based on the intuition of some very smart people on the board, maybe a few focus groups, or some expensive consulting firms), all Netflix had to do was run a pilot of their grand plan in a small portion of the country—say, San Diego—and then study its customers' reactions. The small-scale experiment could have saved the company lots of money without cutting its value.

Netflix might have lost a few customers in San Diego, but it would have had a chance to improve the plan (or maybe cancel it altogether) and remain the market leader. Even if this experiment had stirred up some negative attention, Netflix executives could have explained it was a local snag. The damage would have been much smaller and the experiment worth its weight in gold. Netflix has since recovered, and we expect that, given its product base and strong customer profile, the company will continue to do well, especially if it improves its performance by conducting field experiments.

When we discuss experimentation with business leaders, they usually reply by saying, "Tests are expensive to run." After we point out that they are not, we turn the tables on them by showing how expensive it is *not* to experiment, as the Netflix example shows. We politely explain that every day that they set suboptimal prices, place ads that do not work, or use ineffective incentive schemes for their workforce, they effectively leave millions of dollars on the table.

Of course, many businesses do experiment, and often. Businesses always tinker with the machine and try new things. For instance, Apple's Steve Jobs was constantly experimenting with design and with new ways to sell products. The problem is that businesses rarely conduct experiments that allow a comparison between a treatment group and a control group. Jobs's launch of the iPod and of the iTunes music store revolutionized an industry. But for years, Jobs insisted that recording artists and record companies charge exactly 99 cents per song on iTunes. Defending any justification Apple can offer for this policy is difficult, however. The company never compared the impact of iTunes prices on its sales of songs and iPods. And in the absence of solid evidence, Apple executives turned to their intuitions. They did well with this strategy, but could they have moved "from good to great," as author Jim Collins puts it, through experimentation?

Put differently, say that you have a serious illness. You go to your doctor, and she prescribes a new treatment regimen for you. When you ask what evidence she has for trusting this treatment, she says, "It's my intuition." In such a case, you'd probably leave and never come back, because you prefer to entrust your life to someone whose medical decisions are based on scientific evidence.

How does making the right business decisions differ from choosing the right medical treatment? You might say lives aren't at stake, but executives who are paid millions of dollars a year to sign off on decisions can cost people their jobs and the economy billions. Business experiments are research investigations that give companies the opportunity to get fast and accurate data regarding important decisions. By manipulating various factors in the environment, companies can better understand the causal relationship between a change in strategy and a response in consumers', competitors', employees', or other stakeholders' behavior.

Field experiments in business are also different from other research efforts—say, focus groups—because participants make real-life decisions often without even knowing that they are part of a study. When designed properly, business field experiments can provide invaluable insights and reveal surprising results, which the company can then implement on a larger scale. In this chapter, we tell the story of two great executives who have guided their companies' futures with field experiments. Along the way, we mix in experiments that we have conducted with these and other firms.

Innovation at Intuit

Intuit, the Silicon Valley–based firm famous for its QuickBooks and TurboTax software, has spent years building experimentation into the core of its being. "We used to make decisions through managerial analysis and opinion, and from the top-down," says founder and chairman Scott Cook. "Now we let our small, rapid-fire experiments make the decisions for us."

In the old days, Intuit was run like most large organizations. Product-development folks would come up with ideas. Managers of the business units would pull together data from focus groups and other research, run some analysis, stuff their findings into PowerPoints, disseminate the information to the rest of the company, and their higher-ups would decide whether to fund the project or not. But Cook began to understand that this way of doing work was like walking in concrete shoes. "I started to be convinced that experimentation was the solution to two problems," Cook says. "The first was how to get a large, successful company to be agile and innovative, because the larger and more successful a company it is, the less innovative and entrepreneurial it can become. The second problem was that the decisions made in the old-fashioned way were often wrong."

Intuit trained people in "design thinking," a methodology for investigating problems (especially fuzzy, vague ones), gathering information, and coming up with creative solutions. Design thinkers use a holistic approach, bring creativity to their work, and then innovate new approaches to problems. A small group of design thinkers and executives trained 100 leaders in the organization to run experiments that tested assumptions and hypotheses; they gathered data and came up with solutions. And these leaders taught people who worked for them to do the same. In addition, 150 "innovation catalysts" throughout the organization work in all the firm's departments to drive this culture of experimentation. Today, everyone is encouraged to toy with new ideas using the same, Galileo-like, scientific experimental methods that we use in our work.

In the old days, people in the Turbotax.com division ran seven experiments a year. Today they are running 141 rapid, low-cost experiments during tax season on a weekly cycle, beginning on Thursdays. They test the idea, run the experiment, read the data, tweak the experiment, and the following Thursday they test again. The rapid experimentation cycle "uncorks innovation and entrepreneurship," Cook says.

As a company, Intuit frees its employees to spend 10 percent of their time working on projects of their own invention. Today, Intuit experiments whenever possible on a small, cheap basis as the core of the discovery process. Employees who come up with innovative ideas must prove that the concepts work by tracking results from real customers; the most promising ideas rise like cream to the top. In this way, Intuit developed SnapTax (which prepares taxes on a camera or a mobile phone); SnapPayroll (which enables employers to pay their employees via mobile phone); and an Intuit Health Debit Card, which offers health coverage to small businesses that cannot afford health insurance for their employees; and more.

Very often, such experiments result in new product features. For example, the development team used specific experimental questions about their tax situations; based on the answers, the software could recommend either the standard deduction or the itemized deduction. Testing showed that the feature could reduce the time it took to finish tax forms by 75 percent, so all subsequent versions of the product incorporated the new feature, called "Fast Path," into its free "Federal edition" of the TurboTax software.

Intuit's development teams also created an "Audit Support Center" that helped guide all customers through the audit experience, just as if they received an audit letter from the IRS. Testing confirmed that more customers started and completed their TurboTax filings when the feature was presented on the website. "Our customer conversion rate—the number of people who purchase the product after shopping around on the Internet—is up 50 percent in six years," says Cook.

Employees are also encouraged to come up with solutions to serious social problems. In one instance, a team in India developed a service for Indian farmers called "FASAL" ("harvest" in Hindi). The team members had observed that farm families—comprising half of Indian society—were so poor that they didn't have access to some of the most basic necessities. How, the engineers wondered, could they make these farmers' lives better?

The team from Intuit conducted its own study, observing the poor farmers both in the fields and when they went to market. Most farmers had access to just one or two markets at a distance from each other, and they had to work through one middleman at each market to get a price for their produce. The middleman sat under a cloth and signaled the price through hand gestures. There was no transparent pricing, and the system worked against the farmers. But the farmers had one big thing going for them: they had cell phones.

So the engineers conceived of a cell phone texting application that let farmers know what the middlemen from a variety of markets were offering. In just weeks, the engineers tested the concept with a quick-and-dirty experiment, hand-typing text messages to 120 farmers that told them which markets could secure them better prices for their crops. The test worked, and farmers began adopting the application. Today, the FASAL service is helping 1.2 million farmers out of poverty.

"FASAL is not a charity. We run it as a business, so we can attack head-on one of the most pernicious problems of the developing world, rural poverty," says Cook. "We go out and look for the biggest problems we can solve, and a number of them are social problems. We attack these by running low-fidelity, rapid experiments."

Working with Intuit, we now have dozens of field experiments under way that promise to shed light on what works and why. We suspect many will help move Intuit's bottom line. Intuit is a great company because the field experiment gene is built into their DNA.

Interventions at Humana

Another company that likes running field experiments is Humana, the giant health benefits firm that started out as a chain of nursing homes and hospitals. "I like to know what makes things hum," says Mike McCallister, Humana's affable, mustachioed chairman and CEO. Indeed, McCallister is one of those guys who is constantly thinking about better ways of doing things. In fact, he thinks a lot more like an entrepreneur—or even a field economist—than a CEO. Whereas others may trust their intuitions, he trusts his counterintuitions. "I try to find what is doable," he says. "People assume that things are not doable, but who is to say they aren't? Let's find out!"

For example, in the old days before Humana was a health benefits provider, it owned hospitals and medical buildings, and McCallister was then in charge of the medical offices. The medical offices were money losers; but hospital pharmacies were money-makers. McCallister's bright idea: attach some pharmacies to medical offices and see how they performed financially when compared to medical offices that didn't have attached pharmacies. Lo and behold, the medical offices with the pharmacies proved more profitable. Evidence in hand, Humana expanded the pairing across its medical offices and made money. Nobody had ever tried this kind of thing before. It just wasn't "done" at Humana, or elsewhere in the healthcare industry for that matter. Breaking the mold takes guts, we argue, and evidence from a field experiment that gives you confidence your idea is actually correct.

Once Humana switched to being a benefits provider and McCallister became CEO, he began experimenting with other policies. As an employer, Humana found that its own healthcare costs were out of control, in part because employees weren't taking care of their own health. McCallister is a big believer in personal responsibility, so he told his employees they weren't going to be told what to do. Employees had to work on the problem together. One approach was to run little incentivized experiments. Humana offered a weight-loss program that began and ended with a BMI (body mass index) measurement. Those who lost some of their girth had their names entered in a lottery for a hefty check for $10,000. Not surprisingly, this incentive created quite a bit of buzz around the firm—and, yes, some people lost weight.

The weight-loss experiment is a small one; but consider a large-scale experiment Humana is running today. Although McCallister believes all people should have access to affordable healthcare, he recognizes that the Medicare bureaucracy has very little incentive to invest in preventive care. This, McCallister says, leads to "fraud, abuse, and overuse of services." In the face of a huge generation of rapidly aging baby boomers and ballooning healthcare costs, he thinks there's a much better way of delivering patient care—one that focuses on patient wellness, which he believes saves both money and lives.

To that end, the company recently adopted a mantra: help people achieve lifelong well-being. But what works? To find out, he hired a consultant named Judi Israel to build a "behavioral economics consortium." As part of this consortium, we helped design some field experiments and behavioral interventions. Our common goal was to see what kinds of interventions best helped patients improve or stabilize their health while managing costs.

For example, consider a senior citizen on Medicare who suffers a heart attack. She survives the attack, receives appropriate treatment, and goes home. But then she ends up back in the hospital within a month for some comparatively trivial issue, such as failing to take her prescribed medications. Each hospital readmission averages a $10,000 cost, not including "extras" such as prescriptions, rehabilitative services, and so on. Given that a whopping one in five patients on Medicare is readmitted to the hospital within a month of his or her first admission,[3] these costs can be massive—and readmission is no fun for the patient, either. Humana, which covers the costs Medicare doesn't, has a vested interest in addressing the situation.

So the firm did a little poking around in its databases and discovered that a substantial number of the two million Medicare-enrolled members it insures were being readmitted. The company chartered its analytic team to build a model to address this problem. Among other insights, the team found that members who suffered from chronic health problems (diabetes, obesity, heart disease, pneumonia, congestive heart failure, and so on) were at the top of the list. Accordingly, Humana made a point of following up with patients after they were released from the hospital. All patients receive an automated phone call offering help or advice via a toll-free number, but patients with chronic problems receive a call from a nurse who walks them through the steps of their rehabilitative care and makes sure they stay on track. And patients who suffer from several chronic problems at once receive a home visit from a nurse who monitors and coaches them along. More than 100,000 Humana Medicare members with multiple chronic illnesses receive this kind of help.

Through controlled tests, Humana has discovered that a proactive, low-cost, and simple intervention, such as sending a nurse to visit the patient, can save significant amounts of money while helping the patient. We continue to work with Humana using simple behavioral interventions that we trust will make significant bottom line advances.

From a business and healthcare industry standpoint, these moves all make sense. "Our industry has not been innovative," McCallister insists. "This nation is productive on the back of technology, but there is no innovation in insurance or healthcare outside of products. We are trying to solve a big problem—to control health-care spending and address deteriorating health at the same time. Maybe what we learn from our experiments here can spread."

The Price Is Right

Field experiments focusing on products, services, and prices are not just the domain of big companies such as Intuit and Humana. They may, in fact, be even more crucial for smaller businesses, many of which teeter on the brink of bankruptcy daily.

In the summer of 2009, Uri and his wife Ayelet received a call from a fellow we will call "George," a winery owner in Temecula, California, a lovely, languid town about an hour northeast of San Diego. George asked for their help with pricing his wines—clearly one of the most important business decisions he needed to make. They were delighted to take up the invitation to visit George's winery, taste some of his products, and possibly help him in the process.[4]

When Uri and Ayelet asked him how he'd chosen prices in the past, they heard about the usual suspects: George looked at how other wineries price similar wines, intuition, his last year's prices, and so on. He expected the business professors to come over, look around, do some quick calculations—and come up with the magic numbers that would make him rich. You can imagine how disappointed he was when, after having spent some time with him (and his lovely cabernet), Uri and Ayelet told him they had no idea what the "right" price was, and that the magic number didn't exist. He almost took away the wine he'd already poured for them.

In an attempt to save their drinks, Uri and Ayelet did offer him help, in the form of a method—no magic, no equations, and no superior knowledge—just a simple experimental design. Pricing wines is a particularly tricky task since quality is not objective. We automatically assume a connection between price and quality; all else being equal, if a laptop costs more because it weighs less, people think it's better. And that's how much of the world works—evidence that runs counter to this basic intuition is hard to find.

Is this also the case with wines? You'd assume so, since the price range for wines is so enormous—you can pay a few bucks for a bottle of rotgut, or $10,000 for a bottle of 1959 Domaine de la Romanée-Conti. Research suggests that even when evaluating the quality of a product is subjective (as is the case with wine, since people have different taste preferences), increasing its price may increases its attractiveness to consumers.

Visitors to George's winery, as with other wineries in this region, can taste different wines and subsequently choose to buy from the selection. Consumers typically come to Temecula for wine trips, going from one winery to another, sampling, and buying wine. The wine with which Uri and Ayelet experimented was a 2005 cabernet sauvignon, a "wine with complex notes of blueberry, black currant liqueur, and a hint of citrus." The price George had previously chosen for it was $10, and it sold well.

For the experiment, we manipulated the price of the cabernet to be $10, $20, or $40 on different days over the course of a few weeks. Each experimental day, George greeted the visitors and told them about the tasting. Then visitors went to the counter, where they met the person who administered the tasting and handed them a single printed page containing the names and prices of the nine sample wines, ranging from $8 to $60, of which visitors could try six of their choice. As in most wineries, the list was constructed from "light to heavy," starting with white wines, moving to red wines, and concluding with dessert wines. Visitors typically chose wines going down the list, and the cabernet sauvignon was always number seven. Tastings took between fifteen and thirty minutes, after which visitors could decide whether to buy any of the wines.

The results shocked George. Visitors were almost 50 percent more likely to buy the cabernet when he priced it at $20 than when he priced it at $10! That is, when we increased the price, the wine became more popular.

Using an almost cost-free experiment, and adopting prices accordingly, George increased the winery's total profits by 11 percent. Following this experiment, he happily adopted the results and changed the price of this wine to $20. Since the vast majority of the winery's clients are one-time visitors (this winery sells most of its wines in its store), very few people noticed the change in price.

Be Creative

Finding the "right" price is important. But sometimes you need more. It's not just about the price, but also about how it's collected.

A few years ago, a graduate student at University of California, San Diego, Amber Brown, went to work for Disney Research—a to-die-for kind of job for a young psychologist. Disney has an in-house, interdisciplinary group of researchers that uses science to try to improve the company's performance and explore new technologies, marketing, and economics. As is the case with Humana, this group understands the importance of using behavioral research to simultaneously improve both the customers' experience and the company's bottom line.

At about the same time Amber nabbed her job, we were becoming interested in an emerging behavioral pricing approach: pay-what-you-want. A famous example of this pricing is from the British band Radiohead. In 2007, the band released a CD as a digital download. It encouraged fans to log on to its website and download the album for any price they chose. Fans could get the album for free or pay as little as 65 cents (the cost of handling by the credit card company) or more. But would the fans pay for something they could get for free? And did they pay? Interestingly, hundreds of thousands of people downloaded the album from the band's website, and many of them (around 50 percent) paid something for the CD. (By the way, as our friend, the recent Nobelist Al Roth likes to say, "Columbus wasn't the first to discover America; he was the last." After Columbus, everyone knew about the "new" continent. The same is true here. Radiohead wasn't the first to discover this pricing strategy, but the group is famous enough to be the "last"—no one will ever need to "rediscover" it.)

This example shows that even in markets, people are not completely selfish. But the data from Radiohead's model, and other companies who had used it, left many questions open. Clearly people paid more than they had to, but whether the pricing strategy had positive or negative consequences for the band remained unclear. Did the band make or lose money relative to a standard pricing scheme?

We decided to study the pay-what-you-want scheme in a field experiment.[5] We thought a combination of a pay-what-you-want pricing strategy *and* charity might be an interesting way to go. We called this combination Shared Social Responsibility (SSR) because instead of the company alone deciding how much to give to the charity, customers could share in the donations, too. If people could pay what they wanted for an item, would they pay more if we appealed to the "better angels of their nature"?

So together with Disney Research, we designed a large field experiment that included over 100,000 participants to test the effect of pay-what-you-want pricing combined with charity. We set up our experiment at a roller coaster–like ride at a Disney park where people go on the ride and can afterwards buy a snapshot of themselves screaming and laughing.

We offered the photo either for its regular price of $12.95 or under a pay-what-you-want scheme. We also added treatments in which half of the revenue from selling the picture went to a well-known and well-liked charity. This experimental design resulted in four different treatments that we ran over different days during a month-long period.

The figure below shows the profits per rider:

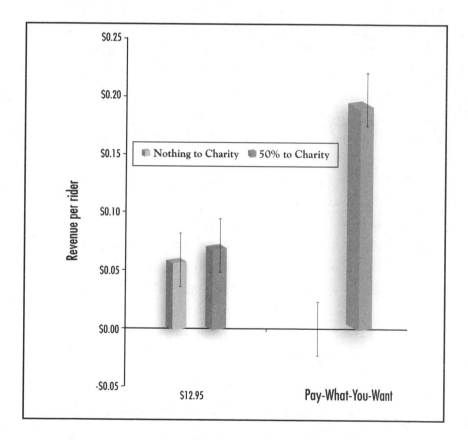

As you can see, we found that at the standard fixed price of $12.95, the charitable component only slightly increased demand—raising the revenue per rider by just a few cents. But what happened when participants could choose their own price? The demand rates went through the roof. Sixteen times more people (8 percent instead of 0.5 percent) bought the photo. But since they only paid about a dollar on average, Disney didn't make any money from them. (Remember: we are interested in running experiments in which we can find a win-win solution for both companies and their customers. That's the best way to make changes that stick.)

And what, in the experiment results, were we most interested in? When we mixed the pay-what-you-want scheme with charity, 4 percent of the people bought the picture, but they paid much more (roughly $5) for it. Adding the charity option proved very profitable. In fact, the amusement park stood to make an additional $600,000 a year by offering the pay-what-you-want/charity combination just in this one location in the park. More generally, making this change also increased the benefit to the charity—and presumably to the customers, who felt they were doing something good.

An important takeaway from our experiment is that if you want your clients to act unselfishly, you need to show you can do the same. When Disney agreed to experiment with the new pricing, the company signaled to its customers that it cared about charitable causes and, more importantly, was willing to share the risk of acting on that concern. More generally, we learned that being creative with your pricing strategies proves you can do good while doing well (as we discussed in Chapters 9 and 10).

How Can We Get You to Respond?

As we mentioned in the previous chapter, we're all used to the piles of junk mail with offers that sound too good to be true (probably because they are not so good or not so true). Many of us never open such mail—we just "file" it in the trash without even looking at it. Those who do open it usually ignore the content or requests.

Knowing this, how can a company get your attention through direct mail (or social media)?

Imagine you open a direct-mail plea and a $20 bill falls from the envelope. Whoever sent the mail likely has your attention now. Curious, you read the enclosed letter. The company is asking you to complete and return a short survey. Would you do it? What if there was only $10 enclosed? Or just $1?

Earlier, we showed how charities like Smile Train and Wonder Work.org have successfully used reciprocity, the basic principle that if someone does something nice for you, you should do something nice in return. But what if you're not a charity?

In this direct-mail case, the company sweetly sent you cash and is asking you to do something for them in return. Let's say you're the chief marketing officer of a big chain store, and you ask yourself whether it makes sense to try to appeal to people's sense of reciprocity when asking them to respond to a direct-mail pitch. Your company has lots of experience in sending surveys and is also good at collecting data. But it isn't very good at figuring out which kind of incentives work best when it comes to direct mail.

With our colleague, Pedro Rey-Biel (of the University Autonoma of Barcelona), we analyzed the results of a large field experiment, comprising 29 treatments and 7,250 "club members" who were already registered customers of a big chain store.[6] The company sent letters asking club members to complete a fifteen-minute survey. The company was interested in the question: Which is better— paying customers ahead of time to respond to a direct-mail plea, or promising to pay them after they've responded?

Put another way: Would more people respond—and would the study be more cost-effective—if the company used the reciprocity angle and sent people money with the survey in hopes that they would fill it out? Or would it be smarter to do things the old-fashioned way? That is, would it be better to treat people more like employees and make the reward contingent on having done the work? Or should the company forget the whole incentive thing and just send out surveys without a reward?

In one treatment, the company sent letters with cash, ranging from $1 to $30 (we called this the "social" treatment, since reciprocity is a social phenomenon), to about half the addressees. In another treatment, the company promised to send 3,500 people checks (with the same amounts as in the other treatment) if they filled out the survey (we called this the "contingent" treatment). In the control treatment, the company just sent the survey to 250 people and asked them to respond. The chart below shows the response.

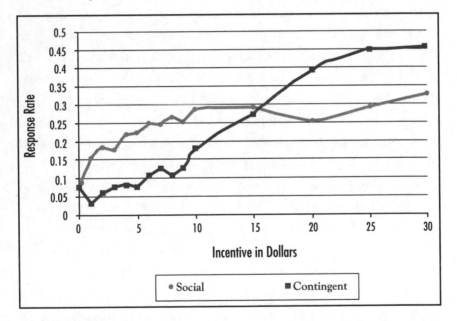

This chart shows the "breaking point" was around $15. Up to $15, we found giving people money up front made them feel like reciprocating and therefore more likely to return the survey, even for small amounts such as $1. In fact, significantly more people responded when we told them: "You'll get a dollar if you'll fill out the survey and send it back." But after $15, more people responded to the contingent, fill-out-our-survey-and-then-we'll-pay-you approach.

Importantly, the contingent was less expensive than the paying-up-front approach. Makes sense: after all, sending money only to those who send the survey back is cheaper than paying everyone regardless of whether they respond. The average cost of a returned survey in the social treatment was $45.40, more than double the cost in the contingent treatment ($20.97). As a result, the total cost in the social treatments was almost three times higher than in the contingent treatments ($38,820 vs. $13,212).

What can companies that send out direct mail learn from this exercise? If your budget allows you to only pay $1 for a returned survey, put the buck in the envelope. People (at least the nice ones) will be happy to get it and reciprocate in kind. But if you can spend enough money per person, you'll be better off paying only people who send the survey back. You might, of course, sample different people in the two cases; our bet is that you'll get more people who think like economists when you make the payment contingent and more noneconomist thinkers when you don't.

A Trip to China

In Chapter 4, we talked about the way framing a bonus as a gain or loss affected teacher and student performance. Framing can be an important tool for businesses, too. Let's say that you are the marketing manager of a product called Sunny Sunscreen SPF 50 Lotion, and you are deciding what kind of spin to put on a campaign. Your "gain-framed," or positive message might go like this: "Use Sunny Sunscreen to decrease your risk of getting skin cancer" or "Use

Sunny Sunscreen to help your skin stay healthy." Alternatively, a "loss-framed," or negative message could be "Without Sunny Sunscreen, you increase your risk of developing skin cancer" or "Without Sunny Sunscreen, you cannot guarantee the health of your skin."

Similarly, a manager can tell employees, "If we boost production by 10 percent this year, we will all be in for a bonus!" Or he could say, "If we don't boost production by 10 percent this year, none of us will get a bonus." Which kind of framing do you think is the better motivator?

To find out, we took a trip with our colleague Tanjim Hossain (of the University of Toronto) to the vibrant, modern city of Xiamen, in Fujian province on the southern coast of China, not too far from Hong Kong.[7]

Xiamen is home to lots of large factories—such as Dell and Kodak. The site of our six-month experiment was a 20,000-employee Chinese high-tech firm that produces and distributes computer electronics. The company—Wanlida Corporation—produces and distributes cell phones, digital audio and video products, GPS navigation devices, small home appliances, and so on, which are exported to more than fifty countries.

Our goal was simple: we wanted to see if we could increase productivity at the plant using simple framing manipulations. So we sent two different letters to two different groups of employees.

Imagine for a moment that you are a twenty-one-year old woman—we'll call you Lin Li—working for Wanlida, and your job is to inspect PC motherboards. You come into the factory on Monday morning, sit down at your desk, and turn on a magnifying light like the kind dentists or surgeons might use. You pull on a pair of lightweight gloves, take a motherboard in your hands, and go over every chip, nook, and cranny, looking for defects. You do this for nine hours a day, six days a week, and, of course, receive a salary for your work.

One day, you receive a letter from management. "Dear Lin Li," the letter says, "You will receive an RMB 80 bonus for every week in which the weekly production average of your team is above 400 units per hour." RMB 80 is about $12, which is a pretty nice weekly bonus for a blue-collar worker in China. Because the average salary of workers in China is between RMB 290 and 375, RMB 80 represents more than 20 percent of the weekly salary of the highest paid worker. None of the 165 workers involved knew they were part of an experiment.

Feeling invigorated, Lin Li goes back to work, smiling. Another young employee—we'll call him Zi Peng—receives a different letter: "Dear Zi Peng, You will receive a one-time bonus of RMB 320. However, for every week in which the weekly production average of your team is below 400 units per hour, the salary enhancement will be reduced by RMB 80." Zi Peng isn't quite sure how he feels about this arrangement, but he goes back to his desk and takes up his work with gusto.

Now, this kind of framing might remind you of the incentives that we tried on teachers and students in Chapter 4, when we said that they would lose their money if they didn't perform well. And as you also probably noticed, this kind of framing combines a carrot ("you will receive a bonus") with a stick ("if you don't produce enough we'll take your bonus away"). The message is clearly—and intentionally—mixed, because we wanted to see the effects of what social scientists call "loss aversion" at work in a real factory scenario.

When we feel we "own" something—say, social media privileges (if you are a preteen), our 1960s-era LP-album collection, our car, home, job, and yes, our bonus paycheck—the prospect of losing it makes us pretty darn unhappy.

So back at the factory, which individuals and teams performed the best? Those who, like your fictional self, Lin Li, received the carrot letter? Or those like your fictional colleague Zi Peng, who received the stick letter? Before you venture a guess, ask yourself what motivates you more: "gain-framing" or "loss-framing"? And if you work on a team with other people, knowing that the performance of each member affects the entire team's bonus, do you work harder under the reward or the punishment framing?

Here's what we found: just having a bonus incentive in place improved productivity. The effect was in the neighborhood of 4 percent to 9 percent for workers in groups and 5 percent to 12 percent for individual workers. These are sizable effects, considering the magnitude of our bonuses. But, more interestingly, although individual workers were not influenced significantly by the loss frame, people who were working in groups increased their productivity by some 16 percent to 25 percent above the workers in the reward framing. And, guess what? Errors and defects didn't rise.

Overall, we found that Wanlida could effectively use simple framing to increase overall team productivity.

Would these results eventually wane over time? Would the workers slow down or stop responding to the punishment incentive? The answer was "No." Week after week, for six months, the punishment framing *increased* productivity.

Clearly, the fear of loss motivated the workers more than the prospect of gain. In other words, carrots may work better if they look a bit like sticks. But who wants to work for a company that gives employees this kind of dual-handed, carrot-and-stick treatment? Well, losses are a fact of life; someone has to bear them. We believe losses are a powerful motivator. Businesses have used the threat of layoffs or firing to encourage productivity, but outside of those large-scale threats, companies rarely use loss-framing.

Of course, if you are a manager, you don't have to use incentives as devilishly designed as the ones used in this study. Remember: it has to do with framing. If you give workers a stake in their production and *then* focus on the losses that could come from their lack of production, you should achieve the effects described above, without scaring employees through manipulative incentives.

So What's the Big Problem?

So why don't businesses experiment more? A number of barriers make implementing experimentation in firms difficult. One barrier, as Scott Cook pointed out to us, is that the people in power like to hold onto their PowerPoints, and they don't want the little guys pointing out that the emperor has no clothes, or that he might run his empire in a different way.

Another is sheer bureaucratic inertia. For example, in the summer of 2009, we recruited some students to help us with a field experiment on incentives in a large company. The company came over to San Diego to meet with us, explained the simple problem they were facing, and agreed to run the experiment within a couple of months. Four years later, the study is still buried somewhere in the big organization, waiting for management approval.

Other times, managers are intimidated by the uncertainty involved in a change and the unknown. Going the traditional route without introducing new methods is familiar, and as long as it works, it seems safer ("if it ain't broke, don't fix it"). Managers also feel they've been hired to provide solutions and make tough decisions to enhance the firm's performance. In other words, they feel they are expected to have ready answers for the challenges the firm faces. Opting for experimentation may appear to imply that they don't, and could compromise the appearance of their expertise—making it look as if they have failed to do their jobs.

One could overcome these barriers in two distinct ways: top-down and bottom-up. First, the company's managing team would need to overcome the typical "short-term earnings first" mindset and encourage (and even reward) experimentation that could improve the firm's performance, as Cook and McCallister have done. This approach requires hiring and training people to design and run experiments, analyze the data, and draw conclusions. Under a bottom-up approach, lower-level managers could conduct smaller-scale field studies and then present the results to the management, providing them with the costs and benefits associated with running the research.

———

Changing a tried—if not so true—mindset is no small feat. In the end, it takes a combination of fearless leadership, training, and hands-on experience to develop an experimental culture. If companies succeed at doing that, they can reshape their industries altogether.

We have seen too many top executives fall in love with their own ideas and then unleash these on an unsuspecting world, generating a big backlash, as Netflix (and other companies before and since) did. We've seen business leaders apply carrots and sticks in an effort to raise productivity, to no avail. We've seen companies try to figure out the right price for a product, without having any idea what it's worth to consumers. These costly mistakes occur all the time, and they are utterly preventable.

By contrast, businesses small and large that *do* run field experiments are making more money and attracting more customers. Intuit has expanded its market by testing out small ideas, and expanding on the good ones. Humana found that by actively helping senior citizens with their prescriptions and self-care, older people could stay out of hospitals and the company could save millions of dollars in the process. A big technology company like Wanlida learned that offering employees a bonus and threatening to take it away raised productivity dramatically. A small vintner in northern California, experimenting with pricing for his wine, discovered that he had been charging half of what customers were willing to pay. And Disney learned that letting people pay what they wanted for a photo taken at the end of a ride worked especially well when half of their donations went to a charity.

The bottom line for business is this: Do you want to make more money? If yes, then run field experiments. Do you want to go down in the annals of great companies? If you do, then run field experiments.

How to Change the World . . . or at Least Get a Better Deal

Life Is a Laboratory

Nearly four hundred years ago, Galileo performed the first recorded laboratory experiment. He set heavy balls on a rolling plank and sent them speeding down to test his theory of acceleration. Since that time, laboratory experiments have been a cornerstone of the scientific method. The principle of science and the test of all knowledge, according to noted theoretical physicist Richard Feynman, is the experiment. "Experiment," he said, "is the sole judge of scientific 'truth.'" Increasingly, economists have turned to the experimental model of the physical sciences as a method to understand human behavior.[1]

To date, this pursuit of the experimental method has taken place largely within the confines of the lab. Lab experiments changed the way economists view the world, as was acknowledged by the Nobel Committee in awarding the 2002 prize to Daniel Kahneman and

Vernon Smith. But the strong reliance on testing behavior exclusively in the lab is changing.

We are part of an emerging group of economists using field experiments to learn about the world. While we are waiting for our economist friends, as well as those in other academic disciplines, to take up the gauntlet we have just laid down, you don't have to sit on your own hands. You can use our tools in everyday life to discover what really works, in everything from potty-training your toddler to running a multinational corporation.

So how do you start?

First, think about the outcome you want to change. Maybe your goal is to increase the bottom line of your business; maybe it's cajoling your child to work harder in school. You may want to help the March of Dimes raise more money in a walkathon, or find ways to cut down on your energy costs. Having a clear-cut idea of exactly what you want to change and how to measure it is crucial. The same is true for businesses: focus in and then measure. For example, grades and test scores can be measured, as can watts of energy and productivity.

The next step is to dream up a few ways to get whatever you're measuring to change. Generally, we start from the premise that incentives matter. Simple financial incentives are great, but nonfinancial incentives can sometimes have a bigger wallop. For example, if your third-grader is obsessed with playing video games, you might be able to use that to your advantage. Offering extra video game time in exchange for higher homework scores might be priceless in the eyes of someone so young. (This approach won't work for all children, though. Our findings suggest that as kids get older, nonfinancial incentives have less power. But use your own experiments to see what best applies to your particular situation.)

Sometimes, removing bad incentives can make a huge difference, too. For example, if in your apartment building there is one electric meter for all residence, and you split the bill equally, then bad incentives are in play. As we noted in Chapter 1, splitting up checks equally may cause people to consume more than they otherwise would. Replacing this incentive with something more sensible (like individual meters) can do a lot to reduce needless expenditures, to say nothing of bad will.

Once you have a plan in place, all you have to do is apply a bit of coin flipping, or randomization. You'll want to compare the difference in results between a "control" and an "experimental" situation. For example, if you devise two strategies for negotiating a lower price with used car dealers, flip a coin before you go to each dealer to choose what approach to use with which dealer. Flip "heads," and you make the first offer to the car dealer. Flip "tails," and the dealer makes the first offer. When do you get better deals? If you want to learn even more, go to a third dealer and make your first offer to him. Or try this: tell some dealers, "I will be visiting five dealerships today." Let others know that "this is the only dealership I'm visiting." Then see what happens.

Alternatively, let's say you like shopping for antiques, and you visit a few places where you can negotiate prices. In one case, let the sellers know that you do not have time to haggle, and you need their lowest price on that nice little 1790s-era dresser, for example. In another shop, let the haggling process proceed naturally. In which case do you get the lower offer?

Or let's say you want to increase donations to the nonprofit for which you volunteer, and you're helping out with a direct-mail campaign. Try randomly sending half the prospective donors on your mailing list a notice of a matching grant.[2] In all these cases, randomization is key; the object of the game is to rule out competing hypothesizes that might influence the results of your experiment.

One of the nicest things about running an economics experiment is that you don't need a Ph.D. to put yourself in the shoes of someone who is participating in your study. Let's say you are on a business trip, and you leave your hotel room for the maid to clean up the day after you arrive. The first day, don't leave a tip, and then do a quick inventory to see how neat the room is when you return to it. The second day, leave a few dollars, and then see whether your room is any tidier when you return than it was the first time. On the third day, leave a larger tip, and so on. You may find that you wind up with a few extra chocolates under your pillow on the third day. This experiment may help you decide how to tip on future trips.

Alternatively, try this experiment when you are hosting a dinner party. Instead of serving wine from bottles, serve different-priced wines from various decanters, and then ask your guests to pick the wine that they think is the best. This experiment is a great way to discover which wines to serve next time—and you may well discover that the less expensive wines are the ones that you and your guests like the most.

As you can see, we believe that the tools of economics can go a long way toward solving important problems in practical ways. When researchers, armed with the methods that we have presented here, get out from behind their keyboards and go into the streets, they discover things that turn previous theories and assumptions on their heads.

Instead of practicing a dismal science, economists can discover that they are practicing a passionate one—one fueled by deep personal interests, dealing with the human emotions, and able to produce results that can change the world for the better. But the opportunity for change goes well beyond economics. We believe that there are massive opportunities for researchers in sociology, anthropology, business, education, and many more fields to use the tools of field experiments in economics in ways that can substantially alter the lives of millions around the world.

Over and over in this book, we have suggested that the reasons why we, as a society, have not made significant progress in battling big, stubborn problems in education, discrimination, poverty, health, gender equity, and the environment, among other areas, is that we have not made a truly concerted effort to leave assumptions behind. We have failed to seek out and discover what works and why. We keep missing the opportunity to bring the tools of scientific research to understand our most pressing problems. Without understanding that life really is a laboratory, and that we must all learn from our discoveries, we cannot hope to make headway in crucial areas.

But to paraphrase John Lennon, we'd like you to imagine an alternative. Imagine what would happen if thousands of researchers all over the world applied the same scientific methods we've described in the preceding pages to big problems. Imagine hundreds of experiments running in tandem all over the world, all dedicated to overturning the rocks and probing inside the closets of the greatest problems we are facing. Imagine what could happen if, once huge amounts of feedback had been collected, we could test, and test, and test again to discover what really works and why. And imagine what would happen if, armed with this knowledge, governments around the world could make broad policy changes based on this solid empirical tests.

So there you have it. You get the idea. Experiment! Go out—white coat and pen-protector are not required—and find out what's really going on. And then let us know what you discover, or how you've begun to think differently.

Conducting field research requires long hours, many spent away from home. The content of this book has been gathered over many years and in many different parts of the world. This book would not have been possible without the support and encouragement of our wives, Ayelet and Jennifer. Words cannot express our gratitude to them.

We also have to come up with theories, make sense of the data, and write long academic papers. For leaving us alone during those long hours at the computer, we would like to thank our children.

It has truly taken a village to produce this book. Although they are too numerous to name here, we sincerely thank our many co-authors, research assistants, and colleagues for allowing us to pursue our dreams. Without your help, none of this would have been possible. For giving us our start in the Academy, we thank our advisers Eric van Damme and Shelby Gerking.

Bronwyn Fryer played a key role in writing this manuscript and breathing life into our research. We learned every day from her writing excellence as she turned our "academese" into something that our neighbors can read. Our agent, James Levine of the Levine Greenberg Literary Agency, provided the professional support and excellent guidance that helped us navigate the many different turns that this book has taken to reach publication. None of this endeavor would have been possible without the great work of Bronwyn and Jim.

Our editor, John Mahaney, provided professional advice and assistance in polishing this manuscript, lending keen insights to sharpen our thoughts. Our graphic designer designed the front cover, which effectively delivers our message. We thank our publisher, PublicAffairs, who believed in us enough to allow us to write this book in the manner that conveys our key message, and for giving us much-needed flexibility.

Finally, a number of people provided comments that helped to shape this manuscript. These include Jennifer List, Ayelet Gneezy, Augie List, Alec Brandon, Molly Wright Buck, Joseph Buck, Winnie Pitcock, David "Lenny" Haas, Michael Price, Anya Samak, Edie Dobrez, Katie Baca-Motes, Sally Sadoff, Jeff Livingston, Steven Levitt, Stephen Dubner, Dave Novgorodsky, David Herberich, Annika List, Sandi Einerson, Jeff Einerson, Ron Huberman, Scott Cook, Freddie Chaney, Michael Goldberg, Pete Williams, Joe Gonzalez, Ryan "Mamba" Pitcock, Eric Faoro, Pete Bartolomei, John Friel, Michael McCallister, Brian Mullaney, Min Lee, Katie Spring, and our friends and associates at Intuit and Humana. Thanks to everyone for all your help and support along the way.

NOTES

Introduction

1. Syed Z. Ahmed, "What Do Men Want?" *New York Times*, February 15, 1994, A21.

2. David Brooks, "What You'll Do Next," *New York Times*, April 15, 2013.

3. When we use the pronoun "we" throughout this book, it means that either or both of us were involved in the experiments described, most often with other researchers as noted. Also, at certain points in the book we use pseudonyms to protect those who preferred anonymity.

4. *All in the Family*, Season 2. Accessed on YouTube, March 25, 2013, http://www.youtube.com/watch?v=O_UBgkFHm8o.

5. Thomas Carlyle, "Occasional Discourse on The Negro Question," *Fraser's Magazine* (December 1849). Reprinted as a separate pamphlet (1853), reproduced in *The Collected Works of Thomas Carlyle* vol. 13 (1864).

Chapter 1: How Can You Get People to Do What You Want?

1. Uri Gneezy, Steven Meier, and Pedro Rey-Biel, "When and Why Incentives (Don't) Work to Modify Behavior," *Journal of Economic Perspectives* 25 (2011): 191–210, http://rady.ucsd.edu/faculty/directory/gneezy/pub/docs/jep_published.pdf.

2. Uri Gneezy and Aldo Rustichini, "A Fine Is a Price," *Journal of Legal Studies* 29 (January 2000): 1–17.

3. Uri Gneezy and Aldo Rustichini, "Pay Enough or Don't Pay At All," *Quarterly Journal of Economics* (August 2000): 791–810, http://rady.ucsd.edu/faculty/directory/gneezy/pub/docs/pay-enough.pdf.

4. As our friend Dan Ariely has shown, the currency with which you are paying is important. In particular, money is different than most other forms of payment. Ariely and his research partner, James Heyman, started by showing that students who got no payment for a task (helping other students load a sofa into a van) invested more effort than people who received just a small amount of cash. Another group received a candy bar. As they expected, they found that people who were paid with candy put in more effort than those who got a small amount of money (and the same effort as those who were not paid). But here comes the interesting part: in a different treatment, they left the price tag on the candy. They predicted that once students knew the retail value of the candy they'd put out as much effort as those who received the cash payment. And indeed that happened. See "Effort for Payment," *Psychological Science* 15, no. 11 (2004).

5. Uri Gneezy, Ernan Haruvy, and Hadas Yafe, "The Inefficiency of Splitting the Bill," *Economic Journal* 114, no. 495 (April 2004): 265–280.

6. Our friends Stefano DellaVigna and Ulrike Malmandier demonstrated this in "Paying Not to Go to the Gym," *American Economic Review* 96 (2006): 694–719, http://emlab.berkeley.edu/~ulrike/Papers/gym.pdf.

7. Steven A. Burd, "How Safeway Is Cutting Health-Care Costs," *Wall Street Journal,* June 12, 2009.

8. See David S. Hilzenrath, "Misleading Claims About Safeway Wellness Incentives Shape Health-Care Bill," *Washington Post,* January 17, 2010.

9. Gary Charness and Uri Gneezy, "Incentives to Exercise," *Econometrica* 77 (2009): 909–931.

Chapter 2: What Can Craigslist, Mazes, and a Ball and Bucket Teach Us About Why Women Earn Less Than Men?

1. *Archive of Remarks at NBER Conference on Diversifying the Science & Engineering Workforce,* January 14, 2005. See also "Lawrence Summers," Wikipedia, http://en.wikipedia.org/wiki/Lawrence_Summers#cite_note-harvard2005%E2%80%9336 (last accessed March 26, 2013).

2. Daniel J. Hemel, "Summers' Comments on Women and Science Draw Ire," *The Harvard Crimson,* January 14, 2005, http://www.thecrimson.com/article/2005/1/14/summers-comments-on-women-and-science/.

3. "Fast Facts: Degrees Conferred by Sex and Race," National Center for Education Statistics, http://nces.ed.gov/fastfacts/display.asp?id=72 (last accessed March 26, 2013); "Women in Management in the United States, 1960–Present," Catalyst, http://www.catalyst.org/publication/207/women-in-management-in-the-united-states-1960-present (last accessed March 26, 2013); and Patricia Sellers, "New Yahoo CEO Mayer Is Pregnant," *CNN Money,* July 16, 2012, http://postcards.blogs.fortune.cnn.com/2012/07/16/mayer-yahoo-ceo-pregnant/ (last accessed March 26, 2013).

4. "Working Women: Still Struggling," *The Economist,* November 25, 2011, http://www.economist.com/blogs/dailychart/2011/11/working-women.

5. See Jeffrey A. Flory, Andreas Leibbrandt, and John A. List, "Do Competitive Work Places Deter Female Workers? A Large-Scale Natural Field Experiment on Gender Differences in Job-Entry Decisions," NBER Working Paper w16546, November 2010.

6. We ended up offering jobs to some applicants.

7. It is not appropriate—and in some cases it's illegal—to ask the job applicant about their gender. So we resorted to a tried and true method to determine whether each applicant was male or female—the applicant's first name. Based on probabilities derived from the Social Security Administration (SSA) database on name popularity by gender and birth year in the various cities, we assigned gender. For any names not included in the SSA database, we used an additional database created by baby-name collector Geoff Peters, which calculates gender ratios by first name, using the Internet to analyze patterns of name usage for over 100,000 first names. Finally, for gender-neutral names, where neither database yielded a large enough gender ratio to make a confident assignment, we searched the Internet for gender identifiers of the actual subjects themselves on their social-networking websites. In the end, we are pretty confident that we had the genders correct.

8. For a laboratory test of this, see Muriel Niederle and Lise Vesterlund, "Do Women Shy Away from Competition? Do Men Compete Too Much?" *Quarterly Journal of Economics* 122, no. 3 (2007): 1067–1101.

9. Uri Gneezy, Muriel Niederle, and Aldo Rustichini, "Performance in Competitive Environments: Gender Differences," *Quarterly Journal of Economics* 118, no. 3 (2003): 1049–1074, http://rady.ucsd.edu/faculty/directory/gneezy/pub/docs/gender-differences.pdf

10. Much has been written about the reasons why girls feel discouraged in math, engineering, and science and are outnumbered in science, technology, and mathematics professions. See Valerie Strauss, "Decoding Why Few Girls Choose Science, Math," *Washington Post,* February 1, 2005, http://www.washingtonpost.com/wp-dyn/articles/A52344–2005Jan31.html; and Jeanna Bryner, "Why Men Dominate Math and Science Fields," LiveScience, October 10, 2007, http://www.livescience.com/1927-men-dominate-math-science-fields.html (last accessed March 26, 2013).

11. Uri Gneezy and Aldo Rustichini, "Gender and Competition at a Young Age," *American Economic Review Papers and Proceedings* 94, no. 2 (2004): 377–381, http://rady.ucsd.edu/faculty/directory/gneezy/pub/docs/gender.pdf.

12. Unlike most of our large-scale experiments—such as one we are currently conducting in the Chicago Public Schools—this investigation in far-flung locations would have to be relatively small in scale and use some of the techniques that might be used in a laboratory setting. We call this kind of research an "artefactual field experiment" or a "lab-in-the-field" study. Uri Gneezy, Kenneth L. Leonard, and John A. List, "Gender Differences in Competition: Evidence from a Matrilineal and a Patriarchal Society," *Econometrica* 77, no. 5 (2009): 1637–1664, http://rady.ucsd.edu/faculty/directory/gneezy/pub/docs/gender-differences-competition.pdf.

13. Dorothy L. Hodgson, "Gender, Culture and the Myth of the Patriarchal Pastoralist," in *Rethinking Pastoralism in Africa,* ed. D.L. Hodgson (London: James Currey, 1639, 1641, 2000).

14. "Male Boards Holding Back Female Recruitment, Report Says," *BBC News,* May 28, 2012, http://www.bbc.co.uk/news/business-18235815.

15. Barbara Black, "Stalled: Gender Diversity on Corporate Boards," University of Dayton Public Law Research Paper no. 11–06, http://www.udayton.edu/law/_resources/documents/law_review/stalled_gender_diversity_on_corporate_boards.pdf.

16. Aileen Lee, "Why Your Next Board Member Should Be a Woman," TechCrunch, February 19, 2012, http://techcrunch.com/2012/02/19/why-your-next-board-member-should-be-a-woman-why-your-next-board-member-should-be-a-woman/ (last accessed March 26, 2013).

Chapter 3: What Can a Matrilineal Society Teach Us About Women and Competition?

1. Garrett Hardin, "The Tragedy of the Commons," *Science* 162 (1968): 1243–1248.

2. This framing manipulation is taken from our friend James Andreoni, who famously introduced interesting variants of the public goods game.

3. Linda Babcock and Sara Laschever, *Women Don't Ask: The High Cost of Avoiding Negotiation—and Positive Strategies for Change* (New York: Bantam, 2007).

4. See Andreas Grandt and John A. List, "Do Women Avoid Salary Negotiations? Evidence from a Large-Scale Natural Field Experiment," NBER, working paper, 2012.

5. "Best Companies for Women's Enhancement," Working Mother, http://www.workingmother.com/best-companies/deloitte-3 (last accessed March 26, 2013).

6. See Richard A. Lippa, *Gender, Nature and Nurture* (Mahwah, NJ: Laurence Erlbaum Associates, 2005).

7. Steffen Andersen, Seda Ertac, Uri Gneezy, John A. List, and Sandra Maximiano, "Gender, Competitiveness and Socialization at a Young Age: Evidence from a Matrilineal and a Patriarchal Society," forthcoming in *The Review of Economics and Statistics*.

Chapter 4: How Can Sad Silver Medalists and Happy Bronze Medalists Help Us Close the Achievement Gap?

1. Thomas D. Snyder and Sally A. Dillow, *Digest of Education Statistics 2010* (Washington, DC: US Department of Education, National Center for Education Statistics, Institute of Education Sciences, 2011).

2. See Richard Knox, "The Teen Brain: It's Just Not Grown Up Yet," National Public Radio, March 1, 2010, http://www.npr.org/templates/story/story.php?storyId=124119468. For a fascinating insight into teenage brains, see *Frontline*'s program, "Inside the Teenage Brain," http://www.pbs.org/wgbh/pages/frontline/shows/teenbrain/.

3. Our friend and colleague Roland Fryer, a coauthor on some of the work discussed here, has made an important effort to implement financial incentives in schools across the United States.

4. Sally is now an assistant professor at University of California, San Diego.

5. To see their stories and learn more about our experiment, watch the fourth episode in the 2010 documentary "Freakonomics" ("Can You Bribe a Ninth Grader to Succeed?"). Note that in the documentary, Urail King wins the lottery and the ride in the limo: it is unclear that this moment was actually supposed to be a dream sequence. Although Urail was not actually chosen, he did improve his grades enough to qualify for the lottery. For the academic paper on which this episode is based, see Steven D. Levitt, John A. List, and Sally Sadoff, "The Effect of Performance-Based Incentives on Educational Achievement: Evidence from a Randomized Experiment," unpublished, 2011.

6. Levitt, List, and Sadoff, "The Effect of Performance-Based Incentives."

7. Steven D. Levitt, John A. List, Susanne Neckermann, and Sally Sadoff, "The Behavioralist Goes to School: Leveraging Behavioral Economics to Improve Educational Performance," NBER Working Paper 18165 (June 2012).

8. This idea comes from Victoria H. Medvec, Scott F. Madey, and Thomas Gilovitch, "When Less Is More: Counterfactual Thinking and Satisfaction Among Olympic Medalists," *Journal of Personality and Social Psychology* 69 (1995): 603–610, http://www.psych.cornell.edu/sec/pubPeople/tdg1/Medvec.Madey.Gilo.pdf.

9. Uri Gneezy, Stephen Meier, and Pedro Rey-Biel, "When and Why Incentives (Don't) Work to Modify Behavior," *Journal of Economic Perspectives* 25, no. 4 (2011): 191–210.

10. See Roland G. Fryer Jr., Steven D. Levitt, John A. List, and Sally Sadoff, "Enhancing the Efficacy of Teacher Incentives Through Loss Aversion: A Field Experiment," NBER Working Paper 18237 (July 2012).

11. See "Teacher Salary in Chicago Heights, IL", *Indeed*, http://www.indeed.com/salary/q-Teacher-l-Chicago-Heights,-IL.html (last accessed March 28, 2013).

12. See John A. List, Jeffrey A. Livingston, and Susanne Neckermann, "Harnessing Complimentarities in the Education Production Function," University of Chicago mimeo.

Chapter 5: How Can Poor Kids Catch Rich Kids in Just Months?

1. See Steven Levitt and Stephen Dubner, *Freakonomics: A Rogue Economist Explores the Hidden Side of Everything* (New York: William Morrow, 2005), Chapter 5: What Makes a Perfect Parent?

2. Joe Klein, "Time to Ax Public Programs That Don't Yield Results," *Time,* July 7, 2011, http://www.time.com/time/nation/article/0,8599,2081778,00.html#ixzz1caSTom00.

3. For a more complete description of the GECC project, see Oliver Staley, "Chicago Economist's 'Crazy Idea' wins Ken Griffin's Backing," *Bloomberg Markets* (April 2011): 85–92.

4. The academic manuscripts are currently in process, with the first prepared study as: Roland Fryer, Steve Levitt, and John A. List, "Toward an Understanding of the Pre-K Education Production Function."

Chapter 6: What Seven Words Can End Modern Discrimination?

1. In the United States, asking such questions would be illegal. This, of course, doesn't mean that US employers don't use such information when making hiring decisions.

2. See "General Orders #11," Jewish-American History Foundation, http://www.jewish-history.com/civilwar/go11.htm (last accessed March 28, 2013). Abraham Lincoln rescinded the order.

3. "History of Antisemitism in the United States: Early Twentieth Century," Wikipedia, http://en.wikipedia.org/wiki/History_of_antisemitism_in_the_United_States#Early_Twentieth_Century (last accessed March 28, 2013).

4. Press Release, NobelPrize.org, October 13, 1992, http://www.nobelprize.org/nobel_prizes/economics/laureates/1992/press.html.

5. Among adults twenty-five years old and older, 10.6 million US women have master's degrees or higher, compared to 10.5 million men.

6. See Kerwin K. Charles and Jonathan Guryan, "Prejudice and Wages: An Empirical Assessment of Becker's *The Economics of Discrimination,*" *Journal of Political Economy* 116 (2008): 773–809.

7. Jeffrey M. Jones, "Record-High 86% Approve Black-White Marriages," Gallup, September 12, 2011, http://www.gallup.com/poll/149390/Record-High-Approve-Black-White-Marriages.aspx (last accessed March 28, 2013).

8. The economics literature refers to this kind of discrimination as "statistical discrimination." See Kenneth Arrow, "The Theory of Discrimination," in Orley Ashenfelter and Albert Rees, eds., *Discrimination in Labor Markets* (Princeton, NJ: Princeton University Press, 1973), 3–33.

9. Aisha Sultan, "Data Mining Spurs Users to Protect Privacy Online," *The Bulletin* (Oregon), September 29, 2012, http://www.bendbulletin.com/article/20120929/NEWS0107/209290322/.

10. See "Web Sites Change Prices Based on Customers' Habits," CNN.com, June 25, 2005, http://edition.cnn.com/2005/LAW/06/24/ramasastry.website.prices/ (last accessed March 28, 2013).

11. This work and the following builds on John's earlier research published in the 2000s. See John A. List, "The Nature and Extent of Discrimination in the Marketplace, Evidence from the Field," *Quarterly Journal of Economics,* 2004, 119 (1), 49–49.

12. Read more at M. J. Lee, "Geraldo Rivera Apologizes for 'Hoodie' Comment," Politico, March 27, 2012, http://www.politico.com/news/stories/0312/74529.html#ixzz1qus Qkm6A (last accessed March 28, 2013).

Chapter 7: Be Careful What You Chose, It May Be Used Against You!

1. At firms with more than 20,000 employees, 24 percent vary premiums based on whether someone smokes, as do 12 percent of companies with 500 or more workers. See "Smokers, Forced to Pay More for Health Insurance, Can Get Help with Quitting," *Washington Post*, January 2, 2012. See also, "Firms to Charge Smokers, Obese More For Healthcare," *Reuters*, October 31, 2011.

2. "Kenlie Tiggeman, Southwest's 'Too Fat To Fly' Passenger, Sues Airline," *Huffington Post*, May 4, 2012, http://www.huffingtonpost.com/2012/05/04/kenlie-tiggeman -southwests_n_1476907.html.

3. See Andrew Dainty and Helen Lingard, "Indirect Discrimination in Construction Organizations and the Impact on Women's Careers," *Journal of Management in Engineering* 22 (2006): 108–118.

4. "Nazi Persecution of Homosexuals, 1933–1945," United States Holocaust Memorial Museum, http://www.ushmm.org/museum/exhibit/online/hsx/ (last accessed April 27, 2013).

5. "The Black Church," BlackDemographics.com, http://www.blackdemographics .com/religion.html (last accessed March 28, 2013).

6. *All in the Family*, Season 2. Accessed on YouTube, March 25, 2013, http://www .youtube.com/watch?v=O_UBgkFHm8o.

7. See Uri Gneezy, John A. List, and Michael K. Price, "Toward an Understanding of Why People Discriminate: Evidence from a Series of Natural Field Experiments," NBER Working Paper 17855 (February 2012).

8. Richard H. Thaler, "Show Us the Data. (It's Ours After All.)," *New York Times*, April 23, 2011, http://www.nytimes.com/2011/04/24/business/24view.html.

Chapter 8: How Can We Save Ourselves from Ourselves?

1. You can watch the video on YouTube if you're desperate to discover what happens next. Perhaps you've already seen it—it was national news, after all. We wouldn't suggest it.

2. The RAND Health Insurance Experiment randomized nearly 6,000 people into different levels of cost-sharing. The experiment is still incredibly influential, and it was frequently cited in the health care debates of 2010. Perhaps the best sign that experimentation is back is that Oregon recently finished a study where researchers randomized individuals into Medicare. For a discussion of the results from the first year of that experiment, see Amy Finkelstein, Sarah Taubman, Bill Wright, Mira Bernstein, Jonathan Gruber, Joseph P. Newhouse, Heidi Allen, Katherine Baicker, and the Oregon Health Study Group, "The Oregon Health Insurance Experiment: Evidence from the First Year," *Quarterly Journal of Economics* 127, no. 3 (2012): 1057–1106.

3. For more information, see "Kanye West," Wikipedia, http://en.wikipedia.org/wiki /Kanye_West (last accessed April 2, 2013).

4. See Dana Chandler, Steven D. Levitt, and John A. List, "Predicting and Preventing Shootings Among At-Risk Youth," *American Economic Review Papers and Proceedings* 101, no. 3 (2011): 288–292.

5. "Jaime Oliver Misses a Few Ingredients," School Nutrition Association Press Releases, March 22, 2010, http://www.schoolnutrition.org/Blog.aspx?id=13742&blogid=564.

6. John A. List and Anya C. Savikhin, "The Behavioralist as Dietician: Leveraging Behavioral Economics to Improve Child Food Choice and Consumption," 2013, University of Chicago working paper.

7. Paul Rozin, Sydney Scott, Megan Dingley, Joanna K. Urbanek, Hong Jiang, and Mark Kaltenbach, "Nudge to Nobesity I: Minor Changes in Accessibility Decrease Food Intake," *Judgment and Decision Making* 6, no. 4 (2011): 323–332.

8. An important effort to increase the supply of such organs is the pathbreaking research of Stanford economist Al Roth, who received the Nobel Prize in Economics in 2012, in part for his contribution to the design of matching algorithms of live donors with people who need transplants. Roth and his colleagues show that simple changes to the procedure used to allocate the organs can make a big difference in outcomes.

9. Eric J. Johnson and Daniel Goldstein, "Do Defaults Save Lives?" *Science* 302 (2003): 1338–1339, http://www.dangoldstein.com/papers/DefaultsScience.pdf.

10. See Dean Karlan and John A. List, "Nudges or Nuisances for Organ Donation," 2012, University of Chicago working paper.

11. See "Federal Advisory Committee Draft Climate Assessment Report Released for Public Review," US Global Change Research Program, http://ncadac.globalchange.gov/ (last accessed April 2, 2013).

12. http://www.energystar.gov/ia/partners/univ/download/CFL_Fact_Sheet.pdf?9ed9-3f06 (last accessed July 24, 2013).

13. See Robert Cialdini, "Don't Throw in the Towel: Use Social Influence Research," *APS Observer*, April 2005.

14. See David Herberich, John A. List, and Michael K. Price, "How Many Economists Does It Take to Change a Light Bulb? A Natural Field Experiment on Technology Adoption," 2012 University of Chicago working paper.

Chapter 9: What Really Makes People Give to Charity?

1. "American Giving Knowledge Base," Grant Space, http://www.grantspace.org/Tools/Knowledge-Base/Funding-Resources/Individual-Donors/American-giving (last accessed April 27, 2013).

2. This research has led us to establish the Science of Philanthropy Initiative (SPI) at the University of Chicago in order to explore the underpinnings of philanthropy by employing an interdisciplinary approach that includes strategic partnerships with the fundraising community. SPI is supported by a $5 million grant from the John Templeton Foundation. Please see http://www.spihub.org for more information.

3. Since John had no resources to run these experiments, it also helped that he could use the sports card collection that he amassed as a kid to pay his experimental participants.

4. While this might seem like a great idea if you are a would-be administrator, it does have some downsides. One is that every person in the department will decide that his or her area should be chosen. People who study the economics of trade want that as the niche area; those who do labor economics think that labor is the best choice, and so on.

5. Prior to this leadership role, John had only coached the men's and women's water ski teams.

6. The paper was published as John A. List and David Lucking-Reiley, "The Effects of Seed Money and Refunds on Charitable Giving: Experimental Evidence from a University Capital Campaign," *Journal of Political Economy* 110 (2002): 215–233.

7. John A. List and Daniel Rondeau, "Matching and Challenge Gifts to Charity: Evidence from Laboratory and Natural Field Experiments," *Experimental Economics* 11 (2008): 253–267.

8. Other economists, most notably our friends Jan Potters, Martin Sefton, and Lise Vesterlund, have found similar insights from laboratory experiments.

9. Kent E. Dove, *Conducting a Successful Capital Campaign,* 2nd edition (San Francisco: Jossey-Bass, 2000), 510.

10. Dean Karlan and John A. List, "Does Price Matter in Charitable Giving? Evidence from a Large-Scale Natural Field Experiment," *American Economic Review* 97, no. 5 (2007): 1774–1793.

11. As a condition of the experiment, we agreed to keep the name of the organization anonymous, so we can't tell you which organization it was.

12. These brackets denote a shorthand (to avoid having to type out the full letter three times for your sake and ours).

13. We essentially rolled a four-sided dice for every one of the 50,000 houses. If we rolled a "1," we assigned that household to Group 1, which was offered a 1:1 match. If we rolled a 2, we assigned the household to Group 2, and offered it a 2:1 match. If we rolled a 3, we offered the household a 3:1 match, and Group 4 was our control group.

14. This result fits well with our intuition.

15. Harry Bruinius, "Why the Rich Give Money to Charity," *Christian Science Monitor,* November 20, 2010, http://www.csmonitor.com/Business/Guide-to-Giving/2010/1120 /Why-the-rich-give-money-to-charity.

16. See the excellent research by economists Rachel Croson, Catherine Eckel, Phil Grossman, Stephan Meier, and Jen Shang showing such insights.

17. See Craig E. Landry, Andreas Lange, John A. List, Michael K. Price, and Nicholas G. Rupp, "Toward an Understanding of the Economics of Charity: Evidence from a Field Experiment," *Quarterly Journal of Economics* 121 (May 2006): 747–782.

18. The solicitors all signed consent forms agreeing to allow this evaluation. The interested reader should see the excellent work of Jeff E. Biddle & Daniel S. Hamermesh, 1998. "Beauty, Productivity and Discrimination: Lawyers' Looks and Lucre," NBER Working Paper 5636 in the area of measuring the value of physical attractiveness.

19. See Craig E. Landry, Andreas Lange, John A. List, Michael K. Price, and Nicholas G. Rupp, "Is a Donor in Hand Better Than Two in the Bush? Evidence from a Natural Field Experiment," *American Economic Review* 100 (2010): 958–983.

20. *The Daily Show with John Stewart,* February 16, 2011, http://www.thedailyshow .com/watch/wed-february-16–2011/you-re-welcome—-balancing-the-budget.

21. Much of this is taken directly from Andreas Lange, John A. List, and Michael K. Price, "A Fundraising Mechanism Inspired by Historical Tontines: Theory and Experimental Evidence," *Journal of Public Economics* 91 (June 2007): 1750–1782.

22. See David Leonhardt, "What Makes People Give?" *New York Times Magazine,* March 9, 2008.

Chapter 10: What Can Cleft Palates and Opt-Out Boxes Teach Us About People's Reasons for Giving to Charity?

1. See "Pinki Sonkar: From School Outcast to an Oscar-Winning Film," *People Magazine*, February 23, 2009, http://www.peoplestylewatch.com/people/stylewatch/redcarpet/2009/article/0,,20249180_20260685,00.html?xid=rss-fullcontent. By the way, Smile Train commissioned the film, and it was the biggest, most effective ad campaign the charity ever ran!

2. There is by now a fair amount of evidence in the literature supporting this viewpoint, including some of our own. See John A. List and Michael K. Price, "The Role of Social Connections in Charitable Fundraising: Evidence from a Natural Field Experiment," *Journal of Economic Behavior and Organization* 69, no. 2 (2009): 160–169.

3. See Amee Kamdar, Steven D. Levitt, John A. List, Brian Mullaney, and Chad Syverson, "Once and Done: Leveraging Behavioral Economics to Increase Charitable Contributions," NBER working paper to be published in 2013.

4. The interested reader should see the psychology and economics literatures, which are full of models and experiments showing that people tend to be nice to those who are nice to them. See, for example: Akerlof, George. 1982. "Labor Contracts as Partial Gift Exchange." Q.J.E. 97 (November): 543–69; Rabin, Matthew. 1993. "Incorporating Fairness into Game Theory and Economics"; A.E.R. 83 (December): 1281–1302; Fehr, Ernst, and Simon Gächter. 2000. "Fairness and Retaliation: The Economics of Reciprocity." *J. Econ. Perspectives* 14 (Summer): 159–81; Dufwenberg, Martin, and Georg Kirchsteiger. 2004. "A Theory of Sequential Reciprocity." *Games and Econ. Behavior* 47 (May): 269–98; Charness, Gary. 2004. "Attribution and Reciprocity in an Experimental Labor Market." Manuscript, Univ. California, Santa Barbara; Sobel, Joel. 2005. "Social Preferences and Reciprocity." Manuscript, Univ. California, San Diego; Falk, Armin. 2007. "Charitable Giving as a Gift Exchange: Evidence from a Field Experiment." IZA Working Paper no. 1148, Inst. Study Labor, Bonn.

5. Belinda Luscombe, "Using Business Savvy to Help Good Causes," *Time Magazine*, March 17, 2011.

6. The charitable-giving deduction is a hotly debated policy. Many in the industry say that getting rid of the tax deduction would ravage the nonprofit sector. This argument is a matter of ongoing research and the jury is still out. But the real impact hinges on determining exactly why people give.

Chapter 11: Why Is Today's Business Manager an Endangered Species?

1. "Netfilx Introduces New Plans and Announces Price Changes," Netflix US & Canada Blog, Tuesday, July 12, 2011, http://blog.netflix.com/2011/07/netflix-introduces-new-plans-and.html?commentPage=25.

2. "Netflix Apology," *Saturday Night Live* video, http://www.nbc.com/saturday-night-live/video/netflix-apology/1359563/.

3. Stephen F. Jencks, Mark V. Williams, and Eric A. Coleman, "Rehospitalizations Among Patients in the Medicare Fee-for-Service Program," *New England Journal of Medicine* 360 (2009): 1418–1428.

4. In the following, we describe our experience in the winery with more details: "Intuition Can't Beat Experimentation," Rady School of Management, UC San Diego, http://rady.ucsd.edu/mba/student/clubs/rbj/rady-business-journal/2011/intuition/ (last accessed April 29, 2013). For a description of the experiment, see Ayelet Gneezy and Uri Gneezy, "Pricing Experimentation in Firms: Testing the Price Equal Quality Heuristics," Rady School of Management, UC San Diego, http://econ.as.nyu.edu/docs/IO/11975/Gneezy_CESS.pdf.

5. Ayelet Gneezy, Uri Gneezy, Leif D. Nelson, and Amber Brown, "Shared Social Responsibility: A Field Experiment in Pay-What-You-Want Pricing and Charitable Giving," *Science* 329 (2010): 325–327.

6. Uri Gneezy and Pedro Rey-Biel, "On the Relative Efficiency of Performance Pay and Social Incentives," Barcelona Graduate School of Economics working paper no. 585, October 2011.

7. Tanjim Hossain and John A. List, "The Behavioralist Visits the Factory: Increasing Productivity Using Simple Framing Manipulations," *Management Science* 58 (2012): 2151–2167.

Epilogue

1. This passage comes from Steven D. Levitt and John A. List, "What Do Laboratory Experiments Measuring Social Preferences Reveal About the Real World," *Journal of Economic Perspectives* 21, no. 2 (2007): 153–174. For an early paper by a pioneer in the field of experimental economics, see Vernon L. Smith, "Microeconomic Systems as an Experimental Science," *American Economic Review* 72, no. 5 (1982): 923–955.

2. For obvious reasons, we encourage you not to deceive your clients. In this case, don't advertise a matching grant if it doesn't exist.

on using framing to increase
productivity, 234–236
Focus groups, 218
Ford, Henry, 111
Fox & Friends (television program), 123
Framing, 80, 84, 130
gain, 80, 84, 233–234, 236
to increase productivity, 233–236
loss, 80, 84, 234, 236
Frank, Barney, 199
Free-rider effect, 179, 180
Friedman, Milton, 112, 113
Friends (television program), 24
Fryer, Roland, 92
Fundraising
beauty effect, 185–187
common assumptions, 175–177
direct-mail solicitations, 177, 203–206
door-to-door, 177
lotteries, 186, 187, 192
lottery effect, 186, 187
matching grants, 175, 180–185, 194
"once and done" campaign, 204–206, 208–209
raffles, 185–187
reciprocity and, 206–207
seed money and, 174–175, 176, 178–180
tontines, 176, 188–192

Gain framing, 80, 84, 233–234, 236
Galileo, 240
Gates, Bill, 192
Gates Foundation, 193
Gay partners, discrimination against, 110, 132–135
Gender
discrimination based on, 109, 110, 115, 116–117, 120–122
price negotiation and, 53–55, 60
responses to compensations schemes and, 36–38
risk for teen gun violence and, 155
See also Men; Women
Gender inequality (gender gap), 1–2, 12–13, 32–48

competitiveness among females and, 33–47
in education, 61–62
in hiring, 46–48, 108–109
in job status and earnings, 57
in labor markets, 34, 35
policy makers and, 61–62
using field experiments to solve issue of, 5
Genocide, 111
Glass ceiling, 35–36
Global warming, 166–169
Gneezy, Jacob, 10
Gneezy, Magda, 10
Grant, Ulysses S., 111
Gratification, deferred, 93–94
Griffin, Anne, 75–76, 92, 104, 106
Griffin, Kenneth, 74–76, 92, 104, 106
Griffin Early Childhood Center, 93–103
early results, 102–103
ensuring attendance, 98–102
student lottery, 96–97
use of assessments in, 102
Griffin Foundation, 93
Gym membership, incentives for, 27–28

Habit formation, incentives and, 29–31
Hardin, Garrett, 55
Harvard *Crimson* (newspaper), 199–200
Hastings, Reed, 215
Hate. *See* Animus-based discrimination
Head Start, 91–92
Herberich, David, 167–168
Hiring, gender inequity in, 46–48, 108–109
Hiring bias, 59–60
Hispanics
discrimination against gay couples and, 134
risk for teen gun violence and, 155, 156
Hodgman, John, 188
Honda, 60

Courtesy of the Author

Uri Gneezy was born and raised in Israel, where he learned applied game theory first-hand in the streets of Tel Aviv. Dr. Gneezy is the Epstein/Atkinson Endowed Chair in Behavioral Economics and professor of economics and strategy at the Rady School of Management at the University of California, San Diego.

Lloyd de Grane

John A. List grew up in a working-class family in Wisconsin—where his father drove trucks for a living—and learned economics in hobby markets. Dr. List is the Homer J. Livingston Professor of Economics at the University of Chicago. He has been a research associate at the National Bureau of Economics (NBER) for more than a decade and served as senior economist on the President's Council of Economic Advisors for environmental and resource economics.